Reflections across

C000062594

EmPower Us!

"EmPower Us! redefines "Value" as purpose-driven, equitable social impact, addressing all stakeholders' needs. It is a roadmap to rise above the individual, national and corporate self-interests to collaborate on human-centered solutions, restoring Trust and Transparency on the impact of emerging technologies."

—Navroop Sahdev, CEO, The Digital Economist

"There are many "fix society" books. This is one of the best that I have read. My own answers to these multiple crises proposed building better systems of capitalism and democracy, all moved by the spirit of the Common Good. But Kaufman and Srića, went much deeper with their analysis of why societies break down. "

—Philip Kotler, *Father of Modern Marketing,* **Confronting Capitalism, Democracy in Decline,** *Advancing the Common Good*

"This "can't-put-it-down" book is a powerful contribution to all the Earth. It shares miraculous solutions inspiring every reader to find their highest life mission—higher than we would dare—to be part of the solution. Do read EmPower Us! now!"

—Susan Davis Moora, *Mother Social Investment Industry,* **Founder, KINS**

"This book is an invitation to look at the world with curious kids' eyes to cooperate and manage social and economic processes differently! It is a call to let love and creativity Empower us to bring Harmony to society! Can the world really become a big orchestra playing beautiful, noble, and human music that turns us all into Catalysts of change? Srića and Kaufman say it is possible. We have to let our soul listen to their New Harmony."

—Prof. Dr. Ivo Josipović, Ph.D., President of Croatia (2010–2015)

"EmPower Us! challenges the reader to embark on a transformational journey. Instead of accepting the world as is, the authors give us a guide to harnessing our passion to be the change we want to see in the world."

—Erik Qualman, Futurist, *#1 Bestselling Author (Socialnomics)*

""*The world as we know it is flawed; Empower Us! encourages readers to not be apathetic, but rather excited in making change."*

—**Ella Feathers, Student UNC, Chapel Hill, Environmental Activist**

"EmPower Us! addresses the root cause of the five global crises, 'dis-eases' beginning with the degradation of values and the breach of trust. We are born hardwired to universal values. Before we are EmPower(ed) we have to be InPower(ed). The power of universal values can act as catalytic forces for transformation."

—**J.E. Rash, President, Legacy International,** *Values-based Leadership*

"EmPower Us! focuses on one of the foundational elements to create a trust economy - the ability to reach, engage and listen to global citizens. Hear the rising voices across geographies, generations, gender and global economies."

—**Irfan Verjee, VP Business Value Group, Sprinklr - Europe & Asia**

"In today's world, people talk to themselves rather than engage in genuine conversation...EmPower Us! stimulates a broader dialogue between generations on the critical priorities of humanity, driving it to reinvent itself."

—**Dr. Joseph O. Okpaku, Sr. CEO, Telecom Africa International Co.**

"EmPower Us! is a wise guide for teams committed to creating a generative future together—starting now! With a melange of passion, wit and poetic wisdom, the book encourages us to action on a very human level, and its apt analytic protocols are immediately useful. It sees reality through a whole-system lens. And through its eyes the reader leaps well ahead on the transition from the profit-primacy business norm toward a paradigm of inclusive wellbeing."

—**Elsie Maio, CEO, Humanity, Inc. /SoulBranding™ Institute**

"A must-read for executives and managers. It provides a comprehensive map of Strategic Transformation, offering excellent insights and practical cases."

—**Dr. Sam Wang, Managing Partner, Kotler Marketing Group China**

"This book provides a leadership model that fosters true values, nourishes a culture of innovation and relies on diversity and inclusion; that is the key for a sustainable value creation in our world that is continuously being reshaped by technology development."

—**Gordana Kovačević, CEO, Ericsson Nikola Tesla**

"*EmPower Us! is a template for sharing the authors' values-based framework for holistic societal growth. It gives readers the perspective needed to interact with the status quo and facilitate sustainable changes.*"

—Emad Davis, Full Stack Software Engineer, FOSTM Agency

"*This book helped me recognize my power within the Gen Z community. I was enthralled by the message of Strategic Harmony in addressing our social inequities by empowering values, including unheard voices and redefining leaders as catalyzers.*"

—Malak Dridi, Writer, Daily Tar Heel, UNC, Chapel Hill

"*It guides each individual to play a significant role in achieving sustainability. It is a practical, easy to follow roadmap revealing the mindset required to design impactful solutions through digital technologies and sustainable business models.*"

—Din Catic, Corporate Sustainability Strategist, Carbon Trust, UK

"*EmPower Us! proposes a new paradigm and manifesto. Time has come to empower us through a non predatory approach to limited resources . Love, harmony and care must be integrated into decision-making. Only redefinition of impact measurement incorporating trust, empathy, and transparency can ensure transformation.*"

—Aïssa Azzouzi CEO, Global Transformation Accelerator, North Africa

"*As a young professional, it can be daunting to think of the responsibility of cleaning up the mess of the past generations. It is time for us to acknowledge our previous wrong doings to the world and work together towards Strategic Harmony.*"

—Musa Khan, Social Entrepreneur

"*EmPower Us! speaks through the language of business, reflecting many of my core values that are grounded in community. It provides a framework to begin folding together the lived experiences of folks along the economic spectrum to get us to the climate win.*"

—Lindsay Harper, Climate Justice Activist, Arm in Arm

"*We need a new generation of human-centered leaders that can establish trust and make decisions grounded in values that take people's future sustainability into account and generate impact for the society at large. These concepts in EmPower Us! enable next generation leaders to achieve Strategic Harmony.*"

—Roberto Croci, Managing Director, Microsoft for Startups, MEA

EmPower Us!

From Crisis
to Strategic Harmony

Ira Kaufman

Velimir Srića

KITSAP
PUBLISHING

KITSAP
PUBLISHING

EmPower Us!
First edition, published 2020
Copyright©2020 Ira Kaufman and Velimir Srića

By Ira Kaufman and Velimir Srića

Cover Design and Interior Layout by Reprospace, LLC
Cover imagess by Unsplash: Amir-Mohammad, Imansyah Muhamad Putera, Joel-Mott-La, John Torcasio, Joseph Gonzalez, Nathan Dumlao, Reza Biazar, Ricardo Velarde

Paperback ISBN-13: 978-1-952685-13-2
Hardcover ISBN-13: 978-1-952685-16-3

20201204

Published by Kitsap Publishing
P.O. Box 572
Poulsbo, WA 98370
www.KitsapPublishing.com

Dedication

To Muhamed Ćatić for your vision and connecting us on the journey to Strategic Harmony.

To my visionary teachers ...

J. E. Rash, thank you for guiding me to discover the essence of my universal values and spiritual being and translating them to the world.

Philip Kotler, many thanks for broadening my understanding of the role of business in changing our world.

To my family–Ashley, Diyaa and Jelal with whom I share love and an imperative for transformation.

Ira Kaufman

To Milan Zeleny, Tom Peters and Jack Welch who inspired me professionally through contact and cooperation.

To my family–Ana, Lana, Luka, Davor and Dario who taught me the importance of Love, Empathy and Harmony.

To my students, coworkers, business and political partners who shared with me passion to innovate and transform.

Velimir Srića

Acknowledgments with Gratitude

We are very grateful for the many inspired people who have supported and contributed to the development of this book during the past three years. Our intention was to be inclusive and listen to the Rising Voices of change globally.

Our 40+ contributors from six continents and across five generations shared their insights and love of the book's purpose; their content is included throughout the text.

- » Abdo Magdy, Principle Coach, Abdo Magdy International LLC
- » Adil Kassabi Ph.D., Managing Partner, Tadafur Consulting Services
- » Aissa Azzouzi, CEO, Global Transformation Accelerator
- » Cassandra Kelly, Co-founder, Pottinger Group, Advisor G20/B20
- » Craig Phillips, Senior Product Designer, Utmost
- » Din Catic, Associate, The Carbon Trust
- » Ella Feathers, Student UNC Chapel Hill
- » Elsie Maio, CEO, Humanity Inc
- » Emad Davis, Full Stack Software Engineer, FOSTM Agency
- » Emir Dzanic Ph.D., Director, Cambridge Innovative System Solutions
- » Erik Qualman, Futurist, #1 Bestselling Author (Socialnomics)
- » Flávia P. Malucelli, Coordinator, Brazilian Permanent Mission to World Trade Organization
- » Frederic Lehrman, Director, Nomad University
- » Gordana Kovačević, CEO, Ericsson Nikola Tesla
- » Hanane Anoua, Principal, Learn and Dare
- » Irfan Verjee, VP Digital Business Solutions, Sprinklr
- » J.E. Rash, President, Legacy International
- » Joe Turek Ph.D., Dean, Business School, Christian Brothers University
- » Joseph O. Okpaku, Ph.D., CEO, Telecom Africa International Corp.

- » Josipa Majic, CEO, Tacit Tech
- » Klaus-Michael Christensen, Principal, SevenBridge
- » Lindsay Harper, Team Coordinator, US Climate Action Network
- » Mark Storm, Custom Program Director, THNK School
- » Michelle James, CEO, The Center for Creative Emergence
- » Miha Žerko, CEO, SRC.SI
- » Muhamed Ćatić, Executive Advisor to Board, IFFCO
- » Navroop Sahdev, CEO, The Digital Economist, MIT Media Lab
- » Noômen Lahimer Ph.D., Founder, Evey Technologies
- » Osama Al-Saleh, Fellow, Forbes
- » Robert Mahavir Homsy Ph.D., Board Director, Legacy International
- » Roberto Croci, Managing Director, Microsoft for Startups, MEA
- » Sam Rasoul, Delegate, Commonwealth of Virginia
- » Shagorika Heryani, Regional Head of Strategy, Grey Group AMEA
- » Sharon McDonald EdD., President, Metatonia Institute
- » Slavko Vidovic, CEO, Infodom
- » Shayn McCallum, Instructor, Bogazici University
- » Stephen L. Gomes Ph.D., President-Corporate Operations, Microstrata Research, LLC
- » Susan Davis, Founder, KINS Innovation Network
- » Tariq Qureishy, CEO, MAD and Xponential Group

Our publication team was committed and deeply shared the vision of Strategic Harmony.

Ingemar Anderson, publisher, was patient, open and supportive of the book's innovative publishing model that reflected the changing digital marketplace and its theme of transformation.

Sharon Lindenburger, manuscript editor, added great insights and refinements throughout the text.

Kristina Bruun-Nyzell, editor, gave direction to the text and shared insights on the impact of the climate crisis as a transformative force for business and the planet.

Jean AbiNader, change management strategist, provided thoughtful insights to clarify the content.

Elsie Maio, thought-leader for social-impact enterprises, provided a continuous flow of wise counsel on marketing of the book.

Saleema Vellani, serial entrepreneur and innovation strategist, collaborated on intergenerational approach to Strategic Transformation.

Maurice Bassett, publishing consultant, was generous with his time, contacts and expertise in advising us on developing a quality publication.

Joni Praded, publishing consultant, was invaluable in designing the new publishing model.

Jennifer Pardee, web developer, designed and built the website www.EmPowerUs.world.

Malak Dridi, writer Daily Tar Heel, UNC, Chapel Hill, developed and managed content for www.EmPowerUs.world

Musa Khan, marketing associate, helped design and implement the social media and network distribution strategy for the book.

Samah Rash, emerging global health researcher, contributed valuable insights on the role of women in the changing world.

Diyaa Kaufman, rising college leader, provided insights on book title and cover design.

Sabreen Rash, Research Assistant International Affairs, contributed to book content and design.

Jelal Kaufman, emerging videographer, provided video design and production.

About the Authors

Ira Kaufman, Ph.D. is a Transformation Strategist, CEO, Social Entrepreneur, and Educator. Ira's 45 years of management experience spans three worlds: business, nonprofit, and education. He challenges leaders, entrepreneurs, and students to reflect on their assumptions and resistances to discover new sustainable solutions and fuel purposeful action. His company, Entwine Digital, works with mid-size organizations and multinationals to design values-based Transformation strategies and train World-Class Leaders. His Catalyzer Lab provides a framework for managing continuous transformation and developing human-centered business models. Drawing upon the strengths of Rising Voices of the Future, he introduced the Catalyzer—a leader that transforms Love of Purpose into a Power that catalyzes the impact of organizations and businesses. As a co-founder of the Global Transformation Corps, he redirects entrepreneurship to a stakeholder-centric model with sustainable impacts. At the University of Lynchburg College of Business, he designed and implemented the Transformative Leadership Lab and Transformative Leadership in the Digital Age curricula. He co-authored *Digital Marketing with Purpose* (now in 2nd edition). His passions are his two children, organic gardening, basketball, and meditation.

ira@entwinedigital.com

Velimir Srića earned an MS in Electrical Engineering, an MBA from Columbia University, New York, and a Ph.D. in Information Systems Management. His education reflects his primary interests: digital technology, innovation management, and creative leadership. His professional life is dedicated to education, research, politics, and consulting. As a member of European Academy of Arts and Sciences, he is involved in teaching and research all over the world from Central and Eastern Europe (Croatia, Slovenia, Austria, Hungary, Montenegro, Bosnia, and Herzegovina) to Asia (Dubai, Beijing, and Shanghai), and to the USA (UCLA). As a politician, he was a member of the Croatian government, a recipient of Eisenhower Fellowship, and Croatian representative to UNESCO and OECD. As a consultant, he worked with many regional and global companies helping them deal with leadership, innovation management, and digital transformation issues. He also served as the World Bank expert on Change Management and is the president of ELITE (Excellence in Leadership, Innovation, and Technology). As an individual dedicated to world peace and sustainability, he is a member of The Club of Rome and an honorary member of the Croatian Helsinki Committee. He published 76 books, over 400 professional papers, and a few hundred columns in popular magazines. He is a proud father of Lana, Luka, Dario, and Davor.

velimir@velimirsrica.com

Contents

Preface

Response to
Global Wake-Up Call
Strategic Harmony

In early 2020, almost everything stopped. What began in the East as a strange new disease, rapidly spread around the world, forcing the World Health Organization to declare the COVID virus a pandemic. Millions of people became ill and hundreds of thousands died. Entire economies ground to a halt. The stock market took a dire plunge. Health care institutions struggled to cope with an emergency situation they had not seen since the 1918 influenza. Distraught leaders conducted frantic searches for equipment like masks, gloves, and protective gowns. Millions were told to work from home. Schools shut down, switching to an online format, expecting overwhelmed parents to become "teachers." Colleges and universities switched their courses and university services to online formats, causing chaos and discomfort for both students and faculty. Thousands of seniors died in long-term care homes that were not equipped to withstand a pandemic. Some government leaders played a blame game; others called for collaboration.

Rates of anxiety, addiction, depression, and other mental health conditions began to skyrocket. The world, as we had always known it, suddenly transformed in ways no one ever expected, and psychologists began talking of the pandemic as an international trauma.

The culprit: an unseen aggressor, a microscopic new virus called COVID-19 cut a wide swath of damage and destruction around the globe. With no sure treatment and no cure, it was a Darwinian nightmare—the power of a force of nature that seemingly had us and all our carefully crafted systems in its clutches, threatening our survival and our way of life.

As devastating as this was, the virus also revealed to humanity that all our previous concepts of "normal" are not working. It showed us the divisions within societies—economic and racial inequality, dysfunctional political systems, preoccupations with violence and power —all of which came into such sharp relief that we could no longer look away or adopt mere Band-Aid solutions to deeply festering wounds. And for those of us who had been sounding alarm bells about the state of our planet pre-COVID, the irony was not lost on us that as COVID shut us down, the Earth began to heal. Air quality improved, the earth's waters got clearer, you could see the night sky, you could hear the birds. And so we began to ask the questions: Does it take a pandemic to show us this stark truth? Or are there things we should have been doing all along? Were new models of leadership accessible, or do we need to reinvent leadership with transformative models to catalyze a Post-COVID-19 society?

These symptoms make it clear that our world is broken! It's been broken for a long time. The need for profound systemic change is no longer an option; it's a necessity. If you disagree, and you like the status quo, put this book aside. Otherwise, join us and we can work to transform it! We must create The New Harmony. Our survival depends on it.

Any book dealing with change can easily get lost in the vast conversations on burning global issues. What's broken, how is it going to be fixed and who is supposed to do it? No wonder we have spent more than a year in deciding *WHY* we are writing this book. Starting with *WHO* is this book for? Is it aimed only at dissatisfied people or all people facing change, wanting to understand it, and more importantly manage it?

This book is a deep dive into our purpose, namely, an exploration of how to fix and transform the broken world. Hopefully, this is not just an idealistic dream of possibilities. It stems from our passion for dramatic change in our current world, combined with our consulting experience, as well as our love for working on transforming executives, managers, teams, students, businesses, organizations, and government agencies in 50+ countries. We began with the book title, the Shattered World. After writing three Guideposts we realized that we were positioning ourselves as victims of the current conditions and not as catalysts for the change. So we had to "transform" ourselves once again. The thread that unifies the book is the call for all leaders to adopt change and act on it.

EmPower Us! is about all of Us! The power of multiple, intersecting generations striving for a sustainable life. It invites the reader to listen for the harmony of the Rising Voices (Next Generation, Women, Marginalized) who demand inclusive impact and equity with the resonant wisdom and expertise of progressive leaders. It guides us to empower our values and purpose; thus reducing the "activation energy" and resources required for adopting new services and transforming our organizations. Each "chapter" is named a "guidepost" to point the reader on the transformation journey.

This book is for those who want to reinvent the world, propel The New Harmony, driven by universal values and a higher ethical compass, emerging technologies, and human-centered business practices. It is for those who want to transform a business or an organization; to catalyze political change; or to disrupt outdated, unresponsive policies in healthcare, ecology, education, government, economics, or other institutions. We mean people of all political persuasions: executives, politicians, educators, profit and nonprofit managers, entrepreneurs, students, change agents, parents, concerned citizens; in other words, You!

Most people see what's wrong and are apathetic or paralyzed. We want to share our passion to transform the world to what it can become, instead of accepting the present situation as the default. We provide a breakthrough in thinking about institutions, and the false "truths" we accept and live by. We offer a resilient approach to managing and innovating, and a roadmap for transformation. We are targeting all generations (Baby Boomers, Gen X, Millennials, Gen Z) across all cultures as the "broken-world-condition" is not beholden to one culture or economic class. And now, the tragedy of COVID has surfaced these new opportunities for transformation.

During the writing of this book, one of us (Ira) became ill with COVID for a month, ending up in a hospital and fighting for his breath. Along with his slow recovery and healing process came an even stronger determination that fixing the broken world is of paramount importance. There is nothing like a taste of our own fragility and mortality to make us realize that time does not wait for anyone, and that if we want to make a difference, we need to do it now, not in some far-off future.

We see that central to all changes are the forces of Power and Love. Dr. Martin Luther King Jr expressed a need to find a balance between the two forces in his famous speech at the Southern Christian Leadership Conference: *"Power without love is reckless and abusive, and love without power is sentimental and anemic."* For our world to change and become more harmonized, our leaders must reflect on their beliefs and actions. Power-driven leaders focus on control and try to achieve goals without considering the impact on citizens, employees, and community, and those focused on love, compassion, and empathy miss their targets by being inefficient. These forces are at present playing a complicated game full of inconsistences and double standards that fertilize our myths and compromise the direction of our ethical compasses. Staying the way, we shatter the world. Daring to dream and enact a more transformed world leads to a more sustainable and harmonious Global Order.

Power and Love are the forces that underlie the existence of every politician, chief executive officer, principal, dean, change agent, and responsible citizen. In times of great challenges, great people are called upon. But are we in search of a realistic saga or a fairy tale?

Since the turn of the millennium, we've witnessed a fascination with the figure of the "superhero" rising all over the world from Spiderman to Batman, from Wonder Woman to Black Panther, from Iron Man to Captain America, from Thor to The Avengers and other Marvel heroes. In the meantime, the NextGen has generated a new genre, young adult science fiction, the technological future animated in terms of Good and Evil. The world is broken, and it seems too complex for a superhero to fix it!

Of course, this book is not a superhero manual aimed only at people with exceptional qualities. The qualities we see in superheroes are innate in all of us. We each have a superhero within us. This book is a template to understand the conditions and *empower us* with the tools necessary to rebuild the broken world.

It begins, integrates, and ends with optimizing VALUES. This is the catalyst for transformation as it permeates every fiber of our body and organizations. Or does it? According to Superman, *"there is a right and a wrong in the Universe. And the distinction is not hard to make."* So maybe it has become hard, and we need to realign our compass. Or according to Black Panther, *"Wakanda will no longer watch from the shadows. We cannot. We must not if we want to be a force for connecting mankind and helping those in need. We must find a way to look after one another, as if we were one single tribe. Or maybe we need to transform!"*

Globally, people are in search of a new balance and meaning, what we call *Strategic Harmony*. We need strategies that align Power, augment Love, and reduce resistance to transformational change. Strategic Harmony is a transformative business model for organizational change necessary to generate a sustainable world. Focusing on integrating mind and heart, it is a blueprint for an equitable economy and society able to overcome the conflict-based corruption and greed inherent in our global environment.

It seems that in the present business and political environment, the needs, concerns, and values of citizens, customers, clients, students, members, and voters are not being met. They are expecting change, and a growing number want to become agents of change. Our book targets entrepreneurs and emerging and current leaders of businesses, nonprofits, and institutions, providing tools to realize sustainable impact on the path to transformation. Our objective is to make this text relevant as a roadmap describing the stages and components of Strategic Harmony.

In order to bring life's lessons to our current challenges, we have interspersed the text with teaching stories from many ancient traditions. This provides the reader the opportunity for contemplation and self- reflection...essential elements in the personal transformation process.

Of course, there is still another essential ingredient to make this book relevant. The path to Strategic Harmony should resemble a creative play. For centuries, philosophers called humans the playful creatures. The concept of playing is responsible for happiness, pleasure, success, victory, exploration, prosperity, creativity, learning, socializing, team spirit, and togetherness. The games we play make us who and what we are, help us evolve, grow, learn, socialize, and change the world.

Our childhood and adolescence are best remembered as the playing time, the beautiful age of innocence and curiosity, the joyful years of discovery, the time to explore endless possibilities of Power and Love, in search of unrestrained joy, freedom, and creativity. The broken world can only be changed by people who are able to look at every challenge and issue with the fresh eyes of a curious child.

One more thing: striving for Strategic Harmony requires collaboration. We are grateful to 40 passionate Catalyzers (you will learn more about Catalyzers in subsequent Guideposts) who joined us and shared insights and resources, making this book possible. They helped to guide the development of this sustainable framework aimed at fixing the broken world. They reflect diverse functional perspectives, generations, and cultures, as well as an unswerving commitment to values-based solutions. Their commentaries are integrated throughout the text.

Many of us have heard the following saying, such that it's become a bit over-drawn, but nevertheless contains some good advice:

» Dance as though no one is watching

» Love as though you have never been hurt

» Sing as though no one can hear you

» Live as though heaven is on earth.

We propose an innovative variation on the saying—one that reflects our model of creating a new generation of Catalyzers all over the globe. This book is dedicated to the searchers for Strategic Harmony, to all the people sharing and living the following set of values:

» Speak out as though everyone is listening

» Serve as though everyone is in need

» Collaborate as though there are no boundaries

» Live as though global survival depends on you.

There is more, in keeping with some solutions we offer in the Guideposts to follow:

» Listen as though you feel everyone's pain

» Innovate as though you're open to limitless possibilities

» Create as though no obstacles exist

» Manage as though sustainability is your bottom line.

There is still more, but you will discover it by reading the 14 Guideposts to the transformation journey. Join us in our modest mission to catalyze transformation and create a world of Strategic Harmony!

Introduction

Navroop Sahdev

Our world is consumed with crises. For some, it's political or misinformation. For others, it's the pandemic, and still, for others, it's economic recovery, or burning forests, or the threat of climate change. It is essential not to address these crises as siloed events but to recognize their global interconnectedness. To generate a sustainable future, we must work together to tackle these global challenges.

To align ourselves and create Harmony, we must rise above the individual, national or corporate benefits or self-interest and collaborate to find human-centered solutions. This imperative is the foundation of *EmPower Us!*—empowering our values and purpose to challenge the crisis and fuel transformation.

To transcend the crisis and achieve Harmony, we must design strategies that define our values, how we live those values, and how we consistently incorporate them to build a sustainable future. This book describes them as TEST Values (Trust, Empathy, Sustainability, and Transparency) as catalysts for leadership and organizational transformation. Transformation requires both internal assessment and external accountability to realize tangible change.

In contrast, traditional decision-makers are focused on maintaining the status quo and hardwired to see risk linearly. The book prioritizes guiding these leaders and emerging entrepreneurs to become Catalyzers aligned with a sustainable plan and the intention to realize it. They must challenge their biases, opening themselves to the emergent possibilities of results that they cannot anticipate.

To achieve Strategic Harmony, we need to empower and reinvent our educational systems to generate Catalyzers across all professional disciplines. They must be agile and develop technologies that are unbiased, inclusive, and transparent. Strategic Harmony requires that we embed each of our value sets into a product or service that is focused on and involving all the stakeholders. Catalyzers require the humility to engage with these stakeholders and the empathy to respond to their needs. We need to restore Trust in our emerging technologies around transparency and the impact of these technologies on people, their consciousness, livelihood, choices, and opportunities.

Finally, Sustainability depends on redefining the role of profit, money, or bottom-line, incorporating core Values and Purpose to address all stakeholders' impact. This is central to the message of *EmPower Us!* and achieving Strategic Harmony.

— Navroop Sahdev, CEO, The Digital Economist

Foreword

Professor Philip Kotler

The world is in shambles. There is a perfect storm of poverty, income inequality, greed, corruption, racial and ethnic segregation, tribalism. The coronavirus pandemic is creating huge levels of infection, death and depression. People are divided rather than united. The planet is dangerously heating up. Business leadership seems largely preoccupied with profits, not social issues. Government is dysfunctional and if anything, showing authoritarian tendencies.

Is there any way to bring order and happiness back into this dysfunctional world?

There are many *"fix society"* books. This is one of the best that I have read. I was pleased when the authors, Ira Kaufman and Velimir Srića, invited me to write the Foreword. My own answers to these multiple crises propose building better systems of capitalism and democracy, all moved by the spirit of the Common Good. But Kaufman and Srića went much deeper with their analysis of why societies break down. They contacted citizens, reformers, businesses, nonprofits and government agencies who showed care and who proposed and experimented with innovative solutions on a micro and in some cases on a macro scale.

The authors expand on Heimans and Timms model of Old Power into New Power. They say *"Old Power favors exclusivity, competition, and authority, while the New Power rests on open source collaboration, sharing, and crowd wisdom. Power affects each stage of the Strategic Transformation process."*

EmPower Us! will fill you with hope, purpose and action. More people are challenging injustice and protest the mismanagement of our shared planetary resources. Young people, women, ethnic and other groups are protesting the broken world condition. You will learn about many Catalytic people and communities. The authors describe the inspiring work and values of particular companies – Starbucks, Unilever, Patagonia, Zappos, Ben & Jerry, Ikea, Nike —in running resilient, caring, and creative enterprises. The authors describe the brilliant work of Catalytic individuals – Richard Branson, Elon Musk, Jeff

Bezos, and many others—in innovating fulfilling enterprises and enriching our standard of living.

EmPower Us! provides a wake-up call with 10 Guidelines to shape and motivate the work of caring individuals and organizations. We need to live TEST Values (*Trust, Empathy, Sustainability, and Transparency*) and drive them into our economic, social, and political interactions with our institutions.

The book describes what it would take to change both ourselves and our institutions to generate transformative decisions that reflect the needs of customers, employees, citizens, and communities. The path for people is to collaborate more with others who are working to create a better world. Values provide the foundation, and Purpose translates these values into action and drives transformation.

The book provides a roadmap to transforming the world into a more loving and caring world filled with Harmony. The authors call for "*a balance between what we think (Head), what we do (Hands), what we feel (Heart), and what we Hope (Purpose and Intent).*" They want to bridge the gap between generations, cultures, nations, leaders and the people they represent. They describe a set of values, models, and best practices to build an equitable economy and a sustainable future.

—Professor Philip Kotler, Father of Modern Marketing
Author of *Confronting Capitalism, Advancing the Common Good*

PART I

Assess Where We Are ...
Where Do We Want To Go?

Guidepost 1

Mind the Gap

Our Broken World

"Most people see the world as it is and get frustrated.
We need people who see the world as it could be and decide to change it!"

Our world is broken!

Yes, greed and corruption and unprecedented disruption dominate. We are not living our proclaimed values. Our institutions are dysfunctional.

Our leaders have failed to address the challenges, and we mistrust them. As a planet, we are facing five interrelated pandemics- health, fear/social isolation, economy, environment and misinformation. Our world is broken ... Yes, you probably agree!

But what are the solutions?

EmPower Us! is the call to action. We must change the way we make decisions. We need to listen to each other, respecting and focusing on our shared values. We have to develop and harmonize collective strategies for our mutual benefit. The outcome is Strategic Harmony—the theme of this book.

1

Rising Voices (Next Generation, Women, Marginalized) demand to be heard and scream for change. They see a careless, unthinking monster like the reptilian Godzilla standing over us, with a footprint large enough to trample the whole planet. More and more, people challenge injustice and protest the mismanagement of our shared planetary resources. Organizations admired for their technology and disruption are increasingly filled with these voices—questioning the values of those in leadership.

These Rising Voices cannot be bought with company perks, questionable leadership, or even good intentions. They want action, accountability, and outcomes that solve problems and impact people's lives. But they need to collaborate with more experienced leaders to develop a common plan, a way to bring Strategic Harmony to this broken world.

Bridging the Gap

A wide gap in perception separates world leaders and those demanding accountability. The former are content with the status quo; the latter are intensely frustrated. Rising Voices channel their frustration and effort into making the world a better place, calling for action now. They cry: "Let us in; let us collaborate; let us work with you. We want to solve the world's problems if you would only let us." A broken world needs bridge builders. Those we see as Rising Voices are more than capable of doing this. But the question remains whether today's leaders will let them participate. And give them the power to transform.

However, before we continue, the word "broken" must be fully understood when it comes to the world in which we live. When something physical is broken, it is damaged, impaired, or destroyed. It is inoperative. Stress points have reached or surpassed critical levels. But "broken" applies not only to physical things, but also to the state of human affairs and our values. Brokenness reflects that leaders are not listening to the voices of their constituencies or building trust in the authority and direction of our institutions. There are gaps between what leaders say and what they do.

This takes many forms. Rather than working together in harmony to solve shared problems, we are polarized and divided into partisan factions. We become tribal in our many battles for personal gain. Our governing values are marred by money and politics. A broken world is characterized by political instability, troubled economies, poverty, injustice, international terrorism, global warming, and epidemic levels of depression and other mental illnesses.

Today, we live in a world where norms, habits, and traditions are in a state of flux. Traditional and modern values, habits, and norms are in conflict. However, paradoxically, they may also be fused or coexist in some manner, as "power and love" or "yin and yang." In today's media climate, a speech or a tweet may signal a sudden change of norms that sends shockwaves through our global nervous system. It can also shift behavior at an unprecedented level. This shifting, chaotic environment makes it difficult if not impossible for leaders at all levels to strategize and operate effectively.

At the same time, Next Generation (NextGen) is attracted to an environment of collaboration and sharing. They are driven by the opportunity to replace traditional goals of shareholder financial success with mutual benefit and equitable generation of stakeholder resources. NextGen feels the need to address deteriorated values and demand action that preserves the planet for future generations. They are motivated to innovate, collaborate, and build a sustainable future for everyone. Not surprisingly, they insist on a moral philosophy as an intrinsic part of economic theory. In a study of Americans aged 18 to 29, Harvard University's Polling Director John Della Volpe[1] concluded: *"Millennials... are becoming more motivated—and I believe the fear that exists today about our future will soon be turned into the fuel that will reform our government. The only question is whether this comes from inside or outside the traditional party structure."*

A New Framework

As almost half of humanity comes online, a drastic restructuring of our collective behavior takes place. The planet-wide digital nervous system brings new challenges to the perennial drivers of change—human needs, politics, ecology, culture, and finance. We need a new framework to build a leadership model that supports the new reality, based on sustainability.

The transformation journey must begin inside ourselves by rediscovering and empowering the core that we call TEST Values: building Trust, propelling Empathy, igniting Sustainability, and living Transparency. We also strongly believe that the basic forces that define relationships are Power and Love. These forces combined with our TEST Values are drivers of action and change. They also serve as foundations of this book, Strategic Harmony.

What is Strategic Harmony? Poetically speaking, it's a balance between what we think (Head), what we do (Hands), what we feel (Heart), and what we Hope (Purpose and Intent). Pragmatically, it bridges the gaps! It's a transforming framework necessary to realign our ethical compass and redesign the broken world by bridging the gap between generations, cultures, nations, leaders and the people they represent. It outlines a set of values, models, and best practices to build a sustainable future. We need to look at the challenging conditions in the world through new lenses and mobilize radical, yet collaborative solutions to assess and evaluate our impacts.

However, we need to remember the future is already here in the form of the Rising Voices and catalytic leaders. They *empower us*, sometimes in the streets, sharing their concerns and willingness to sacrifice status and titles to solve the challenges facing humanity. Let's take a closer look at the current state of affairs.

The State of Affairs

Lebanese-American scholar, Nassim Nicholas Taleb, the author of *The Black Swan*, once noted that *"humanity has never faced such deep social and economic problems, and, at the same time, was equipped with such a low level of understanding of the scope and reach of these problems."* Here are some striking examples of these interrelated, conflicting realities.

Managerial economics, as proposed by Milton Friedman in 1970, is built on maximizing shareholder value. From 1980 to 2013, the global economy, driven by that goal of maximizing profits, tripled in size. However, one result has been the rise of income inequality and a rise in poverty. The most opulent 1% of the population control 90% of private wealth. However, the definition of value may be changing. In the past five years, the long-term value of a company has been redefined by digital technologies and eco-innovation. Eco-innovative companies are growing at a rate of 15% per year, while their respective markets have remained flat. Such a transformative, stakeholder-centric economy, built upon core values, will drive greater inclusivity, equality, and opportunities for sustainable prosperity. Despite the current stock market recovery, economic problems are deep-seated in many regions of the world. This has resulted in the collapse of social programs, higher unemployment, and the impoverishment of millions of people. We need a global strategy and programs to address these issues and bridge the fundamental gaps.

Global System Change provides a holistic approach to achieving sustainability and transformation. It is based on Einstein's idea that we must think at a higher level to solve our most complex challenges. All major aspects of human society are interconnected parts of the whole Earth system. We cannot effectively address them in isolation. However, considering all parts of society at once can be highly complex. To simplify the processes, we often break society into parts and study them without adequate reference to the larger system that contains them. This reductionism ignores relevant factors and produces often unintended consequences, such as widespread environmental and social degradation. And some of the damage is, unfortunately, not unintentional because many companies and governments are aware of the damage caused by some of their practices, but they may opt instead to cover it up, or perhaps they don't care. The solution is to think at a higher, whole-system level. Global System Change integrates all major aspects of society and provides effective, systemic solutions to the major challenges facing humanity.

Political gridlock also inhibits innovative, collaborative action. Many of the world's most influential politicians are rightly seen as untrustworthy, corrupt, and unethical. Even though they keep talking about change, they are nothing but bureaucrats fighting for power. We need a critical mass of hero-innovators to displace these influencers—trustworthy and ethical leaders dedicated to sustainable change. We need persistent idealists ready and able to transform the world into a better place.

Global nutrition, or the lack thereof, is a major concern. Many people either starve or practice unhealthy lifestyles. One-fifth of the world population faces obesity while one-fifth suffers from malnutrition. Conversely, a third of all food produced for human consumption—about 1.3 billion tons annually, at a value of more than $1 trillion—is thrown away. Living our core values more consistently, including prioritizing a healthy, less wasteful lifestyle, could potentially allow us to feed all people.

Global cultural ecosystems have turned into bad taste, mass consumerism, a marketing-driven swamp, instead of promoting values-driven purposeful products and services that increase the quality of life and sustainability of our planet. Digital technologies and shared value for all stakeholders can serve as a bridge to diffuse a more sustainable global culture.

Education as a global standard is still engaged in regurgitation of content and striving for grades instead of cherishing creativity and breakthrough transformative learning. Education must go back to its roots as stimulating learning and discovery. Lifelong learning and digital collaboration ignite opportunities to address the challenges faced by humanity.

Global media are easy access sources of real-time information, but can they be trusted? Often our daily feed is biased or sometimes fake, and thus does not provide access to trusted, dependable sources. We have the technology and resources to provide authentic news that will rebuild the trust in our media.

Anthropocene era is it the current historical epoch which human activities (technology, governance, business, climate change), became the primary driver of many existential threats on our planet. Our business and political leaders are challenged to live their proclaimed values and transform their decisions and investments to support the achievement of Agenda 2030 Sustainable Development Goals.[2]

Rising Voices are echoing globally their demand to be heard and included. Following the footsteps of Greta Thunberg, the Next Generation is taking to the streets protesting the unwillingness of politicians, businesses, and global organizations to take control of global climate change. Women are outspoken as both elected representatives and directing initiatives that tackle the challenges of humanity. While the Marginalized, those who live on the fringe of a country (e.g., America) and are excluded from the "American dream," demand equal opportunity, rights, and universal access.

Why, despite our access to powerful technological innovations, are we unable to address most of these burning issues?

Why are we still pursuing questionable goals, trusting the same unsustainable pathways and accepting the old excuses that block purposeful action?

The problem lies in our deteriorating values and unwillingness to empower our core values. Because of these conflicting realities or Gaps, we allow the health and direction of our planet to deteriorate, even though we have the potential to reverse this process.

The Solution ... Address the Gaps

Empower Us! with *Strategic Harmony* looks through new lenses at the challenging conditions and mobilizes radical, yet collaborative solutions, to assess and evaluate our impact on the future.

We must self-reflect on how: (1) we live our core values, (2) we use/misuse our resources, (3) we engage our communities, and (4) our leaders direct our institutions. Change begins with transforming our mindset. Let's take a closer look at the Gaps.

1. Core Values

We are and do what we believe. Our core values drive mindset which leads to action and creates outcomes. If we reject the outcomes, we must question the values, beliefs, and mindset. As Albert Einstein[3] noted: *"We cannot solve our problems with the same thinking we used when we created them."* It is obvious that the values we preach are not the values we live by. John Steinbeck[4] defined the Gap as *"…the things we admire in men [indeed all of humanity], kindness and generosity, openness, honesty, understanding, and feeling, are the concomitants of failure in our system. And those traits we detest, sharpness, greed, acquisitiveness, meanness, egotism, and self-interest, are the traits of success. And while men [indeed everyone] admire the quality of the first, they love the produce of the second."*

2. Resources

We have vast resources including capital, technologies, knowledge and expertise. Most of these resources are focused on ourselves, our businesses, and our personal success, and not serving others, our communities, or the sustainability of our planet. Herein lies the Gap: we must transform these resources into assets and optimize them for all stakeholders, empowering innovation and synergy to create sustainable outcomes and harmony for our failed systems.

3. Communities

We are networked to local and global communities of resources and people. Thousands, even millions, of people may know and interact and share our interests. The Gap is: how are we leveraging these connections to foster trust and real collaboration for scalable sustainable impact? In reality, most networks are not relationship-focused, or built upon the principles of sharing and scaling global solutions that benefit all.

4. Leaders

The majority of executives, businesspeople, administrators, and managers don't interact with or listen to the stories of their constituencies. They do not have the courage and flexibility to act upon what they see, hear, and feel. It's also a common perception among many workers or constituents that executives, managers, chairpersons, and the like, do not care about those under their direction, and that not caring leads to not listening. This one-way, top-down communication has created a Gap in trust between elected leaders and citizens, and between executives and their stakeholders and employees. The Edelman Trust Barometer 2018[5] supports these conclusions as it reveals reduced trust across the institutions of government, business, media, and NGOs. The credibility of leaders dropped to an all-time low of 37%, plummeting in every country studied. Trust in media is at an all-time low in 17 countries, while the government is the least trusted institution in half of the 28 countries surveyed. There is a steep decline in the United States, with a 37-point aggregate drop in trust across all institutions. At the opposite end of the spectrum, China experienced a 27-point gain. The Gap is the discrepancy between public trust and trust in Chinese brands abroad. These statistics reveal a growing polarization between citizens and market economy.

We are surrounded by conflicting realities and linked dualisms, e.g., polarized citizens protecting their turf vs electors striving for harmonious/sustainable solutions; egotistical leaders vs empathic "servant leaders;" concentrated wealth vs efforts to reduce poverty; escalating unemployment vs expanding high tech jobs; radicalized alienated youth vs inspired millennials; exploding technologies healing the planet vs destroying the world order. By connecting and linking these opposite forces, we accept their divisive nature as the norm that continues to influence our thoughts and our actions. These less than value-neutral dualities and polarities accentuate the Gap in our minds, hearts, actions, and intents widening the fissure in our society between leaders' promises and people-action.

In each case, the different situations are outcomes of conflicting values and mindsets that drive behavior.

> » If we want new outcomes, we need to transform our mindset.

> » If we want organizational transformation, we must acknowledge and challenge the Gaps between our words and actions.

> » If we want to build the systemic change, we need to challenge the linked polarities in society that have become the norm and myths they have created that underpin our thinking.

The importance of a mindset shift is reflected in the following story.

The Monkey Cage Lesson

This classic study demonstrates the empowering of a false narrative as the basis for myths.[6]

Imagine a cage with five monkeys. You hang a bunch of bananas at the cage top and place a ladder nearby. Soon, a monkey climbs the ladder, trying to get some bananas. The moment the monkey touches the ladder, you sprinkle all the animals with ice-cold water and they quickly back off. Soon, another monkey goes for the ladder, just to find out that the ice-cold-water situation is still there. From that moment on, you don't need the sprinkler anymore. If a monkey even tries to get close to the ladder, other monkeys are sure to knock him or her flat.

Now, you remove one monkey from the cage and replace him or her with a newcomer. Seeing the bananas, he or she tries to reach for the ladder, only to find his or her ass kicked by all others. You replace another monkey with a new one. If that monkey tries to reach for the ladder, he or she is severely beaten by all, including the former newcomer. Repeat the procedure until the initial five are removed from the cage. Regardless of the fact that none of the remaining monkeys has ever been sprinkled with ice-cold water, none of them ever tries to get the bananas because, if he did, he would immediately be stopped by all the others. Why? They have learned the way things are done here. And who are they to question the common practice?

The monkey cage metaphor explains how values and beliefs lead to behavior. Also, it perfectly describes nations, tribes, employees, politicians, or citizens who accept the prevailing norms and values without questioning them. Remember the Germans under Hitler? The Soviets under Stalin? The Founding Fathers of the USA, many of whom were slave owners? And the tale of the Emperor who had no clothes? We know what happens when people just accept the existing values and don't question the inherent contradictions, limitations, and shortcomings of a simple story.

Isn't the world broken because we are trapped in the monkey cage of the old economic, social and political values? Strange, crazy, even outrageous things are constantly taking place around us, and we are treating them as normal. Expanding polarization and feelings of hopelessness have translated into a world suffering from epidemic depression and growing numbers of people turning to false narratives, conspiracy theories, opioids, and even violent acts of opposition as a response. At the same time, NextGen screams to have their voices heard. They want to work for and purchase products and services from companies that respect and live their values.

Most politicians try to persuade us that the world is not broken. With 60% of the global population relying on social media as the only source of news, many cannot determine the difference between real and fake news. It is this Gap in critical thinking that politicians exploit. We must be patient and learn to live with all the discrepancies while vigilantly taking action to remove their root causes. Like in a joke about a guy, falling from a twenty- story building. As he passes by the tenth floor, his phone rings, and a friend asks him: How are you doing today? So far, so good, replies the guy.

Global Cage of Myths

So what is the result? We have adjusted to the myths that reinforced our broken world and misaligned our ethical compass. We have engendered a mindset where billions of humans and our leaders are trapped in what we believe to be a global cage of myths—a web of interconnected half-truths, misinformation that remains unquestioned and supported by a false narrative that elicits strong polarized emotions in people. Myths may seem unconvincing and harmless; however, when we think of them as emerging from a bombardment of images and news, the effect of their impact heightens, creating strong emotions that linger in our mind for a long time. Myths add color to false narratives that become solidified into commonly accepted truths, based on the body of untrue statements that become absolute truths.

The real threat here is that such "myths" are the stories and ideas that lead our behavior, and create (both undesirable and desirable) outcomes that influence our actions in three ways: positive, negative and neutral (even neutral carries a value as in chemistry).

When myths are used by leaders as truths, they become trust breakers. Myths create a Trust Gap in society between the original false narrative and the lesser audience that carries the voice of the legitimate news. In this context, we generated 20 myths that guide our broken world, related to leadership and organizational transformation. They are by no means exhaustive:

1. Successful leaders must control information and decisions in their interest.
2. We are happy and secure only with people we are familiar with, in terms of religion, culture, ethnicity, and gender.
3. Nobody is unbiased, and everyone has an agenda; so don't trust anyone.
4. Asking forgiveness is a weakness; empathetic people are lame.
5. Sustainability is just focused on our environment. Our resources are constantly growing and being replenished; there's no need to be restrained.
6. You can lie about anything, as everyone does it and as long as you don't get caught.
7. Admitting you're wrong or made a mistake or don't have complete knowledge is not acceptable and needs to be covered up.
8. Taking a risk and failing is bad; it's not a learning experience.
9. Strive to win, be right and in control; compromise is a sign of weakness.
10. A successful product is based on sales revenue only.
11. It's a waste of resources to collect data that you don't have any use.
12. The experience of senior executives is the key to success in the complex world.
13. Efficient, profit-centered departments increase business innovation in digital age.
14. We have done things for many years quite successfully; there is no need to change.
15. Customer satisfaction is a very good intention, but shouldn't be expected.
16. You are what you "possess;" money opens all doors and is the key to success.
17. Sharing of ideas and collaborating is dangerous; it's better to exploit ideas by yourself.
18. A university degree prepares you for future jobs in the growingly complex world.
19. Innovation is determined by the capacity of the current team.
20. Return on Investment (ROI) is the best tool to measure success of businesses and organizations.

Now you've considered these 20 myths. Take a moment to think of which of these myths you have adopted in your daily life, and a few more we haven't listed here.

Behind each of these myths, there is a belief underpinning a resulting action to bridge the gap between acting with purpose and acting only with financial progress. The climate crisis is caused by the Gap between siloed, traditional decision-making leaders vs. sustainable impact-driven, decision-making leadership that is at the foundation of transformative solutions.

The Gap exists between the ambiguity and the tension between action and inaction; between promises and real performance; between inclusion and exclusion; and between the culture of control and a culture of change. It is Strategic Harmony that is required to bridge these Gaps.

Throughout the book, we share how these myths are associated with solutions or values from our Strategic Harmony five-stage model to align purpose and progress with the sustainability goals.

Of course, in order to realize a more sustainable world, we must replace these and similar myths. But, first, we must transform ourselves, our mindset, and values. We must strive for Strategic Harmony. Is it possible? How does it work?

EmPower Us! provides a road map for transformation. It proposes a breakthrough in thinking about institutions and the false "truths" we accept, take for granted, and live by. It offers a resilient approach to managing and innovating.

We believe that the journey toward transformation must begin internally with rediscovering the TEST Values. Also, we strongly believe that the basic forces that define relationships, once again, are Power and Love. These forces combined with our values are drivers of action and change serving as the foundations for Strategic Harmony.

Guidepost 2

Strategic Harmony
ABCD's of Transformation

In Guidepost 1, we have outlined the conditions and myths that reflect that our world is broken. We may agree or disagree with some details, but concur on the need to address the global condition of brokenness. The established rules and norms are disrupted; economy inequitable; governance corrupted; and citizen dialogue entrenched and partisan. There is a lack of trust in our major institutions, a deterioration of our values, and conflicting ideologies between generations.

For the most part, we are stuck in stale and outdated thinking, facing the results of unsustainable choices made by our business and political leaders. Why has there not been a response to the changes called for by the NextGen, students, women, employees, voters and connected consumers globally?

However, before we discuss a solution, let's gain some insight by combining Sleeping Beauty[7] with an old Chinese story[8]. A King and Queen celebrated the seventh birthday of their young Princess. They invited four fairies to present the child with a magic gift. Each brought a box with the name of the gift. The first was Wealth, the second Success, the third Well-being, and the fourth Harmony. "You can pick only one of the four," the fairies explained. "That's our rule."

The King said: "Surely you pick Wealth, and then you will have a good life!" The Queen was unsure. "No, choose Success! We want to be proud of our daughter!" The King was still in doubt, and said, "Or maybe well-being is the most important!" The Princess looked at the parents in distress. "You seem to disagree. I will pick Harmony then."

When she said that, the fairies handed her all four boxes. "How come?" asked the King and Queen, "Isn't that against the rule?"

"Oh, we have another rule," replied the fairies. "If you pick Harmony, you also get Well-Being, Success and Wealth." In other words, the model of Strategic Harmony.

In this Guidepost, we introduce you to the basic mind frames necessary to achieve Strategic Harmony.

The condition of our world reflects the misalignment and abuse of two forces— Power and Love, and the deterioration of our will to bridge the gap between our intentions and sustainable actions.

We corrupt Power for own self-interest, while twisting Love as an infatuation with money, fame, and greed. The remedy is to flip the broken model and transform these forces.

Transformative Power is anchored in higher purpose; Transformative Love emanates from consistently living our highest values. The book strategically analyzes the gaps between: what we intend and what we say; what we value and how we expend our resources; and how we act and how we impact our community. Reconciling these gaps creates harmony, direction, and sustainability.

Strategic Harmony is a transformative blueprint for an equitable economy and sustainable society. It harmonizes two disparate forces, Power and Love, through values-driven strategies to generate workable outcomes. Focusing on integrating the mind and heart, Strategic Harmony is a model for organizational transformation that results in mutual stakeholder benefit, well-being, and sustainability. It requires collaboration to implement and scale.

Beginning ... Point of No Return

Strategic Harmony begins with *empowering us*, the mindset transformation within each of us. It translates to the organization and its culture, is transmitted to its stakeholders, and then scaled to communities and networks.

Why do we need a new mindset? Transformation is so broad in scope; it requires expanded thinking and a new strategic business model that reflects the challenges of today's world. We can't base our actions on an old mindset, one based on premises that don't work. We are immersed in a digital global economy facing an acceleration in the speed of innovation, changes in climate, and digital transformation with unexpected outcomes and exponential scale that we've never experienced. Therefore, our approach to transformation must reflect the flexibility and power of our current challenges.

The metamorphosis of a larva into a butterfly is a metaphor that provides context. This transition is sometimes defined as the moment of singularity. It's a space of total openness to change and complete transformation when the changes in civilization are so vast or different that previous generations would not have been able to comprehend them. Historians often call this a point of no return. Thomas Kuhn would call it a new paradigm that manifests a better framework containing new assumptions, ways of thinking, and methodology that replace the old mindset that no longer explains the world around us and no longer deals with its problems in an efficient way.[2]

New paradigms have always depended on new leadership. As suggested by John F Kennedy, *"It's time for a new generation of leadership because there is a new world to be won."* In the emerging world order, the Rising Voices must be incorporated in the leadership determining the solutions for the future. They are the bridge between Old Capital and New Capital. These Rising Voices redefine Power as passion and Love, as well as the equitable use of resources.

If we think the same, we act the same, and we accomplish the same. If we think differently, we act differently, and we change. If a "point of a no return situation" takes place in our private or business life, or on a global scale, it means that we need different leadership, bringing along a different mindset and values to address the challenges we face today that impact us tomorrow.

Today, all leaders, executives (e.g., business, government, and social sectors) in particular, are positioned to play a major role in defining this transformation. They need to face that we are in a historical position which requires a new action paradigm. Many of the new rules and technologies are "incomprehensible to old generations." We must let go of the myths that control our "opening up," and keep us "caged" in an old world order. Like the caterpillar, we need to develop new capabilities to prepare for the transformation of the larva into a beautiful butterfly—a totally new, "strategically harmonized" being with open wings that can fly!

Revolution Becomes a "Refolution"—a Brand New World

Are we talking about a revolution? Yes, as Marianne Williamson suggests *"There is a revolution occurring in the world today, but it is not fought with armies and it does not aim to kill. It is a revolution of consciousness."* Yes, we are experiencing dramatic changes in the way our world works. Witness the converging of six "revolutions in mindset" that is taking place globally:

» Revolution in Values reflects the growing lack of Trust in leaders and institutions. Organizations must rewrite and strengthen the trust equation for each stakeholder and integrate it as its DNA.

» Purposeful Revolution reflects a shift among employees, customers, and investors to become a force for good in society and the environment. Purposeful companies perform better on every traditional metric: greater customer loyalty, higher retention, more innovation, and a healthier bottom line.

» Sustainability Revolution reflects a recent manifesto[10] issued by Lombard Odier Bank, first established in Switzerland in 1796. *"It's a revolution that touches every aspect of all 7.6 billion lives on this planet: energy, transport, food systems, population growth, healthcare, education, data management. We believe it represents the biggest investment opportunity in history."*

» Revolution in Stakeholder Value reflects the transition to Responsible Finance. Bankers, investors, and fund managers acknowledge that sustainable financial models can secure future prosperity. Impact investing is more than a fad; it's a movement that brings Value to all stakeholders.

» Digital Revolution reflects the global imperative for all organizations (politics, business, nonprofits) to transform, to leverage the power of digital to listen and respond to their constituencies; to connect globally in real time; and to use data to personalize content.

» Silent Revolution reflects the confrontation of the silence of business and political leaders on climate change. It speaks to the alternative imperative: the Rising Voices of youth climate activists protesting for immediate collaborative action to address the threats of climate change.

We have already mentioned less quiet "revolutions" happening in various parts of the world, from yellow vests in France to movements fighting against arms, for climate change, or for women's rights all over the world. In all these cases, people are dissatisfied with the values preached and even more with the values lived. They are walking the streets in protest.

It has become clear that we need politicians and businesspeople who listen and serve, who represent their markets' needs and not the selfish desires of the few driven by money, power, and greed. It's a revolution for those positive, humane values calling out for a more ethical, just, and caring world order. However, we don't advocate force or violence; hence, we call it refolution[11], a combination of revolutionary change in mindset and constant, gradual reforms.

The Model

You might still think that "Strategic" and "Harmony" don't fit together. Let's view the Strategic Harmony Map (Figure 2.1) to address how transformation occurs. Personal Transformation drives Strategic Transformation, merging the mind and the heart; Power and Love; analytics with sustainable outcomes. So: let's examine how strategic interfaces with harmony, and why we use that expression.

» *"Strategic"* because it's driven by specific intentions to create a values-driven plan that is inclusive and trusting, empathetic, sustainable, and transparent. It is Strategic as it must adjust the response to the forces affecting "refoulutionary transformation" (e.g., values, purpose, stakeholders, digital, impact investing, sustainability).

» *"Harmony"* because it is a congruent combination of varied cultural values and mindsets resulting in win-win outcomes, and shattering our status quo. Harmony unifies the Love and Purpose of all stakeholders to generate alignment. It is collaborative, empowering well-being, and strengthening sustainability efforts.

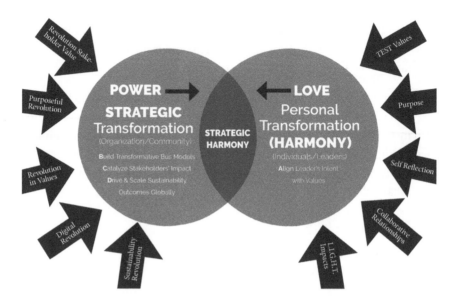

Figure 2.1 Strategic Harmony Map

Strategic Harmony defines the intersection between Transformation (both Personal and Strategic) and the ABCDs of Transformation (how it is implemented).

» Align values and intent with leaders

» Build transformative business models

» Catalyze stakeholder impact

» Drive and scale outcomes globally

The Application

How do change leaders (or as we call them Catalyzers in Guidepost 5) to transform these forces into strategies that fuel sustainable social impacts?

Our journey is circular with five values-driven modules (Figure 2.2). Each supports the objective of attaining Strategic Harmony and builds upon one another. It starts with Drivers and ends with L.I.G.H.T. Impacts. Our approach balances Power and Love and applies the TEST Values to drive the transformation process.

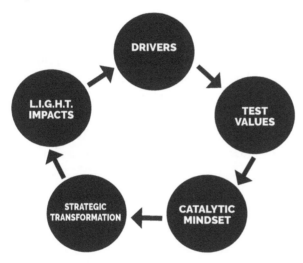

Figure 2.2 Strategic Harmony Model

Let's take a short dive into each module. Our goal is to demonstrate that elements of this model are operational in diverse sectors and organizations globally. The model is a testimonial that a purposeful, Quadruple Bottom Line approach to transformation works and is sustainable. Their best practices can be translated to every organization and all conditions.

Drivers

Our model starts with the Drivers, the ignition of the Strategic Harmony process. Since everything that we do is 'driven' by a constant balance between Power and Love, we use these two forces as the focus to the catalytic process that fuels transformation. The organization's values and ethics influence the transformation as the framework expands outward, powering the direction of the organization and impacting institutional societal/outcomes.

What drives individual and organizational change?

We had a chat with Dr. Joe Turek, Dean of the Business School of Christian Brothers University (a values-based institution) on understanding why peoples' values and actions are changing in the current Information Age. As an economist, he sees behavior through the lens of "self-interest." Or as Adam Smith posited, "rational" self-interest explains the actions producers and consumers take, making exchanges that leave both parties better off than before the exchange; both sides benefit, either intrinsically, financially, or both.

The lively discussion challenged us to reflect and expand our thinking on what are the real drivers of transformation. Our Strategic Harmony model begins with two internal factors (based on Love) driving transformation and two external factors (based on Power) affecting leaders and organizations. Leaders must leverage these Drivers to ignite transformation (Figure 2.3).

Internal Driver - Spiritual Connection

» Transformative Love – self-reflecting on values and purpose directing actions

» Good against evil – striving to "conquer evil" (higher calling of a super-hero)

» Self-actualization – acquiring material possessions is replaced with sustainable priorities

Internal Driver - Self-interest

» Self-preservation – leaders fear the loss of job, company, and viability for future generations

» Self-worth – people lack confidence in traditional institutions such as higher education, economic systems, career mobility

» Powerlessness – NextGen, Women, and Marginalized feel excluded, and this drives action to be heard and involved

External Driver - Digitization

» Transformative Power – leverage digital resources (unlimited search, easily publish content, access abundant data, crowdfund support, mobilize networks)

» Business Transparency – respond to social distrust and gap in values and business decision-making

External Driver - Leadership

» Transformation – fueled by disruption, changes in mindset

» Customer response–driven by feedback

» Disruptive environment – ignited by social movements, environmental disasters, technology

The Drivers reflect the Chinese *yin/yang* that describes how the opposite forces give rise to each other as they interrelate to one another. It is important to note that Love and Power can be labeled as positive and negative and internal and external.

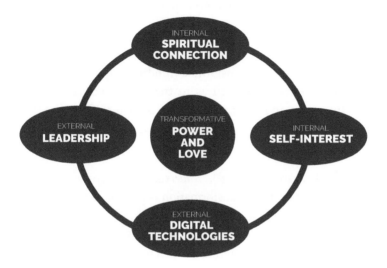

Figure 2.3 Drivers

New Power is a major motivator in 21st Century organizations. We contrast Old Power, garnered from outside sources (position, family, money) and controlled, with Transformative Power generated from both inside (beliefs, values, ethics, and purpose) and outside (information/data and digital assets) and the resulting Transparency.

Furthermore, we contrast the Old Love which is selfish and controlling with the Transformative Love which is supportive and enriching. The Old is like a chain; the Transformative gives you wings. According to Nicholas Sparks,[12] *"The best love is the kind that awakens the soul; that makes us reach for more, that plants the fire in our hearts and brings peace to our minds."* Obviously, we (the authors of this book) are strong believers in Transformative Love and Transformative Power. Combined, they are the heart and soul of transformation that will fix our broken world.

The idea behind our Drivers is that transformation is driven from within and from without—from within by our spirit; our struggle and self-reflection with values, ethics, morality (good and evil) and priorities; and by our self-interest, including factors that affect our security, career, and lifestyle. These Drivers are not new to this age; but in World 4.0 they are significantly affected by explosive digital technologies, and transformed by our access to vast volumes of real-time information, instant transparency of data, how we reflect on it, leverage it, and judge it, giving powerful feedback to our institutions and leaders.

Digital technologies are coupled with Leadership as the Drivers from without, initiating change based on a transformed mindset, responding to market and environmental disruptions, as well as to the Rising Voices of citizens and customers. Internally and externally-driven change is faster, constant, and overwhelming; it disrupts us from within and transforms how we think and act!

According to W. Edwards Deming[13], "*leaders and their organizations are designed to get the results that they get.*" Transformation is possible only if the executives, the leadership team, and the organizational culture allow themselves to be "vulnerable," striving for Strategic Harmony. Leaders who are intimate with the focus of the change, transparent and open to that change, and listening to their constituencies, will drive harmonious solutions, based on a common and agreed-upon purpose. Strategic Harmony is driven by Transformative Love and Transformative Power!

TEST Values

How will the Drivers initiate transformation? Where will Leadership take us? It depends on their values. Transformation starts when an organization manages to pass the TEST (Trust, Empathy, Sustainability, and Transparency). These values must be aligned to an ethical standard, a compass that goes beyond local cultural morals. The TEST integrates values and ethics to benchmark the strength and potential of an organization to bring forth change in the marketplace or society. The values of each team member should be congruent, harmonizing to build and sustain the organization's culture. (See Guidepost 3)

Let's look at examples of how these values drive transformation.

Catalytic Mindset

Catalytic Mindset consists of four "think lenses." Each lens demands us to reset the way we think about and approach a threat or opportunity. The Catalytic Mindset (see Guidepost 9) is authentic, open, and values-driven, focusing on organizational purpose. In contrast, the traditional company's mindset is driven by Old Power controlling communication, consumer and employee input, market strategies, and product design.

In organizations facing transformation, the executive team must determine a clear purpose to define its goals and direction. In our Strategic Harmony framework the organization's, WHY becomes the soul and spirit of the organization, generating Transformative Power.

Strategic Transformation

The next module generates a roadmap for Strategic Transformation (See Guidepost 10) to design, guide, and support initiatives to fix what is broken. These activities—organizational change, purposeful design, digital transformation, and social impact, must be aligned with the values and mindset. They drive the concentric circle of operational activities that lead to total transformation.

L.I.G.H.T. Impacts

The integration of values with the mindset and operational activities is reflected as purposeful solutions at the societal level. We call it the principle of LIGHT. There are five L.I.G.H.T. Impacts (see Guidepost 12) that bring harmony and sustainability to any organization or business:

1. Lifelong Learning
2. Innovation Engine
3. Good Governance
4. Holistic Living
5. Transformative Economics

These five impacts define the action steps and sustainable solutions necessary to fix the broken world and transform organizations. They reflect the assets of the organization manifested at the community or societal level. Each of these impacts works both independently and interactively to propel change, heal, and illuminate organizations through the TEST Values. If we "place LIGHT" on our darkened (broken) organizations, transformation begins realigning their values and actions with purpose, reenergizing them, and bringing them to life. The principle of L.I.G.H.T. brings balance and sustainability to organizations; thus, organizations need to incorporate these impacts into the design of social ventures, businesses, community action groups, and institutions as they strive to transform.

It's the Journey, not the Destination that Counts

Strategic Harmony is a goal in the transformation journey, not a destination in progress. It is a model for personal and organization transformation. Our present culture is dominated by Old Power, competition, conflict, and the Darwinian survival of the fittest. It forces companies to do whatever it takes to make profit and grow, be it cheap child labor, wars to protect economic interests, or ecologically disruptive resource utilization. It makes the whole society insensitive to a growing gap between the rich and the poor, and leads to an overall lack of humanity and solidarity.

Strategic Harmony is a blueprint for an equitable economy and society able to overcome the conflict-based and anarchic nature of capitalism, and shift the focus from competition, growth, and profit toward mutual benefit, Love, well-being, and sustainability.

So how do we realize this goal?

Socrates shares his insights, "*The secret of change is to focus all your energy not on fighting the old, but building the new.*"

To achieve the purposeful impact necessary to sustain our planet, we propose to transform our emerging and current leaders into a cadre of Catalyzers (see Guidepost 5) with the required agility and laser-focused direction. This new generation of leaders must expand their capacity to apply four core actions: the ABCD's of Strategic Transformation.

Align leader's intent with values

We begin with Harmony through aligning leader's intent with TEST Values. As leaders transform into Catalyzers, they are anchored by their Purpose and empower their operations and strategies through living these values. Consistently embedding these values generates the power to impact a genuine stakeholder experience and achieve sustainable outcomes. Harnessing strategic skills (inclusivity, collaboration, targeted disruption) allows Catalyzers to realign blockages in the ecosystem by consistently harmonizing their values with their customers and organization culture.

Build transformative business models

As the Catalyzer applies these different lenses, the business model is transformed: new catalytic strategies evolve and produce new outcomes. The rules of the enterprise change! It is driven by all stakeholders' rather than shareholders' interests – translating purpose and values to reflect social needs and business priorities. The corporate strategy paradigm must shift transforming the predatory business model into models that support and sustain harmony. These models incorporate human-centered business practices, ESG (Environmental, Social, and Corporate Governance) criteria and circular/regenerative design to achieve win-win social impact as well as profit.

Catalyze stakeholders' impact

Driven by a Catalytic Mindset, sustainable ventures harmonize profit with achieving the 17 UN Sustainable Development Goals. They mobilize stakeholders across sectors to collaborate and catalyze investment to generate a Quadruple Bottom Line (explained in Guidepost 3). Systematic monitoring and holistic assessment of impact is vital and necessary to reduce risk and bridge the gap between available capital investment and the exploding need for impact investment to drive system change.

Drive and scale sustainable outcomes globally

Sustainable ventures with proven impact must be scaled to fuel Global Social Change (GSC). Catalyzers must ignite "this sustainability revolution...as the largest investment driver in history" by confronting outdated mindsets and resolving existing gaps between words and actions. They require new integrated venues/networks and funding sources to drive and scale regenerative solutions that "*fundamentally rethink established norms in areas including transport, food systems, healthcare, education, data management, and infrastructure*"[14] They must lead in the current world and beyond.

The ABCDs are designed to harmonize strategic inputs to achieve successful sustainable impact. They are not siloed, but build upon each other to generate the required and intended outcomes. Critical to GSC is building networks of Catalyzers, anchored in purpose, who will collaborate across sectors and functions to access the impact investment required to implement Strategic Transformation.

Our model presents a set of solutions and tools that require strong leadership throughout the organization aligned with values and intent to accomplish the goal. There is no alternative to individual initiative and collaborative action. Each of us must live our values to start this process; take the initiative, and contribute through our actions. We must build transformative business models and organizations that challenge/disrupt the traditional business rules that accelerate transformation. These business models catalyze impact among all stakeholders. They expand the intent and purpose of the business beyond just investors to all those that connect with the product or service, including customer, employee, partner, and community. Finally, the model develops and scales the digital media and communications to spread the message and transform broken values on which many of our institutions, products, and services are built.

This book has five parts to reflect the ABCDs of Transformation.

Let's conclude the Guidepost with yet another poetic discourse. Our model ends with L.I.G.H.T. Impacts that have a great influence on every individual, business, and society. They are ongoing, transformative, and synergistic.

- » <L> earn as if there are no boundaries.
- » <I> nnovate as though you're open to limitless possibilities.
- » <G> overn as though you feel everyone's pain.
- » <H> eal as though no obstacles exist.
- » <T> ransform as though sustainability is your bottom line.

PART II

Align Values and Intent with Leaders

Guidepost 3

Values Matter

Where Have All Our Values Gone?

"Your beliefs become your thoughts, your thoughts become your words, your words become your actions, your actions become your habits, your habits become your values, and your values become your destiny."

Mahatma Gandhi

A teacher of Zen noticed that some of his students had a habit of constantly complaining about the same problem. One day he told them a joke and everyone roared in laughter. A couple of minutes later he told them the same joke and only a few of them smiled. In half an hour he repeated the joke and no one laughed. Then the teacher said: You can't laugh at the same joke all the time. Why do you keep crying about the same problem?

Despite the story, we typically pursue the same problem. Why is the world broken? Globally, voices are "screaming" for solutions, but sustainable actions are sporadic. But to break the cycle, we need to address the root causes!

What is fueling this problem? The deterioration of values and institutions! We see the signs of distorted behavior and broken rules everywhere.

The Value of VALUES

Today's global imperative is to aggregate diverse populations for the common good, affirming universal values. We must use these core values to neutralize the growing tribalization and nation-centric mentality that seeks to impose doctrine and ideology upon individuals and groups who appear culturally and ideologically different from those that embrace extremism, outmoded hierarchal social and business models, and who abjure collaborative and open source design thinking What used to be 'faith' in a product, institution, or a moral or ethical imperative for social responsibilities has degenerated into being self-centered, narcissistic obsession with "I" and "mine"; again abandoning the core human imperative to care for others with the same concern and effort one cares for themselves. So the compassion and love and duty at the basis of virtually every major faith have become transformed into a selfish affirmation that elevates suspicion or fear of 'the other' over human concern.

Universal values are the foundational architecture of human beings. That means that the road to adopting and sustaining positive transformative value-principles, of absorbing and reflecting them, lies in the transcendental realm of spiritually grounded ideas and practices, not in religious or secular dogma and ideology. Values are the foundation of profoundly humane actions, values that transcend a tribal survival mentality that eventually gives rise to demeaning 'the other'...whether the 'other' is a different human being or a competitor in commerce. Affirming and articulating love and compassion, peace and patience, justice and equality is the beginning of transformation. In the world of commerce and social action, it applies equally to the need for strategic planning, economic development, and transformation of whole societies.

We are at a crossroads in history, a global society where individuals are influenced moment by moment by material and emotional attractors. The future demands that this process becomes more and more conscious lest we are more and more misled by the attractor that feeds our negative fears and prejudices and not our natural inclinations toward harmony and goodness. Our purpose is to present the questions and the illustrations

---

that reinforce and transform others, that affirm the core values of being part of a global transformation (for the good or for the bad). Nations are no longer only physical entities; how can we assure or even influence its citizenry toward positive values and Strategic Harmony? That is the only question to ask of our higher self.

J. E. Rash, Founder and President, Legacy International

Here is a futuristic story by Tariq Qureishy that points to the possibility of integrating values and ethics in our decision-making.

"Everything will change ... Nothing will change!"

The "child of the future,", Ayesha was born on 00:01, 2001, at the stroke of midnight. This is the turn of a new millennia, a new century, a new age, a new vision for the world we live in.

As Ayesha prepares to go on a journey into the future, in a majestic time-machine she sits with a wise "sage and his students" before they fly away into the future. He sat them all down and gave them the following guidance as they go on their time travels. The sage said that the pillars on which the future will thrive are "trust, ethics, humanity, values, and empathy".

Technology is important but always subservient to these core values and life principles. He said, just keep these in mind first, look at everything, through this lens, particularly technology and science, and you will always find your way through the maze of future transformation. If you forget or ignore it, the intended and unintended consequences could potentially be catastrophic.

Therefore, our basic core values and life principles will define the future of the world and Ayesha's place in it. Technology and other developments will essentially be there to serve the nation. Therefore, embrace technology, use it but always keep in charge of the AI, data and the processes.

It is like riding a horse. The horse is 10 times stronger, faster and bigger; however, we ride it and manage it with a bit of discipline, love, and empathy. That is how we manage science and technology in the future.

Then they took off into the future, rather bemused, a bit confused and quite curious about the unexpected advice that they received. They looked back. Then they looked forward. From a different perspective, a new lens. This was a bit counter-intuitive; however, it served them well as they went through time.

When they returned from their long journey over time they felt that "everything had changed … while nothing had changed," when they looked around the family gathering, with kids running around and the aroma of wonderful food and coffee. They all sat together and chatted about our memories and experiences through time.

Epilogue

Upon their return Ayesha and her peers sat with the wise old man alone, in the deep future, to synthesize and understand all these things and put them into context. It was evident that some of the big discussions and challenges of the time were based around ethics and values.

Tariq Qureishy, CEO, MAD and Xponential Group

The first value that seems to be disappearing is *Trust.* The Survey on the Global Agenda[15] reported that 86% of global executives suggested that the world is facing a major leadership crisis, with executives having less than 50% confidence and trust in the leadership of business, media, government, education, and religious institutions. More specifically, when people around the world were asked how much they trusted other people, great discrepancies were found. On one extreme, in countries such as Norway, Sweden, and Finland, more than 60% of respondents believed that people can be trusted. On the other extreme, in countries such as Colombia, Brazil, Ecuador, and Peru, less than 10% believed that people can be trusted.[16]

As far as the average trust in national governments in OECD (Organization for Economic Cooperation and Development) countries is concerned, it has declined every year between 2009 and 2014 from 44% to 38%. The 2019 Edelman Trust Barometer[17] (edelman.com/trustbarometer) finds that two-thirds of the countries surveyed are "distrusters." It means that under 50% of their population trust in the mainstream institutions of business, government, media, and NGOs to do what is right. The profound crisis in trust obviously gained momentum after the Great Recession of 2008. As far as the public trust in U.S. government is concerned (% of people who trust government in Washington always or most of the time), it dropped from 48% in 2001 to 19% in 2015.[18]

The 2017 Edelman Trust Barometer suggested[19], *"trust in institutions has evaporated to such an extent that falsehood can be misconstrued as fact, strength as intelligence, and self-interest as social compact."* This has been a slow-motion meltdown, an angry delayed recognition of permanent decline in economic and social status by those who have not kept pace with globalization and dramatic technological change. We are witness around the world that as faith in the system continues to fall, rising populist movements could wreak unimaginable havoc, with resurgent nationalism and divisive rhetoric moving to dangerous policies.

The report points out that *"the onus is now on business, the one institution that retains some trust with those skeptical about the system, to prove that it is possible to act in the interest of shareholders and society alike."* Workers are looking toward their CEO's (76%) for leadership and "My Employer" (75%) as most trusted institution rather than government, NGO, or media.

Not living the values

There is an ongoing debate about the need to examine the values of the changing global culture. But what are they? A classroom experiment at a small liberal-arts college sought an answer, and presented students with a simple question: What are the qualities of a superior organizational leader in our changing world? The students from European nations favored qualities they believed would make the leader a better person (e.g., empathy, honesty), whereas those from USA focused mainly on productivity (e.g., teamwork, charisma, knowledge), though they eventually recommended some personality traits near the end of the two hour experiment.

Tenzin Priyadarshi, founding director of the Dalai Lama Center for Ethics and Transformative Values, posed the same question to executives around the world during his leadership seminars. He noted that executives became defensive when confronted with their values. It took them an average of 83 minutes to include values (e.g., honesty, integrity) on their lists. He attributes this defensiveness to the fact that many businesspeople live in conflicting realities. At home, their intention is to provide guidance based on universal values. But in the work environment, their intention is to meet their company's profit objectives most efficiently, often sacrificing their core values.

Living in the world of shattered conditions and broken values, we can get confused. To clarify the issue on a personal, as well as on an organizational level, we need to track the discrepancy between our "preached" values and our actual behavior. The method we propose to reflect and confront discrepancies is called Transformative Values Gap Analysis, on both the personal and organizational level.

Keeping in mind that consistent values are a key power driver in any organization, there are several value gaps that seem to need our consideration. For example:

> » value gaps between message and action
>
> » value gaps between employee and company culture
>
> » value gaps between baby boomers and millennials
>
> » value gaps between product design and marketing
>
> » value gaps between customers and company

Many analyses[20] indicate that high level of such value conflicts can negatively affect sales as well as job satisfaction. The late Jack Welch, the "manager of the 20th century" and visionary leader of General Electric, continuously pointed out that if "*he had to run a company on three measures only, those measures would be customer satisfaction, employee satisfaction, and cash flow*"[21]. Therefore, the consistency of personal and organizational values in any organizations cannot be overemphasized.

But many examples of companies and organizations have failed because they preached one set of values and lived another, including well-known cases of Enron, Arthur Andersen, WorldCom, and Lehman Brothers. As a typical energy company, Enron valued hard work, honesty, and quality. After shifting focus from energy production to speculative trading energy contracts, their values were compromised. As a result, management began cheating the stockholders. Their accomplice in "outrageously fraudulent" accounting practices was Arthur Andersen, at the time the world's most highly respected auditing company. Interestingly enough, one of their corporate values, carved on the wall, stated that each employee must "stick to the truth even if it makes him lose a client." In reality, the company followed the myth that white collar crime pays even if you get caught. Any Andersen professional would have been fired if he lost Enron as a client.

So, what is our lesson?

We always do best when we consistently live what we believe. If there is a conflict between individual and organizational values, there seem to be three options :

» If the individual stands up for his/her beliefs, and refuses to engage in actions that he/she thinks are wrong, there is a high possibility to lose his/her job.

» If the individual compromises on his/her beliefs by turning a blind eye to what he/she believes is wrong or even accepts to comply, he/she might feel guilt and remorse.

» If the individual challenges the norms and organizational politics, he/she takes a chance to confront the discrepancy and possibly suffer the consequences or retribution. And, in particular, whistleblowers tend to pay the highest price of all—the loss of their career and reputation.

The first two choices are commonplace. The last is rarely considered. However, the best practice is not to make the confrontation between the individual and the company. Rather work with the leadership to strategize how focusing on values would enable the organization to fulfill its business goals[22]. For example, Apple computers built its business on the back of its commitment to the values of "passion" and excellence. The growth of "Fairtrade" products in Starbucks coffee shops has been based on the fair treatment of people. Now 99% of their coffee is ethically sourced, helping small-scale farmers sustain their quality of life. In both cases, companies have subscribed to strong principles as a basis of their brand; it propelled a distinct market advantage.

Today, purposeful values-based companies are becoming a standard with the growing personal responsibility of the Next Generation. In the Harvard Business Review[23], such companies are called "the organizations of your dreams." They support "superior values." For example, individual differences are nurtured; information is not suppressed or spun. The company adds value to employees rather than merely extracting it from them; the organization stands for something meaningful; the work is intrinsically rewarding; and there are no senseless rules.

In the last decade, the B (Benefit) Corps has become the global model of companies dedicated to being not just "best in the world" but "best for the world." They consider not only shareholders, but also employees, the broader community, and the environment. B Corps use profit and growth to make the world sustainable. The movement has gained momentum with 3000 certified businesses worldwide. Significant companies like Patagonia, Unilever's Ben & Jerry's, Brazil's Natura, and Danone's North America operation are now B Corps.

Unilever, a British-Dutch transnational consumer goods company, under former CEO Paul Polman, has become a symbol of ethical business practices and what it means to be truly sustainable. Polman maintains that being a good leader means taking risks, being accountable for those risks, and putting the greater good above your own needs. *"If ultimately the purpose of a company is maximizing shareholder return, we risk ending up with many decisions that are not in the interest of society."* It is this ethos that has shaped him into one of the greatest business leaders of our time.

Recently, we hear a lot about "empathic" organizations. Research from the Hay Group[24] finds that *"highly engaged employees are, on average, 50% more likely to exceed expectations than the least-engaged workers. And companies with highly engaged people outperform firms with the most disengaged folks—by 54% in employee retention, by 89% in customer satisfaction, and by fourfold in revenue growth."* Research by London Business School[25] has stressed emotions as sources of competitive advantage. It demonstrates that *"employees who feel welcome to express their authentic selves at work exhibit higher levels of organizational commitment, individual performance, and propensity to help others."*

Bastian Lehmann, as the co-founder and CEO of Postmates, a logistics company that operates a network of couriers who deliver goods from 100,000 retail locations, launched his start-up using core values as guide to decision-making. He explains that *"...core values are powerful because they serve as reminders to everyone inside the company. They are hard to argue with once they are part of your company's culture and will help you form an ideology that will ultimately find its way through every part of your organization and to your customers."* The company has been very successful in working with local businesses to meet the needs of the consumer, and empowering "mom and pop" retailers to compete in a digital economy.

Basketball star Lebron James lives his values. He recently established a public school for at-risk students, and is yet another great example of new values and their power to change the world. The I Promise School, which opened in James' hometown of Akron, Ohio in summer 2018, welcomed 240 third- and fourth-graders for the inaugural class. It is a public school formed in collaboration between James' philanthropic foundation and Akron Public Schools. The plan is to provide 1,100 kids with scholarships with the support of his foundation at U.S. $41.8 million. The school's unique offerings include a long school day (eight hours); a "support circle" for students after lunch; and GED courses and job placement for parents. All are driven by James' mission to help children and youth overcome the problems and difficulties that he faced as a low-income student in Akron.

Values have changed their position in an organization's business strategy from a personal belief of the founder or leadership team to a strategic imperative to compete in the marketplace and attract talent.

Leaders must be open to integrating values across an organization's operations. The values we preach must be the values we live. Our head, heart, and hands must be aligned: what we think must be in harmony with what we feel, and what we do. Otherwise we may end up in the previously depicted monkey cage, doing unwise things (or not doing clever things) without even asking ourselves why.

Here is an interesting example of how a family-led company includes values in its ways of doing business.

THP[26] is Vietnam's largest privately owned (Dr. Thanh Tran) fast-moving consumer goods company that applied values, purpose, and mindset to guide its growth. The company's success led Coca-Cola to offer a $2.5 billion buyout deal (but THP turned it down). Behind THP's success, there is the Tran Family's story, based on the idea that purpose drives all operations. The Tran Family aspires to live life to the fullest; boldly building worthy, memorable achievements that are respected by families and communities at home and globally. This is how Dr. Thanh Tran reflects his company vision: *It is critical for our family and our employees to make a lasting contribution to our communities, particularly young people, so that the next generation has as many opportunities as possible.*

Phuong Uyen Tran maintains the family vision as Deputy CEO with seven core values that form a cohesive company culture. These clearly incorporate elements of our TEST Values and Catalytic Mindset:

1.   Put customer satisfaction first —THP sees all stakeholders as "customers" requiring respect and involvement in goalsetting.

2. Adhere to international quality standards—THP maintains a high bar with regard to standards, technology, and operating systems.

3. Behave responsibly toward your community and society—THP sees itself as a citizen of its local community and of society at large, making sustainable development a priority when choosing business partners.

4. Believe that nothing is impossible - THP's team always focuses on results; they dare to think differently and approach problems with a willing spirit to conquer challenging goals.

5. Keep the spirit of entrepreneurship alive—They are proactive in making decisions, managing risk, carrying out their duties, and inspiring collaboration.

6. Maintain a forward-looking mindset—THP encourages the spirit of learning, sharing, and innovative thinking. They strive to improve working methods, processes, and technologies to increase efficiency and quality.

7. Act with integrity—At THP Integrity and Transparency lie at the foundation of the culture. It's a must to rise to the occasion by remaining respectful and committed, choosing to do the right thing at the right time.

Explaining their superior corporate culture, Ms. Tran[27] suggests: *"We strive to ensure our employees live and breathe these core values every day.... They can recite them by heart, and the ideas are woven into songs. They have had a powerful impact on our ability to sustain growth over time."*

TEST Our Values

In the first Guidepost we presented 20 myths that influence the behavior of a majority of human beings on the planet. The prescription for extracting us from the cage of these myths and healing ourselves is simple. We believe values have the power to attract, engage, and transform. The journey must begin with a TEST to align and harmonize four core values—building Trust; propelling Empathy; igniting Sustainability; and living Transparency as the foundation of Catalytic Mindset. You can personally enlarge the list of values, but living the TEST Values is an important step to achieving Strategic Harmony. It is worth noting that a variation of these values has been used to define the Customer Experience Principles for Artificial Intelligence.

These values seem to be attractive to the global "connected" generations independent of age and location. Studies[28] pinpoint that these values have recently deteriorated, yet are essential for realigning our moral compass.

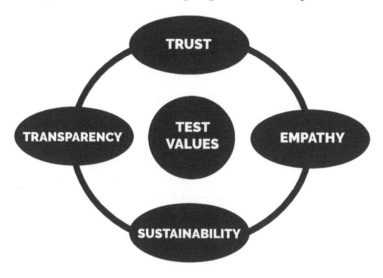

Figure 3.1 The TEST Model

Since the broken world needs to be transformed, we propose the TEST model as the foundation of change in applying values across the organization. Your values must be aligned and tested along the entire path to transformation.

How to use TEST in Transformation path?

The TEST model requires a consistent reinforcement of these values to generate the power and direction for the transformation. Often organizations question why their change efforts are stymied or blocked. They should frame the challenge in the context of values. They need to regularly TEST the application of their agreed-upon values and resulting actions across all operations. As they raise the bar for consistency (for each value among the leadership team and the company culture), the organization's teams get more focused and gain power. When all four values gain consistent application, they synergize. In order to achieve that consistency, the leadership team should regularly TEST six areas for values consistency.

1. TEST your leader's mindset
2. TEST your culture
3. TEST your innovation process

4. TEST your business model
5. TEST your execution and communications strategy
6. TEST your sustainable impact among all stakeholders

Whenever the executive team notes a gap between what they say and what they do, they need to agree upon a strategy to resolve the conflict and harmonize the values. Let's take a deep dive into each of the four TEST Values.

Trust

Imagine the ideal world in which two people decide to work together, and they know they can completely trust each other. They openly discuss everything, exchange all information, and resolve disagreements for mutual benefit. They collaborate to deliver what was promised and strive to gain the trust and satisfaction of their customers and employees. The outcome is that they need no contracts, lawyers, or courts, to settle disputes. Their decision-making is efficient, and transparent, not to mention lowering the costs of "unnecessary legal infrastructure."

According to recent studies[22], Trust is quickly becoming the global—the most-valued currency of modern time. Trust generates the power to transform stakeholders and institutions. If we are not working to build and gain the trust of all stakeholders, then the future might be about to leave us behind.

Trust is a form of energy that changes over time. It is something committed to one's care for use or safekeeping, as a responsibility. Trust is both an emotional and logical act.

We feel trust. Emotionally, it is where we expose our vulnerabilities to people, but believing they will not take advantage of our openness. Emotions associated with trust include confidence, companionship, friendship, love, agreement, relaxation, and comfort.

We sustain trust. It is the ultimate human currency. It impacts our environment at every level, from brand and organizational loyalty to community sustainability. It transcends relationships, institutions, and markets.

We build trust. Trust is built on intent or motives, actions, capabilities, and results. In a business model, we access forms of energy that are exchanged, aggregated, augmented, and leveraged. Energy can come in the form of money, trust, resources, and harmony (people). When energy is harmonized and aligned, its direction is focused and provides more power. In the case of Trust, the individual's and organization's objective is built upon to develop value. Reputation is built on trust. Leaders require trust to lead and govern. A start-up must generate trust in the company, the team, and the business model to attract investors and other stakeholders. Building Trust among all stakeholders is the cornerstone for success in the Post-COVID recovery.

Trust builds harmony. Trust is the basis for movements, religions, and political parties. Trust in one's mission and business model is the force behind all institutions, organizations, and businesses. Trust in mindset facilitates change. Trust in products and services generates value. Trust in people builds relationships. Trust in customers, employees, and managers build powerful business systems. Trust in technology builds networks and online communities. Trust in customer experience drives advocacy and champions. Trust in organizational culture builds employee loyalty and productivity. Trust between departments generates collaboration and innovation. Trust within a supply chain develops efficiency and generates performance. Trust between stakeholders generates results and sustainable outcomes. Trust in economic relationships drives the shared economy.

Trust is mutual and binary in nature. It's like virginity or pregnancy. One cannot be a little pregnant or a little virginal. Take a look at the following story[30]. There was a farmer who sold a pound of butter to a baker. One day the baker decided to weigh the butter to see if he was getting the right amount, only to find out that he wasn't. Angry, he took the farmer to court.

The judge asked the farmer if he was using any measure to weigh the butter. The farmer replied that he had a scale. He explained that every day when the baker brings him a pound of bread, he puts it on the scale and gives in return the same weight in butter. If anyone is to be blamed for the wrong weight, it is the baker.

Trust is built upon mutual agreement and accountability.

Today we are trust-ranked as individuals and as organizations from Airbnb and Uber to social media and career websites. China plans to assign each citizen a trust score as part of its Social Credit System. Even our devices are now assigned trust scores, an example being Apple iPod's device trust score based on our calls and emails[31]. The power of trust becomes accentuated when *Loss of trust = Loss of revenue*. Accenture's *The Bottom Line on Business Trust*

Study[32] of 7000 businesses globally found that the companies that experienced a drop in trust projected a loss of revenues equal to at least US$180 billion.

The study analyzed companies across three interdependent dimensions of competitiveness: growth, profitability, sustainability, and trust. The analysis revealed that 54% of the examined companies experienced a material drop in trust at some point during the past two and a half years. For example, a $16B B2C company launched a sustainability-oriented publicity event that backfired, breaking trust with their stakeholders. It's trust score significantly dropped while revenue declined by US$400 million.

The study concluded: *"Managing trust cannot be relegated to simply addressing individual incidents with public relations as necessary. Instead, companies need to intentionally create a culture that builds, maintains, and preserves trust. They must bake trust into their DNA, strategy, and day-to-day operations ... Trust must permeate relationships with stakeholders, from employees, to customers, suppliers, investors, analysts, and the media. To be competitive in today's environment, companies need to execute a balanced strategy that prioritizes trust at the same level as growth and profitability."*

On the other hand, transformation and change requires trust as the generator in an open environment with as few rules as possible, leaving room for initiative and freedom. To transform our broken world and all its institutions, we must discover the deficient and weak linkages of trust among our stakeholders and provide correctives.

Trust is the foundation of Strategic Harmony.

Empathy

Empathy is the ability of getting in tune with another person and learning to be in his or her shoes. It is the capability to feel and comprehend another's emotions, while imagining what someone else is feeling. Empathic people listen attentively to others and can facilitate communication. They tend to be more generous and concerned with others' welfare.

In our broken world, "radical empathy" is gaining traction as a deep commitment to changing the world, one person at a time. It is getting to the root of relating to and caring for each other through shared experiences. It generates a more compassionate and connected world.

Empathy is the core ingredient in designing and sustaining a purposeful brand. Companies must obsessively focus on user experience to build successful, responsible brands in our transparent world. Also, empathy is trending as "essential learning" at major business schools (e.g., Harvard) and becomes critical in developing a purposeful business. Companies focused on actively listening to employee and customer feedback develop sustainable relationships based on employee loyalty and customer experience. Empathetic boards incorporate company values in expanding Return on Investment to include both profit and social impact.

Here is a Zen story on empathy[33]. Dissatisfied with his progress, a student decided to leave the temple, situated at the top of the Ping Mountain. One evening, he knocked on his teacher's door to say goodbye. "Leave if you want to, but let me accompany you tomorrow on your way down the mountain," responded the teacher.

When they set out in the morning, the teacher asked the student to look around and tell him what he saw. "I see the valley, encircled by mountains; in the center there is a lake and an old city," said the student. When they were halfway down, the teacher repeated the question. "I see the walls of the city, the brown rooftops, the port and many boats sailing on the lake" answered the student. When they arrived at the city walls, the teacher repeated the question. "I see dogs and children playing, a group of traders taking livestock to the market, a few sailors loading wooden boxes onto boats, and a bunch of noisy children throwing rocks into the lake," answered the student.

"The path to knowledge is like a journey down the mountain," said the teacher. "Wisdom can be attained by understanding that what we see from the top is not identical to what we see from the mid-point, or from the bottom. Knowing this helps us reject prejudices, opens our minds to learning, feel compassion for others, and teaches us to respect what we don't see from where we stand."

Empathy is essential as the ability to look at the world through the eyes of others, as well as to reconsider and change one's point of view. It is rooted in humility, and serves as the second building block of Strategic Harmony.

Sustainability

What does sustainability really mean? The Great Law of the Iroquois (the Haudenosaunee Confederacy, made up of six indigenous nations in North America) states that today's decisions must benefit our children seven generations into the future. Few people on the planet will disagree with the requirement to meet today's needs without compromising our collective future. However, there are many different interpretations of sustainability and how it competes with self-interest.

Sustainability[34] is living within the resources of the planet without damaging the environment now or in the future. Sustainability is creating an economic system that provides for quality of life while renewing the environment and its resources. In a sustainable world, everyone can have fulfilling lives and enjoy a rich level of well-being within the limits of nature. Sustainability means taking a long-term view of how our actions affect future generations. Therefore, it means living a life of dignity in harmony with nature. Still, another definition of sustainability focuses on using resources efficiently, working to preserve cultures, protecting natural eco-systems, raising aspirations, and extending opportunities for all. Finally, "sustainable relationships" are the foundation of brand and employee loyalty, as well as sales and financial interactions. They reflect the needs of all stakeholders.

Sustainability is both a value and behavior. It interconnects all eco-systems and how they affect each other. We can base sustainability on a spiritual view of the circular use of all resources - mental, physical, environmental, financial, and social. Initially, we temporarily borrow materials from nature, and use them as goods and services, and then return them to the natural environment through a continuous circular process. For example, in the forestry industry, forestry companies with a commitment to sustainability make sure that they practice re-planting and re-forestation. Sustainability creates[35] a positive future for the climate, our planet, our organization, and our life.

Once the organization is functioning in harmony with its values and stakeholders, it is on the journey to sustainability. This journey involves a commitment to view sustainable principles as a lens for all the business interfaces with the external environment, including purposeful design, community, and impact. Here are four aspects of sustainability to consider:

1. Environment

Most people understand environmental sustainability as being green, and most business leaders globally are aware that environmental issues are becoming a mainstream priority. However, we all must implement the concepts throughout the social and ecological vectors. It involves adopting the UN Sustainable Development Goals (SDGs), a universal call to action to end poverty, protect the planet, and ensure that corporate behavior makes all people enjoy peace and prosperity. Finally, it is a commitment to protecting our world by promoting a Circular Economy[36]. A circular economy is an alternative to a traditional linear economy (make, use, dispose of) in which we keep resources in use for as long as possible, extract the maximum value from them while in use, then recover and regenerate products and materials at the end of each service life.

2. Design

To adopt circular economy practices, organizations must evaluate the impact of their products on the world. (e.g., waste, pollution). Based on their analysis, they redesign ingredients and packaging to incorporate performance goals and impact. They transform packaging that pollutes landfills to design re-usable products and services. They re-invent their product to have a dual purpose as a necessary product and serve the greater good. William McDonough, the father of sustainable development, suggested Cradle to Cradle (C2C)[37] or regenerative design. It is a biomimetic approach that forces all industries to mimic nature's processes, viewing materials as nutrients circulating in healthy, safe metabolisms. The C2C designers seek to create systems that are not only efficient but also essentially waste-free. The term is based on the popular phrase "*Cradle to Grave,*" implying that the C2C model is sustainable and considerate of life and future generations.

An extreme example of the C2C thinking is Capsula Mundi[38], a sustainable graveyard (it works for some religions and cultures and not others). Instead of being buried, our loved ones are placed in an egg-shaped pod (ashes are held in small egg-shaped urns while bodies are laid down in a fetal position in larger pods). The Capsula is then buried as a seed in the earth, with a tree, chosen in life by the deceased, planted on top as a memorial for the departed and a legacy for posterity and the future of our planet. It might provide cemeteries with a new look: grey tombstones replaced by living trees, creating a "*holy forest.*"

3. Community

Purposeful businesses consider the ramifications of their business decisions on local environment, jobs, social and economic development. In principle, sustainable businesses address multiple goals: economic prosperity and continuity for the business and its stakeholders; social well-being and equity for both employees and affected communities; and environmental protection and resource conservation on local and global levels. An intriguing example is Dancing Rabbit Ecovillage in northeastern Missouri (USA), an entirely self-reliant town that practices "radical environmental sustainability." The ecovillage has established a set of guidelines on its way toward achieving sustainability: (1) no vehicles are to be used or stored in the village; (2) all gardening must be organic; (3) all power must come from renewable resources; (4) no lumber from outside the local area is allowed unless it is recycled or salvaged; (5) organic waste and recyclable materials are to be reincorporated into usable products through composting methods. It was one of the first plastic-free environments. Clearly, most communities are not ready to adopt such radical standards, but it serves as a model in designing sustainable communities. For example, a coastal town in England achieved "plastic-free" accreditation in 2017; since then more than 100 other communities have done the same.

4. Impact

Sustainability is based on the assessment that a project or business venture will be optimized for its impact on all stakeholders. Furthermore, it will have sufficient funds to meet all its resource and financial obligations, whether the funding continues or not. Organizations should not be judged just on their financial performance. Sustainable projects are those that provide stability for all the stakeholders now and in the future, based on a so-called Quadruple Bottom Line. Their goal is to integrate and optimize the outputs in the context of four factors: People (customers, employees), Planet (local/global environmental considerations), Profit (positive financial and social impact) and Prosperity (growth and prosperity of all the members of the community). A company's impact is evaluated on performing well financially, environmentally, socially, and in how they treat all their stakeholders. They must become "stakeholder centric"—engaging and optimizing the experience of customers, employees, suppliers, investors, and community. One such company is Tentree, that sells clothing made of natural fibers, and also plants 10 trees (anywhere in the world) for every article of clothing the company sells.

Sustainability is the cornerstone and outcome of Strategic Harmony.

Transparency

For many years, transparency was a term used in science to mean a material that one could totally see through. As the financial crisis hit the global markets, major financial institutions were confronted with their breach of ethics, hidden data and information, and the illegal actions of some executives. As a result of the corruption of Enron executives (noted earlier) and other financial leaders, transparent financial transactions and governance were demanded. During the same period, social media began to thrive based on open, candid exchanges and content sharing. Every connected individual could publish content and influence the connections in the network. Thus, by design, social media requires transparency, and we must be vigilant that this tremendous potential does not get misused by biases or spread of misinformation.

Every person's honesty and credibility is transparent when it is established in the eyes of others. The prospect of being open and vulnerable is a necessity for survival in the digital age. For some organizations, the transition to digitalization and transparency is a major benefit, but to others it threatens their culture and business model generating a threat and greater risk.

Transparency invites trust by revealing that there is nothing hidden or altered. It allows objects, data, information, and people to be seen clearly through integration. It reveals all facts and actions taken, even when some of them are uncomfortable. It enables open dialogue in areas of disagreement to facilitate mutual understanding. Transparency calls for "democratization of data," expanding access to business information from traditionally coveted sources, providing the tools to analyze it for a broader audience. The #MeToo movement is a manifestation of the call for transparency and the demand for women's equality in relationships and the workplace.

A culture of transparency requires a purposeful and methodical system-wide process with real time monitoring and open dialogue. As such, transparency is the cornerstone of trust. It insures accountability as it makes people and their skills, knowledge, and ideas visible and accessible to all their colleagues. It helps to build interpersonal trust, which is vital for people to share and collaborate with each other.

In today's ever-changing environment, it is essential that organizations make full use of their assets—information/data and people—to improve their responsiveness, productivity, and ability to constantly innovate. It is easy to use social software to increase "technical transparency" across an organization. But to create a culture of transparency requires changes in mindset and the related behaviors and practices.

The global environment of social connectivity and real-time news updates increases external and internal pressure on organizations to become more transparent. This pressure is not only coming from customers and employees, but also from stakeholders (investors, media, community, and government). In such a setting, the culture of transparency is the only sustainable strategy.

Transparency is the thread entwined through all interactions that generates Strategic Harmony.

Synergy

It is obvious that the four TEST factors are not independent as the values interface and augment each other. The result is synergistic (e.g., two or more agents work together to achieve something either one couldn't have achieved on its own). Synergy of all the four TEST Values is a powerful benchmark for individuals, organizations, and governments engaged in transformation. It's the concept of the whole being greater than the sum of its parts.

TEST the Values with Amazon Go

The future can be scary because it is different. Amazon Go is an innovation that goes beyond the normal when it comes to grocery shopping. This concept of walking into a store, grabbing what you want, and just walking out has never been done before. As a new idea it deserves to be carefully TESTed for values it should stand for:

Trust-It is fair to say that customers can be cynical. It is extremely important to ensure customers that Amazon Go is honest, trustworthy, and real. One way this can be achieved is by collecting feedback from customers and replying to that feedback. Statistics show that 61% of customers read reviews before making a purchase. Looking at feedback and responding in an honest way is a great way to make corrections and excel.

Empathy-Amazon Go must walk in the shoes of the customers in order to understand their experience and how we can better help them get what they want. Find out problems that they may have and work to correct

---

them. If a customer is having technical issues with the app, ensure that there is someone in the store that can fix the problem immediately. It is important to understand that Amazon is trying to make the customer's experience easier rather than just gaining data and benefit ... not the other way around.

Sustainability-This company has to realize the importance of making the world a better place. This is how the company operations affect the environment, and community, as well as the finances of the company. These means can be shown through using fully recyclable containers of all food. This shows that Amazon Go is thinking more than just about money. It is thinking about making the world a better place.

Transparency-The old way of tricking your customers into buying products is fading. Amazon Go must remain open and honest with its customers. Making their practices, policies, operating data, or future plans of the company available to customers is paramount. This shows that the company isn't hiding anything, but is presenting the product that is promised.

Amazon Go is a futuristic idea that can shine among all businesses. By focusing on TEST Values, it may gain and retain more customers than all other competing grocery stores combined.

Trammel Robinson, student, University of Lynchburg

Living your values

Transformation is rooted and fueled by living and "performing" the underlying values. Our TEST Values determine the agreement and synergy of the team in charge of transformation. It is a set of ideas for judging the leaders' experience and performance at each level of the organization, and a way to evaluate sustainable impact.

Translating the TEST Values into action is the real challenge. Resolving the Gap between what we proclaim and what we live in the organization's culture lies at the heart of Strategic Harmony. A purpose-driven culture requires core values that will serve as standards and aspirational goals, and ultimately help drive productivity. While aspects like perks, benefits, and employee-centered policies can play a role in fostering a positive environment. Your company's core values should go much deeper in expressing your mission.

According to a LinkedIn study, 71% of employees would consider taking a cut in pay to work in an environment harmonized with their values. Yet, a 2019 Gallup survey revealed only 25% of a company's employees believed in the company's stated values with conviction. This survey reflects a drop from earlier surveys that showed a propensity for employees to trust the companies they work for. A decline in that trust is a warning to executives to pay close attention.

To sum it up, here is another story. A father and his son climbed a mountain. Suddenly, the son stumbled and fell. Angry and humiliated, he screamed "Ouch!" To his surprise, the mountain replied with "Ouch!" Curious, the boy asked, "Who are you?" "Who are you?" answered the mountain. "You are creepy," cried the boy. And the mountain responded, "You are creepy." "A coward," cried the boy. "A coward," the mountain was sure to reply. "What is it, Dad?" the boy asked his father. "Watch this, son," said his father and shouted: "You're the best!" The mountain replied: "You're the best!" Then the father explained: "People call it an echo, but it's actually life itself, as it returns everything you say or do."

If you want more love in the world, create more love in your voice, in the things you say. If you want trust, empathy, sustainability, and transparency, live it every day. They are the key ingredients that *EmPower Us!*

The broken world requires these four values to achieve Strategic Harmony. If they are lived consistently in our organizations and personal lives, we will experience major positive change and a realigning of our institutions.

Guidepost 4

Transforming Power and Love
Igniting Action

*"To create lasting change we have to learn to work fluidly with two distinct, funda-
mental drives that are in tension: power - the single-minded desire to achieve one's
solitary purpose; and love - the drive towards unity."*

Adam Kahane

A well-known American entrepreneur, author, and motivational speaker, Jim
Rohn[39], said: *"You cannot change your destination overnight, but you can change
your direction overnight."* So far, we have detailed the nature of our broken
institutions and reflected on the myths behind them. We have outlined the
TEST Values and mindset required among leaders and organizations to begin
to rebuild and generate Strategic Harmony. In this Guidepost, we look at the
myths of our broken world through Power and Love and how we can transform these forces into Strategic Harmony. It's now time to contemplate how to
change the direction and the destination.

Where are we going? After describing and understanding the chaos and deterioration of our institutions, how can we solve all the problems? How can we
change the living reality? Our answer is quite simple: by striving to rediscover
and align our values and ethical compass on the path to Strategic Harmony.
As a starting point, Power and Love must be re-imagined entirely as forces for
change and as powerful tools for transformation.

Let's describe The Power of Love in a real example of a penguin that was saved
by a fisherman in Brazil after being covered by the oil of a local spill. Since
then, before heading to the Antarctic to mate, the penguin swam 5000 miles
every year to spend time with his Brazilian savior[40].

Power and Love are the forces that drive all changes. At present, they are
playing a complicated game full of inconsistences and double standards that

fertilize our myths and deflect our ethical compasses. Power and Love are complementary forces that motivate all our individual and social endeavors. They are the key drivers of transformation; the abuses of Power and Love may well be the key contributors to our broken world. Their harmony can contribute to "fixing" our situation!

TESTing Power and Love

As already pointed out, Strategic Harmony is aimed at discovering and incorporating TEST Values into organizational life and culture. We need to redefine our mindset toward building an open, tolerant, and unbiased view of the world. Let's briefly discuss the role of TEST Values as they synergize with Power and Love. The key word that brings them together is the need to transform the existing broken world into a new strategically harmonized planet.

We have recently witnessed value-based movements worldwide, from Climate Strike, yellow vests in France to #MeToo and #NeverAgain in the U.S. Initially, this Transformative Power gets ignited within the individual (e.g., Greta Thunberg). Greta's inspiration was focused on her love of the environment and our planet. Her actions gained traction, and others responded. Her mission and life translated into the Power of those who adopted and harmonized with the immediate need for climate change action. The aggregate of that energy generates a Transformative Power. When it spreads from person to person, from organization to organization, it becomes a movement. The excitement and enthusiasm of Transformative Love for change permeates those who connect and work together, and the result is a unified response, namely Strategic Harmony.

TEST Values are a vital driver of Transformative Power. Each value generates power when it becomes fulfilled within the individual and then becomes reinforced within the organization or through relationships.

When we feel Trust among ourselves, our colleagues, and our leaders, we become energized. The power of that relationship can change us personally as well as all members of our organization. Trust is the fulcrum of personal and organizational transformation. In the political environment when the candidate speaks to the highest values of their constituency, the harmonization of values engenders Trust among voters. They feel empowered and motivated to vote as they feel heard and their needs are being represented.

When the relationship becomes compromised, breaking down Trust, it results in a *"divorce."* The citizens, feeling powerless, have little trust in the candidates. People become apathetic, not voting in elections or voicing their concerns. In companies with a lack of trust, the employees' motivation deteriorates to perform and innovate; they leave the job. In order to create sustainability, the harmony must be realigned between our core values and how they're manifested in our lives. As for Empathy, it allows us to listen to and walk in the shoes of others, and it brings forth the love and understanding for their situations and points of view. When we come into harmony, we generate compassion, and we feel moved to change by empowering individuals and organizations. The recent U.S. immigration crisis reflects the Transformative Power of compassion. It was exemplified by the plight of refugees and migrants entering the United States and being separated from their children. Millions of people were emboldened by this Love and compassion to speak up against injustice by demanding a change in the U.S. immigration policy toward children and separation from their parents.

The third TEST Value, Sustainability, is the Power realized from the harmony of our environment with the community, the harmony of our financial situation with our organizational goals, and the harmony of our leadership with our employees to allow us to fulfill those goals. The sustainability of our organization is often seen as an outward manifestation of feeling secure and sustained internally. When there's a disharmony between our personal core values and those manifested by our relationships, organization, or country, there is degradation and loss of power and energy, and such systems are not sustainable.

The current global climate crisis poses an existential threat to our planet's sustainability. This threat has empowered youth to challenge our leaders to face their gap between words and actions.

The last TEST Value, Transparency, means open and honest communication, living our values internally and manifesting them in outer experiences. This consistency translates to harmony and creates power, as our values become reinforced in our actions. Transparency gives us the strength to speak truth to power. Transparency based on the consistency and harmony of values in relationships, media, businesses and other organizations generates Transformative Power.

However, we are still living in the paradigm of the Old World with Old Power and Old Love, a far cry from Strategic Harmony. In the vacuum of the deterioration of our values and ethical compass, we have filled the void with myths, falsehoods, and incorrect anchors to our thinking. Now many of these myths are used to guide our actions and determine our decisions.

Transformative Power

So far we have used the concepts of Transformative Power and Transformative Love without clear definitions. Let's dive into both ideas a little deeper. As for Power, we live in the age of global shifts that are dramatic, the old being challenged by the new. According to Heimans and Timms in their book *New Power*[41], "*the Old Power works like a currency. It is held by few, and when gained, it is jealously guarded. The powerful have a lot to store and to spend. So they keep it closed, inaccessible, and leader-driven. It enslaves and captures, makes the power-less majority feel miserable and unhappy. On the other hand, New Power operates like a current. It is available to many; it's open, participatory, and peer-driven. It empowers and connects. It is not supposed to be kept and abused but channeled and distributed.*"

Heimans and Timms[42] focus on how to make Power work for building movements and spreading ideas. We suggest that *Old Power* favors exclusivity, competition, and authority, while the *New Power* rests on open source collaboration, sharing, and "crowd wisdom." The Old Power is protected by secrecy and confidentiality, while the New Power requires radical transparency. The practices associated with Old Power are managerialism, institutionalism, unquestioning loyalty, and long-term affiliation, while the New Power relies on self-organization, networked governance, conditional affiliation, and participation.

Power affects each stage of the Strategic Transformation process. So what is Transformative Power? If you "*Google it*," there are many descriptors of the venues that feature it (e.g., storytelling, Declaration of Independence, education, environment), but no explanation of what it is, how to access it, or how to accelerate or increase the power. We define it as the passion and commitment to one's values that potentiates and increases the power of the transformation that leads to Strategic Harmony.

We see Transformative Power as a tool based on self-reflection, values, and an ethical compass, used to transform culture, mindset, and decision-making. This integration is essential in shifting from Old Power to Transformative Power.

Guidepost 4: Transforming Power and Love

Old Power is derived or gained from resources, status, and position in the organization. One strives to gain "capital" of money and rank. It generates a competitive social order and win-lose work environment. Transformative Power is based on values such as trust, empathy, respect, and openness to change, and it is earned from relationships with all stakeholders through a loving, open two-way channel. Capital is earned in facilitating understanding, creativity, solutions among coworkers, instead of power over somebody. According to Abraham Maslow[43], *"the more influence and power you give to someone else in their team situation, the more you have for yourself."* Transformative Power is based on 'equal' sharing of power and being responsive to other stakeholders' needs. This model challenges the competitive *"Win-Lose Model"* in favor of a collaborative approach. If one partner wins and the other loses, both lose because the loser always makes the winner pay.

Old Power is based on scarcity, derived from closed relationships, resources, status, rank, and position in an organization. It is cold and calculating, forcing a position and point of view. It is negotiated, promoted, defended, anchored, and tied to its scarce source and self-interest. It reflects strength, influence, money, and might. Like Capital, it is owned, coveted, and protected. Old Power is control over someone or something.

The world is mostly broken because of such use of Power. In order to fix it, traditional leaders must be willing to self-reflect and transform, giving up exclusive control to encourage inclusive participation and nurture Transformative Power. In contrast with the old model, the new one is driven by abundance, earned from open relationships, accomplishments, and ethical actions; it's based on respecting people, networks, and entrepreneurship; and is driven by the consistency of ones' values.

As an example, look at the former U.S. prosecutor and CIA agent[44], Chris Hunter, who ran for Florida's 12 Congressional District seat. He focused his campaign on the power of values, explaining that *"voters are ready for honest leadership and a renewal of an American service ethic that really has the power to be transformative."* He also added that *"the Transformative Power is something that can get us through a very difficult time. It has a power that has potential to be unifying."*

The following table contrasts the values and expression of Old and Transformative Power.

CHARACTERISTICS	OLD POWER	TRANSFORMATIVE POWER
Visual	Currency	Current (open source, grows with connections)
Control	Held by few, closed, captured, protected	Generated by many, trusted, distributed, transparent
Source	Money; family; position	Earned; peer driven
Target	Control of others	Democratize input
Availability	Scarcity	Abundance
Rewards	Money, position, fame	Mutual benefit
Context	Coveted, exclusive, restricted	Unlimited, inclusive, expansive
Focus	Maintaining SELF	Sharing with OTHERS
Principles	Greed. ends justify the means	Generosity, value of deeds based on intention
Communication	Top-down hierarchy	Collaborate across silos
Exchange	Expand transactions	Network relationships
Outcomes	Material success	Harmony, sustainable impact
Purpose	Enrich shareholders	Enrich all stakeholders
Methodology	Assert pressure	Empathize and respond

Figure 4.1 Old and Transformative Power

(Expanded from Heimans and Timms: New Power[45])

All stakeholders gain "power" by contributing value to the organization and feeling integral to the whole. It is supported and granted by the "grass roots," facilitating transparent communications and sustainable decisions, and tied to mutual benefit. It is humanizing, reflecting trust, shared value, and humility. Unlike the traditional view, behind Transformative Power there is Social Capital which is earned, "organically grown," and shared. Transformative Power is expansive, nourishing, fulfilling for individuals, and harmonious for organizations.

So, why are we still enslaved by the forces of Old Power? In a Zen story[46], a horse suddenly came galloping down the road. It seemed as though the rider had somewhere important to go. The crowd standing alongside shouted: "Where are you going?" The rider replied: "I don't know! Ask the horse!"

Of course, the horse symbolizes the power of habits. We live at the mercy of our old habit energies which are based on prevailing values and culture. Like the horse, Old Power is pulling us along, making us run and hurry on our road to a local disaster or a global catastrophe. This book aims at guiding us how to take back the reins and use Transformative Power to fix our shattered institutions and the broken world.

But it's not just habits; maybe it's also human nature. According to Maslow[47], *"the person who seeks for power is the one who is just exactly likely to be the one who shouldn't have it, because he neurotically and compulsively needs power. Such people are apt to use power very badly."*

Game of Power

Our Next Generation has a passion for seeing our community and the world in a more sustainable state. More importantly, we have access to the tools and knowledge of what needs to happen to take decisive action. As the founder of an online community in an emerging economy generating growth by thousands weekly, I realized the power and scalability of networks.

As I strived to meet the challenges of development, I often faced the "political power game," based on exclusivity and control, which contrasted the online community encouraging inclusivity and openness. Rarely, everyone shares the same intentions and values or wants to steer the community in a sustainable direction. Often forces are trying to dictate the course, putting us in confrontation with powerful entities that seek to possess and control the community for their benefit.

If you work in development with a "sense of community," I doubt that navigating interpersonal power struggles comes naturally. When such "games confront your dreams and passion for change," it challenges your problem-solving approach and the expected outcomes.

As the rules of the "power game" change, the community developers must courageously maintain their values in striving for sustainability. Often these groups retreat, not seeing a need to engage in confrontation with these powerful entities. It is sad to see the resistance to build capacity and capability to face these games.

How many initiatives and entities only reach a fraction of their potential impact when its owners refused to face the "power games" head-on?

> *I keep the Queen of Hearts in my pocket as a reminder of values of love, community, and forgiveness, for which the "real game" needs to be played. And while doing all that's possible to avoid "power games," you must be ready for it when it comes.*
>
> *Abdo Magdy, Social Entrepreneur, Egypt*

Transformative Power comes from within as a result of self-reflection. The only problem is that most people are slow learners. Namely, at some point in time we want to change the broken world, but sooner or later give up. This book points out that we can do it by changing ourselves. It's never too late to start, especially if we are driven by Transformative Love.

Transformative Love

The word, "*love,*" has many different meanings depending on the culture, language, and context. Love has been limited to focusing on personal relationships, but its roots found in the texts of world religions, convey a more expansive vision. For example, the Bible says: *We wish for others that we wish for ourselves; and Do unto others as you do unto yourself.* The Quran says: *Love for your brother what you Love for yourself.*

In his already quoted book on Management[48], published back in 1965, Abraham Maslow defines *"love as the happiness of the other that makes you happy."* The happiness of the other, including the broken world and its institutions, is the clearest reflection of Transformative Love.

Love is based on uniting with those we respect, trust, and are attracted and committed to. We love whatever we are dedicated to, a mate, our creator, our leader, our friend, our country, or religion, a favorite brand, sports team, film, book, idea, and so forth.

Love is based upon empathy, the ability to look at the world from other people's shoes. It means caring and thinking of the other person as a priority. It is about removing the obstacles in front of another person and about achieving trust, equity, justice, and equal opportunity in a healthy, secure, and sustainable environment.

Love can easily be abused as we rush into relationships for sex, or sell unhealthy goods to make a profit, or make false promises to constituents to get their votes. These contradictions are ingrained in today's market-driven economy and digital relationships. We must not forget the power of feelings because people may support the best charity and the worse terrorist organizations out of love, passion, and commitment.

In organizations, Love enables Power and catalyzes change. How can we adapt an organization's culture without Love? How can we facilitate transformation without compassion for others? How can we solve intractable problems without empathy for other stakeholders? In answering these timely questions, Beatrice Ungard[42] (Benne), a specialist in regenerative development points out: *"We need love as the new Transformative Power to develop higher level of consciousness. We need love to create a generative field and awaken our collective wisdom. We need love because these are times when the most accomplished rational mind is helpless to find solutions because they require us to change our long-held mental models and values and to take a leap of faith into the unknown. We need love to believe in a world of possibilities, abundance, justice, equity, peace, and harmony with the environment and with other living species."*

Like Power, there are also the Old and the Transformative Love. The Old is selfish and controlling; the Transformative is supportive and enriching. The Old is like a chain, the Transformative gives you wings. According to Nicholas Sparks, *"The best love is the kind that awakens the soul; that makes us reach for more, that plants the fire in our hearts and brings peace to our minds."*

The contrast between Old and Transformative Love can be seen in the following table:

CHARACTERISTICS	OLD LOVE	TRANSFORMATIVE LOVE
Visual	Two halves make whole	Integral
Target	Personal relations, soul mate, directed to another person	Interpersonal relations with purpose, colleagues, company, community
Availability	Scarcity	Abundance
Currency Exchanged	Affection, emotions	Shared values, principles
Context	Coveted, exclusive, restricted	Unlimited, inclusive, expansive, open
Focus	On self, to be loved	Share love, concern with others
Feeling	Excited, satisfied (short-term)	Nourished, fulfilled (long-term)
Expression	Passion, attraction	Loyalty, commitment, devotion
Communication	Top-down hierarchy	Collaborate across silos
Exchange	Expand transactions	Network relationships
Vulnerability	Weakness, fear exposure	Strength, key to freedom, authenticity
Place	Private	Public
Outcomes	Divorce, abusive, relationships	Harmony, transformation, collaboration

Figure 4.2 Old and Transformative Love

Transformative Love is realized through values—compassion, empathy, understanding—with clients, employees, other leaders. Even the human body is designed to thrive on love[50]. It's a feeling that makes people more positive, resilient, optimistic, persistent, healthier, and happier. Conversely, the body's biochemistry is negatively affected when love is not present.

Transformative Love is a solution and salvation to any discord, organizational conflict, or other source of broken institutions, and relationships involving humans. It starts as self-reflection aimed at bridging the gap between our proclaimed values and innovative actions to achieve our goals. As such, it is a vehicle for achieving better collaboration. Transformative Love is placing others above us or putting our Purpose above proving to be right or above our desire to achieve something.

Transformative Love has many faces; it can be seen as Love of Purpose and values; Love of the mirror or feedback; Love of the challenge; Love of our constituency, other people's needs; Love of right action; and Love for change. Transformative Love is based on passion, commitment, heartfelt energy, and openness. As a creative expression of Harmony, it provides a model from the best of our emotional and romantic relationships to use that force for tolerance, compassion, and understanding in driving transformation. It is based on the inner trust and confidence of just being you without masks. This translates to your message being genuine and authentic, leading to Trust.

A critical key to Strategic Harmony is the Transformative Power of Love. We need to create a mindset of Love for all stakeholders. Customers must love our brand, products, and services. Employees must love the organizational culture and work environment. Suppliers/Wholesalers/Partners must love and feel engaged with the distribution of the product and efficiency of the supply chain. A community must love and support the business's local impact. And Investors must love and thrive on the sustainable outcomes of the business.

Transformative Love can change the global culture through passionate commitment to our values and purpose. It means to love the opportunities generated by high velocity exponential change. It means to love the equality of opportunity for all people. It means to love honest, open, accountable communication as the basis for trust in relationships. In the end, it means having love and tolerance for all people experienced through compassion and relationships.

Balance between Power and Love

An interesting struggle to strike a balance between Power and Love is seen in a well-known book by Dr. Martin Luther King Jr[51]. He wrestles with how Power and Love connect to deliver justice and says: *"Power without love is reckless and abusive, and love without power is sentimental and anemic. Power at its best is love implementing the demands of justice, and justice at its best is power correcting everything that stands against love."*

Ideally, our world is about using Power to build and manage institutions, businesses, and movements that are caring, transparent, and sustainable. But many leaders are abusing their Power and not acting ethically. Many constituencies and targets are disgusted, and fed-up; they feel unrepresented as their leaders deliver products and policies that only serve their own personal goals and those of their investors. This practice makes them richer, concentrating their Power and catering to the few.

We have broken our world by abusing Power and Love. The abuse can be seen in many different shapes and forms, for example:

» Power of money controls leaders, decisions, and communication

» Abuse of resources threatens and challenges local and global sustainability

» Domination and authoritarianism supersede equity and democratization

» Control of communications media enables manipulation and creation of biased news

» Public lying replaces integrity, trust, and transparency

Old Love means affection for money, material things, and consumption; its manifestation is greed. Transformative Love is based on generosity. Old Love means only loving yourself which is narcissism. Transformative Love brings forth compassion and humility. Old Love is exclusive affection for one's culture over another. Transformative Love means tolerance and respect. The Old Love is exclusive; it protects borders, builds walls, and promotes fear. Transformative Love is inclusive; it builds bridges, fosters variety, and compassion for others.

Changes and transformations can best be catalyzed by a "relevant" Love and Power interaction. Before we can initiate change, in a movement or an institution, there must be a gathering of energy, inspiration, and intention for change. Participants need to catalyze a vision to imagine the possibility for change and success. As tools, Transformative Love and Transformative Power combine, serving as an inspiration and hope that initiates the change.

Take as an example the #NeverAgain anti-firearms movement in the USA. Why did it fail in the past, but is now much alive? Before, it was the time of Old Power and Old Love, and the "activation energy" (the bar of resistance) was too high! But the times are changing. Now, NextGen is not only talking with their hearts, but also with the passion and skill to speak the truth to both political parties through the connected networks and in real time. They are leveraging social media to position their Transformative Love to overcome the controlling Old Power of business, interest groups, and government lobbying for NRA.

The interplay between Transformative Power and Transformative Love has always been a problem, as in the story about President Lincoln. Countering a radical Senator, committed not merely to abolishing slavery, but to racial equality, President Lincoln[52] explained his own lack of radicalism by saying:

"A compass, it'll point you True North from where you are standing, but it's got no advice about the swamps and deserts and chasms you'll encounter along the way. If in pursuit of your destination you plunge ahead, heedless of obstacles, and achieve nothing more than to sink in a swamp, what's the use of knowing True North?"

Lincoln had to come to the realization of why he needed to do the right thing, but these insights did not come easily to him. His struggle within himself to resolve the Power/Love continuum, helped to transform him as a catalytic leader. Lincoln was able to balance his Power as Commander in Chief with his Love and dedication to abolition of slavery. As a Catalyzer, he combined his strategy, political savvy, and agility with his values and faith to achieve his goal of Harmony in the form of racial equality.

Strategic Harmony Transformation Process

Needless to say, the key to *Empower Us!* is the transformative forces of Power and Love resulting in Strategic Harmony. We've developed a four quadrant snapshot to tell the story of the Strategic Harmony transformation process. The quadrants are Transformative Love and Old Love, and Transformative Power and Old Power. Each quadrant is described by a condition, objective, mindset, and lead.

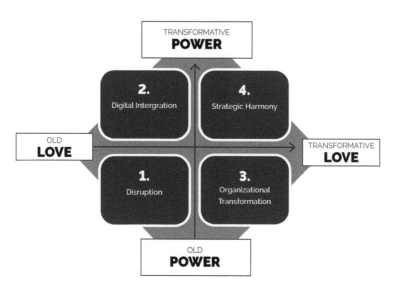

Figure 4.3 Transformative Power and Love Matrix

The lower left Quadrant 1—Disruption is the condition of a traditional business or organization governed by Old Power and Old Love. The mindset is based upon scarcity, controlling power and information. Decisions are driven by self-interest, profit and economic efficiencies. These businesses face the conditions including disruption, changing technologies, and younger and digitally savvy target markets. They are led by transactional executives with a focus on the short-term impact and return on investment.

With their survival at stake, the traditional organization looks to adopt digital technologies. Their objective is to "move" into the second Quadrant - Digital Integration. It is governed by Transformative Power and Old Love. The organization is reaching out to its constituency and attempting to listen, be more transparent, and have empathy for their target markets. The organization is challenged to integrate the customer experience into its new business model. Such organizations face exponentially changing technologies, but most of them have leadership rooted in Old Love. Thus, the staff don't have the skill sets necessary to execute and implement the transformation. They struggle to integrate a digital mindset and customer-first orientation into their current organizational culture. As reported previously, the outcomes for digital transformation have been disastrous, with 84% of them failing on a global level.

Some organizations choose to move from Quadrant 1 to Quadrant 3 and engage in a process of Organizational Transformation governed by Transformative Love and Old Power. In this context, the leadership focuses on transforming the organization and developing a mindset that is anchored in love of values and purpose that are driving cultural change. But this organizational transformation is not accompanied by changes in structure and communications hierarchies necessary to facilitate continuous innovation. Thus, functional silos (marketing, finance, HR, IT) remain, reinforcing Old Power and a competitive, solely profit-driven internal environment.

If we look at the corporate response to climate change, we see the conflict between Transformative Love and Old Power. The third TEST Value, sustainability, must be redefined as the power realized from harmonization of the ecology of our environment, the harmony of our financial situation with our organizational goals, and the harmony of our staff employees to allow us to fulfill those goals. Corporations retaining the Old Power resist changing their design, manufacturing, and distribution decisions to reflect a "greener "policy and maintain the status quo. They fear the introduction of restrictions on their Power. They are missing the opportunity to channel empathy toward the effect of climate change on all stakeholders and reframe their decision-making to sustain their company and the environment. The sustainability of our organizations and our world can be seen as an outward manifestation of feeling secure and sustained internally. When there is disharmony between our personal core values and those manifested by our organization or country, degradation of our relationships results in loss of power and energy. It's not sustainable!

Finally, as the mindset and culture changes, the organization is able to move from Quadrant 3 to Quadrant 4 - Strategic Harmony, governed by Transformative Power and Love. The objective is sustainable growth with a "stakeholder-centric" mindset of abundance. In this quadrant, leaders act as Catalyzers of the transformation process: optimizing the needs of all stakeholders; breaking down silos inhibiting collaboration; integrating values and purpose and new digital technologies across all operations; developing fully open channels of communication-facilitating innovation; generating intergenerational multi-functional teams focused on designing and implementing purposeful business models; and generating sustainable impact and growth.

Jack Ma, the founder of Alibaba, began as an English teacher who visited the United States and became infatuated with the Internet and its commercial applications. Upon his return to China, he began building an e-commerce system with some of his colleagues. Alibaba has grown to become one of the top three e-commerce delivery systems in the world.

Through its impact and Transformative Power, it has become a major force for social change and economic development. We personally witnessed this four years ago, talking to the CEO of the largest food distribution chain in Central Europe. He told us that a member of the Chinese visiting delegation had offered a support to economic development in Croatia. In lieu of foreign aid, he suggested to choose two or three food products which would be sold through Alibaba's Global Network and bring in revenue and jobs for Croatia. Alibaba offered its network as a creative way to change the model of economic development.

Jack Ma likes to point out that he built his company on customer service and universal values. Speaking at the World Economic Forum in Davos 2018, he emphasized that, to be successful, it's not enough to have high personal capacity (IQ) or high emotional intelligence (EQ). The key ingredient that makes companies and organizations grow and sustain is a high Love Quotient (LQ), universal capacity for empathy, compassion, and generosity. In his words: *To gain success, a person needs high EQ; if you don't want to lose quickly you would need a high IQ, and if you want to be respected, you need high LQ - the IQ of love.* In the context of Strategic Harmony, he is talking about Transformative Love and its impact on people and organizations.

When announcing that Daniel Zhang will succeed him as Chairman of the Board of Alibaba Group in September 2018, Jack Ma pointed out that a sustainable Alibaba is built on sound governance, culture-centric philosophy, and consistency in developing talent. The company is particularly successful because of its partnership system, a creative solution to good governance and sustainability, as it overcomes the challenges faced by companies of scale: continuous innovation, leadership succession, accountability, and cultural continuity. Over the years, they have experimented with a management model based on the right balance between systems and individuals. Simply relying on individuals or blindly following a system would not solve problems. In order to achieve long-term sustainable growth, Jack Ma relied on the right balance among system, people, and culture. He had full confidence that their efforts to safeguard the company's unique strategically harmonious culture will in time win over the love and support from customers, employees, and shareholders.

If we want to better measure the achievement and position in the Strategic Harmony quadrant, we may use Sustainable Impact Indicators in both short and long-term perspectives. Such indicators help us evaluate and address the issues of scarcity or abundance mentality, community, prosperity, and social impact, including more traditional Key Performance Indicators (KPI) such as customer loyalty, employee engagement, and business profit. When we harmonize our personal values with those in our organization, this Trans-formative Power is ignited within the individual; that new energy becomes aggregated as powerful corporate culture. When that harmonization spreads from person to person and from organization to organization, it becomes a movement. Enthusiasm and Love encourage businesses and organizations as well as employees to connect and augment this sustainable direction.

Another concept similar to our fourth-quadrant Strategic Harmony has recently been adopted by the former Japanese Prime Minister Abe and his Cabinet. It is called *Society 5.0* and describes the future that Japan aspires to achieve.

Society 5.0 is the fifth step in the evolution of the human society[53]. After being hunters, people settled down in the Agricultural Society. The next Industrial Society provided products for everybody based on mass production. Currently, we live in the Information Society, preparing for the fifth stage with humans coupled with machines, or Artificial Intelligence. The building of Society 5.0 (Super Smart Society) was initiated in April 2016 by the Japanese government as the country's *5th Science and Technology Plan*. It covers many aspects, including innovation promotion and internationalization, focusing on new values, namely Power and Love.

The underlying idea is that the rapid development of information technology allows the combination of cyber space and the physical space. The combination is expected to help create a sustainable society for human security and well-being through a cyber-physical system. It is defined as[54] human-centered society that balances economic advancement with the resolution of social problems by a system that highly integrates cyberspace and physical space. It will achieve a forward-looking society whose members have mutual respect for each other, transcending generations, and a society in which each and every person can lead an active and enjoyable life.

It is worth noting that Society 5.0, just like our "World of Strategic Harmony," focuses on optimizing the impact for all stakeholders, as well as on promoting values that are compatible with our TEST Values.

Power and Love in Strategic Harmony

Transformative Love, Transformative Power, and TEST Values are just a starting point. Strategic Harmony will be sustained through reinventing out-of-date educational systems; stimulating constant innovation with a collaborative engine; democratizing citizen participation and all institutions to be more reflective of the needs of all stakeholders; and balancing work and lifestyle with health systems replacing convenience and disease-promoting alternatives. Finally, there is a need for transformation of the global economic system into a comprehensive, sustainable approach to our people, our communities, our globe, and our ecology

Our model points out that a search for Strategic Harmony will change the global culture through Transformative Power and Transformative Love. As nicely put by the great rock star Jimi Hendrix[55], *"When the power of love overcomes the love of power, the world will know peace." EmPower Us!* and the new values will bring new reality!

Another provocative attempt to discuss the interplay between Old Power and Old Love[56] is the superhero film "Black Panther." The story takes place in Wakanda, a technologically advanced African nation hiding its vast resources and advanced technology from the rest of the world. They are aware that their assistance could provide a lot of good worldwide, but they are afraid of the implications of sharing. In the end their unwillingness to utilize their Power may leave their Love for the rest of the world harder to implement.

In a world of Transformative Power and Transformative Love, their dilemma would be easily solved. Strategic Harmony calls for action to fix what is broken and create balanced, trustworthy, sustainable, and empathic organizations aimed at collaboration and win-win. Speaking with the words of Mother Teresa: *"If we have no peace, it is because we have forgotten that we belong to each other."*

Why does EmPower Us! refer to superheroes? For two reasons: first, they are a popular method to talk about values; second, creating a world of Strategic Harmony is such a challenging task that maybe the insights of superheroes could live up to the challenge. The 2017 release of "Wonder Woman" was crowned the highest-grossing superhero original film of all time. But its impact can eclipse box office receipts; it is a timely metaphor for the Transformative Power of women. It is a movie about Wonder Woman's overwhelming faith and commitment to save the broken world. She was prepared from her child-hood to respond as a warrior with superpowers and skills to the most extreme trials in the best way possible. However, it was only through her experience of Love that her abilities and strength were enhanced to defeat evil! After experiencing Love, she was transformed—protecting humans unconditionally, even though some have been corrupted, greedy, selfish, and evil.

Here are a few Wonder Woman quotes as valuable lessons for those on the Path to Strategic Harmony:

> » "We can't change what happens to us eventually, but we can change the way we respond to it!"

> » "If only we would unite to our similarities instead of dividing because of our differences!"

> » "You can choose to do nothing about the wrong that's happening in the world, or you can choose to do something, no matter how much or little it helps."

As we complete this Guidepost, you can ask yourself:

> » Are your goals (endpoints) imbued with the feeling of Love?

» How are you strategically integrating Love and Power to balance the constant barrage of disruption, vulnerabilities, and threats?

» Are your endpoints driven by compliance with past strategies or by implementation of Transformative Power and Love to generate new ways and sustainable solutions?

» Is the Power balanced between stakeholders with active engagement and mutually beneficial strategies that fulfill the organization's purpose?

In Sanskrit the word *Upeksha* stands for equanimity. It describes the balanced approach we should take to all things in life, including Power and Love. Though political love and power are often deadly, and business love can turn into something lethal, and romantic love has its roller coaster moments, all real love must be balanced with power in its utmost aspect. Without Upeksha, Love and Power become possessive. It's like trying to forcefully put a summer breeze in a tin can. If it is left to be free, it stays a breeze; in the can, it dies.

This book is dedicated to a transparent application of Transformative Power and Love as tools to imagine, create, and (re)build a world of Strategic Harmony. It's the path to defining our purpose and objectives integrated with a carefully designed plan to realign the socio-economic forces in such a way to achieve balanced and sustainable outputs. We see Strategic Harmony as a state of constant change resulting in dynamic equilibrium among individuals, organizations, and society. It is based on common TEST Values and driven by Transformative Power and Love. One of the key reasons why our world and its institutions are broken lies in the fact that the roles of Power and Love are completely confused and abused. We must *empower us* to transform.

Love and Power are like the breeze. The more we control them, the less pleasant they become. We need Love and Power that are shared and used to transform the broken world to achieve Strategic Harmony.

Guidepost 5

From Leader to Catalyzer

"You must be the change you wish to see in the world."

Mahatma Gandhi

According to Harold S. Geneen, the legendary CEO of ITT, leading change is not so much in words, but in attitude and in action. Peter Senge, a legendary organizational behavior expert at MIT, suggests that our systemic global challenges require a unique type of leader, one who catalyzes collective leadership.

In this Guidepost, we will look at values and attitudes that challenge the myths and fuel the Catalytic Leadership necessary to initiate change.

What is driving the unprecedented chaos and deterioration of our institutions? At the same time, what are the drivers of transformation? As mentioned previously, we see four driving forces – Values, Power, Love, and Leadership. In this Guidepost, we add an adjective to the fourth force, and we call it *Catalytic Leadership, a key to EmPower Us!*

From Leader to Catalyzer

During the past four years, we have consulted with leaders in businesses, nonprofits, and government across the world; they are confused and overwhelmed with the vast changes. They are searching for the keys to successful transformation. What they need is exemplified in a popular story about Jester Nasruddin, a thirteenth-century mystic and story-teller, and his approach to searching for solutions and different ways to find them.

A man walking home saw Nasruddin out in the street searching frantically on his knees for something. "What are you searching for," asked the man. "I've lost my key", replied Nasruddin. The man decided to help him and joined the anxious search. After some time and no results, the man asked Nasruddin, "Where exactly was the key lost?"

"I think I lost it in the house," replied Nasruddin quite matter of factly. The man was quite shocked. "Why are we searching for it in the street?" "Because it's better light here," replied Nasruddin.

This story gives us an opportunity to reflect on how and where we search for solutions. Often, we spend time looking in the wrong places to solve our problems. We turn outside ourselves or organization to address challenges, just because "it's better light" there. We are more comfortable in the material arena of hiring new experts, investing in new technologies, or changing our marketing strategies. But the search must begin "Inside" with self-reflection on our values, assumptions, confirmation bias, and organizational culture. That is where the best answers lay.

Most leaders aren't prepared for the journey to Strategic Harmony. In the 21st century, leaders will face the equivalent to 20,000 years of progress at today's rate; they will operate in a hyper-connected environment where exponential changes build upon each other to generate unpredictable outcomes.

Traditional leaders see disruptive (technological) change as chaos. They strive to manage and bring order to it. They default to comfortable decisions because these have worked before. The result is that leaders look for solutions in wrong places. For example, they hire a new CXO (Chief Transformation Officer), establish an innovation unit, or invest in new technologies. But these siloed add-ons are mere "window dressing" to the total transformation required for success. These responses are referred to as "Innovation Theater," not a sustainable, impactful solution.

To truly address this imperative, leaders need to commit to uncharted business environments requiring transformation and adopting new rules for decision-making. These vital changes must be pervasive across all organizational functions.

Drastically new environments call for total organizational transformation. Like the above story, change begins "inside" with people and values. Leaders must redefine how they interact, think, gain power, and see change as a threat. They must reinvent their role to reinvent their organization. They must clarify company values and how they are incorporated in company culture. Functional teams must integrate mindset, digital literacy, and strategic muscle to collaborate on leveraging opportunities.

Most executives do not recognize the relationship between the changing environment, their role in the company, and the requirement for radical change. This gap leads to executives feeling unprepared and companies not ready to take on the challenge of Strategic Transformation.

What is to be done?

An executive's thinking must change from managing the current situation to creating a catalytic change in their environment, both internally and externally. They must be self-reflective and humble, striving to become more agile and flexible. They need to be prepared to dismantle their assumptions and confirmation bias as well as to break the "rules" and beliefs of the current organization. They must leave their comfort zone and be ready to change and learn. In one word, they must become Catalyzers for a comprehensive transformation in the organization including strategy, culture, organizational structure, stakeholder experience, product design, finance, marketing, and IT.

Exponential change seen as disruption and chaos must be redefined as a strategic opportunity. The Catalyzer is no longer a victim of the chaos but a master of transformation, searching for sustainable solutions. Opportunities and challenges are everywhere. Let's take a look at just two examples. Currently Kenya has a 7% smartphone penetration. However, in three years, it is expected to jump to 90%, exponentially impacting every person and institution. Dubai, in quest to become the world's innovation capital, faces heavy construction; 25% of cranes worldwide are operating in that city resulting in various building-related records: the world's tallest tower (Burj Khalifa), the world's largest shopping mall (Dubai Mall), the world's largest fountain (The Dubai Fountain), the world's tallest hotel (the Gevora Hotel), and Dubailand, twice the size of the Walt Disney World Resort. Business and government must transcend their linear models to anticipate and design solutions for the future that employ human-centered strategies considering social impact.

According to Judith Rodin, president of the Rockefeller Foundation, *"in much of the world, markets must be built before they can be served. Forward-looking business leaders who embrace this reality make explicit commitments to enter new global markets both as economic opportunity zones as well as community spaces requiring nurturing and support."*

Fixing the broken world means developing and nurturing new leaders, Catalyzers, masters of transformation able to lead organizations toward Strategic Harmony.

What is a Catalyzer?

Traditionally, leaders are people who take responsibility, inspire, and enable their team. This works in the world when the leadership team understands the variables, can project a decision path based on experiences, and can observe and respond to their competitors' outcomes in the marketplace. Today, most leaders live in an "outdated" world of unknown drivers and non-causal relationships. Their role and business models are anachronisms reflecting a past set of conditions. Executives must redefine their role to be a "Catalyzer" of change.

Why a Catalyzer? The executive's first task is to reflect on his or her identity, on what value they bring to his or her organization. Twenty-first century management is still based on the method invented by French philosopher, René Descartes, and later expanded upon by physicist, Isaac Newton. The management is there to research a problem, create a tool to fix the problem, test the hypothesis, and evaluate if there is a relationship between the solution and outcome. Based on reductionist thinking, we break down issues into component parts, then isolate them and measure them for the cause and effect. Managers direct tasks. Leaders orchestrate. Catalyzers transform.

Catalyzers initiate and increase the velocity of transformation while leveraging disruption. In the world of chemistry, the Catalyzer is a "matchmaker." In a test tube environment, the catalyst grabs the desired reaction partners, dissolves the old bonds, and brings about the right partners to make a new chemical compound. It speeds up the process, increases the rate of chemical reactions, and saves energy without being consumed itself.

Much of contemporary management theory owes a great deal to Peter Drucker. During the last half century, the entire world has dramatically changed. The command-and-control economy has evolved toward a shared economy. Hierarchical management structures have yielded to broken down silos and open communication channels. Incremental change (10%) is scaled to exponential change (10X). Gen Z (26% of population) is now the largest consumer segment. It's globally connected, sharing the same digital culture. According to the World Economic Forum, 65% of children today will end up in careers that don't even exist yet. A global survey[57] points out a lack of belief in contemporary leaders. More than two-thirds of citizens don't have confidence that current leaders can address the global challenges. Survey suggests that the credibility of CEOs fell to 37%, and trust in government officials is down to 29%.

Leaders must reinvent themselves to tackle the above challenges and disruptions. They must accept their responsibility as Catalyzers. The executive's choice is not to be a *"Leader"* or not, but instead to acknowledge a commitment to the transformation process and the executive's new role as a catalyst for change.

The practical dilemma starts with a need to, on one hand, optimize the existing system while it still functions, and, on the other hand, transform it, in order to build a better system. Mastering the present means to manage all existing organizational processes in such a way to ensure their quality and efficiency. The existing processes are not designed to last forever, but until changes take place, they must remain as profitable and successful as possible. In order to deal with this problem, two strategies must be developed in each system. The first is aimed at ensuring the optimal performance of the existing system, while the second means the demolition of the existing system in order to introduce a better system. The first calls for traditional managers who are able to do things right; the second calls for Catalyzers who are ready to do the right things and ignite transformation.

According to Stephen Covey[58], one person can be a change catalyst, a transformer in any situation, any organization. Such an individual is the yeast that can leaven an entire loaf. It requires vision, initiative, patience, respect, persistence, courage, and faith to be a catalytic leader.

Traditional managers are trained and able to work within the business environment of mostly known variables; a Catalyzer is challenged by revolutionary technologies, market disruptions, and new expectations of connected consumers and citizens. Catalyzers are working in a sped-up time implementing Lean methodologies, while traditional leaders operate within a limited scope and efficiency. Traditional leaders and Catalyzers can share values but have a different focus on actualizing them. Leaders strive to translate them into each functional area; Catalyzers base strategies and operations on values to ensure transparency and consistency. They gain Power by fully implementing their values across all operations. While the Catalyzer's team is interdependent and collaborative, drawing on each participant's strengths, the traditional team is often struggling to break through an old siloed mentality to form a cohesive group. Peter Senge proposes collaborative competition as a way to address the global challenges: we compete with one another, and at the same time, share research and findings. It's an interdependence coupled with action on multiple fronts.

The traditional leader is interested in addressing questions about the system as it is. On the other hand, the task of the Catalyzer is to deal with the future, describing where to go from here and how to get there. His/her primary interest is the system as it could be. The Leader deals with what the present system looks like, while the Catalyzer wants to transform the current system or build a new one. In practical terms, it means that the Leader is the chief organizer, and the Catalyzer is the chief "disorganizer." The organizer makes sure that every facet of the existing system functions as it should; the disorganizer wants to transform the existing system in order to introduce a totally new system.

In the framework of our book, the leader who takes over the role of disorganizer is the change agent, the Catalyzer. Such leaders existed from the early history of mankind, and are epitomized in The Great Man theory[59], a 19th-century idea according to which all progress can be explained by the impact of "*great men*," or heroes (and also women); highly influential individuals who, due to intelligence, wisdom, personal charisma, or political skill used their power in a way that had a decisive historical impact.

Leadership Challenge – Climate change

The crisis of leadership is constantly defined as "global problem no. 1". Let's review the challenge to address the global threat of climate change.

As a planet, we have passed the 10th anniversary of the complete disintegration of climate negotiations at the UN Climate Change Conference in Copenhagen. In December 2019, at the UN Conference of Parties 24 in Madrid, history repeated itself. Once more, heads of state and corporate leaders left the world without a roadmap to combat climate change. As a planet, we have failed to address the necessities of Global System Change. It is our responsibility to look at the role of our leaders in failing this challenge.

Our leaders failed to respond.

What has emerged is a clear scientific case for urgent action on climate change; however, global leaders seem not to be prepared for practical action. They are locked into a dated, defensive mindset focused on restraint and sacrifice, rather than an expansive approach to the vast business and investment opportunities that the necessary social transformation could generate.

Our leaders failed to recognize the warnings and opportunities.

"*The new normal*" and "*unprecedented*" became the buzzwords of our global community. We are facing depletion of scarce resources at alarming rates; massive migration of refugees; dangerously high unemployment; underutilized youth talents in developing countries; and increasing concentration of wealth. These unprecedented impacts have exacerbated inequality and the climate crisis. There is much conversation in the media, business roundtables, and political debate, but little action.

Our leaders promote short-term "wins" but don't generate game-changing impact.

Traditionally, leaders face such challenges with reductionist, siloed thinking by investing resources to increase their short-term profits and value to the shareholders. Our 'broken" world demands integrated, holistic, and complex solutions. When faced with exponential change on all different fronts, leaders move from inaction, to overwhelming confusion, to accessing their power interests, and then acting for the status quo. When these leaders awaken to the global threat, they default to comfortable models of vested interest. The Gaps between their words and actions block creative agreements and movement required for Strategic Transformation.

Our leaders failed to truly prioritize sustainability and resolve the gaps between proclamations and action.

As a globe we face this overarching challenge. Are emerging and current leaders prepared to act decisively to create a more just and sustainable world?

The fact is, for the most part, No, they aren't. Most leaders are trained in traditional business schools with one dimensional and dated curriculum. Targeted advanced trainings/certificates focus on one aspect of the necessary transformation. For example, entrepreneurial incubators are focused on profit-only outcomes, while leadership trainings improve emotional intelligence. Accenture's *New Rules for Engagement Research*[60] suggests *"leaders will have to embrace a more balanced approach blending left and right brain skills if they are to be successful ... Further, 65% of the C suite surveyed is weak in empathy, self-awareness, intuition, and relationship building. If they harness these skills, then they can expect, on average, 22% higher revenue growth and 34% higher profitability growth."*

Our leaders don't have the skills or holistic training required to fuel sustainable ventures that meet the Quadruple Bottom Line!

Catalyzers must lead!

During the last five years, with the newfound sources of digital power and the heightened awareness of climate change threats, the mindsets of emerging leaders have undergone a transformation. Rising Voices are demanding a sustainable future and have the insights and courage to disrupt the structures and systems which block this necessity. These agents of exponential change must be empowered and given access to collaborate with current leaders on a roadmap to regenerate our global ecosystem. Catalyzers must transform the use of capital resources to mobilize action strategies that fuel sustainable impact. For example, the adoption of circular business models driven by a Quadruple Bottom Line will impact people, planet, profit, and prosperity of all stakeholders.

Here is a consultant's view[61] on that issue: With people in private enterprise or in government, there is a common refrain: *"no leadership at the top."* This has created an interesting dynamic. True leaders are emerging from the middle, bottom, or outside of organizations. These are people who are focused on solutions and simultaneously unaccepting of the gridlock. These are people who do not allow accepted expectations to define the limitations of what they can do, change, or influence. These leaders emerge from the private or public sector and create impact in areas that would not be top-of-mind for most people.

Viewing leadership through the lens of Transformative Power, another consultant[62] suggests that every player on the team can be an initiator. We need to empower those that will make the change happen, NextGen, women, those historically marginalized. In other words, we all need to become change makers because we have to support those who need to change the world. It is a survival imperative. No more questions about "why" and "when" and "what for." The only question is "how" to make change happen now, not tomorrow.

Leadership means guidance and direction. Traditional Leaders base their decisions on the past, personal experience, and historical evidence. Catalyzers must anticipate. It's hard to lead without the knowledge of the future in a state of change and ambiguity. As a consequence, new enterprise leaders must become constant innovators adjusting to the necessities of the environment. However, most managers do not recognize the relationship between the changing environment, their role in the company, and the requirement for radical change. This gap makes them feel unprepared and their companies unready to take on the challenge of Strategic Transformation.

Catalyzers must act to fill the leadership gap!

What's required to transform? Our global priority is to transform current leaders and these Rising Voices into Catalyzers. We must be laser-focused on four transformation forces to meet the 2030 climate change goals: personal transformation of leadership team; inclusive transformation of Rising Voices; digital transformation of organizations' strategies (connectivity) to scale outcomes; and stakeholder transformation of organization's impact on Sustainable Development Goals (SDGs) to regenerate the planet. Each force is linked to a TEST Value to empower the transformation. The synergy of these transformational spaces is required for emerging leaders and executives to leverage exponential changes and generate sustainable outcomes.

Personal transformation is based upon the value of Trust. Leaders must incorporate values and purpose as a compass for the organizational culture. Their self-reflection and consistent application of values across the organization generate Trust among all stakeholders. Trust releases the potentiality for transformation, changing the business model and framework for decision-making. It unlocks the dimensions of catalytic thinking, reframing the previously unmovable dots in a decision matrix, and unlocking digital perspectives, networks, value engagement, and sustainable impact criteria.

EY[63] worked with a major home appliance brand in India to revamp their business model. They challenged management ... *"Is trust your most important deliverable?"* The team realized Trust ultimately helped to drive profitable growth in innovation by engaging and empowering the stakeholders throughout the supply chain.

Inclusive transformation is based upon the value of Empathy. Organizations must collaborate across generations and listen to and engage the Rising Voices to fuel equitable and just outcomes.

Catalyzers must be equipped to leverage vast sources of information and data-diverse mindsets. They need to be guided to include five generations of our workforce to transform the gaps in intent and action while uniting the C suite[64]: *"Everybody comes in with a different version of the truth...different perspectives on where you are today, on what the KPIs are based. And we haven't united the language of leaders ...and what they hold people accountable to."[65]*

Digital transformation is based upon the value of Transparency. Organizations must incorporate the three digital differentiators (network connectivity, rich data, and exponential technologies) to effectively deliver and scale outcomes to the community and globe. Digital transformation is a strategic priority for 80+% of the C suite, yet 42% do not know where to start and 40+% of senior leaders said they believe their business transformation efforts have been "a waste of time" and failed. The World Economic Forum suggests *"With increasing pressure on the world's resources and an urgent need to cut emissions, digital transformation can help set the world's economy on a sustainable footing."* Catalyzers must incorporate the pervasiveness of digital in the organization and work to leverage to it globally.

Stakeholder transformation is based upon the value of Sustainability. All stakeholders strive for Harmony in a dynamic environment of change (resources, investments, technologies, and institutions) that enhances their potential to meet human needs and aspirations. Sustainability requires a high social sustainability standard for due diligence of impact-driven ventures. It depends upon transparent communications, data, information, and financial accountability.

Transparency powers the economic engine. *"Without it, investors are unable to make informed decisions about where to allocate their capital, which hurts companies' ability to attract it and puts a drag on economic growth."[66]* Stakeholders must have open access to critical factors (e.g., talent recruitment and retention and constraints on natural resources) to make informed investment decisions.

Leadership Challenge: Overcome Limited Thinking

Throughout the path of digital era towards the so-called new industrial revolution 4.0, information is somehow considered a currency, more than just a competitive advantage. It has a direct impact on how leaders are going to share knowledge and data, due to uncertainties about the use of transparency for virtuous or corrupt purposes. This fear can be observed in both macro and micro levels, from governments to corporations. Leaders have a huge challenge in understanding the impacts of digitalization in a human dimension.

The impacts of real-time communication require quick and proper answers to demands that can only be reached if leaders decentralize the decision-making authority. However, to empower their team with the ability to take actions, leaders have to share their knowledge, their privileged information, and their power to influence—i.e. the media, sectors, policies, standards, politics, and many others. The diplomatic art of selecting the appropriate way to inform, and what to inform, together with the authority that leaders have to command, hides a subjective seduction for keeping this hegemony over information.

Somehow, the digital era deconstructs this model. There is a hidden fear of leaders that shared information could become an 'out of control' empowerment of others. Maybe it would, with not enough engagement, transparency, open interaction, accountability, and consequently, trust.

Trust is actually a big issue. Even to allow data access, you need trust. But to trust, one needs to feel safe; and to feel safe it is imperative to stimulate comprehensive dialogues, debate risks, map solutions, and reach understandings. There is no need to fear change: big data, 3D printing, IoT, AI... the natural process of progress. If the world changes, we have to change. These ideas lead humans to evolution. Probably, there would be no evolution without the courage to accept the challenges of changes. To be constructive, evolution requires new leaders committed to overcome their own limitations with the audacity to guide our society in a meaningful direction.

Flávia P. Malucelli, Senior Program Coordinator, Brazilian Mission to World Trade Organization

Leader's Self-Reflection

So far we have talked about Leaders and Catalyzers. Based on the (r)evolution of the global digital marketplace, there is still another role, one of Navigator. The key difference lies in their purpose and openness to disruption and change. The Leader works in a bureaucratic organization with a transactional mindset and is driven by profit. The Navigator works in a digitized organization with a digital mindset and is driven by optimization of the results for investors, customers, and employees. The Catalyzer is a revolutionary type, searching for exponential growth, disruption, and radical innovation through networks, participative decision-making, consensus, and Quadruple Bottom Line.

In order to better understand the challenges and issues associated with their role, all potential managers and executives must be able to monitor the transition from a Leader to a Catalyzer. The following table (Figure 5.1) is a powerful tool to determine how they currently approach transformation and change.

Each (prospective) leader can self-reflect on the 20 factors from the left column and observe the difference between the three approaches (bureaucratic Leader, evolutionary Navigator, and revolutionary Catalyzer). Then each leader can self-reflect and note the factors that require work and adjustment.

APPROACH	BUREAUCRATIC	EVOLUTIONARY	REVOLUTIONARY
Executive	Leader	Navigator	Catalyzer
Mindset	Transactional	Digital	Catalytic
Goal	Status quo	Incremental increase -10%	Exponential increase-10x
Objective	Growth, profit	Customer/ market value	Social impact
Change	Slow, resisting	Intermittent	Continuous
Focal point	Product/service	Customer	All stakeholders
Approach	Follow rules	Change rules	Reinvent procedures, fit culture
Power	Old Power	Hybrid	Transformative Power
Decision-Making	Outvoting	Business model	Consensus
Problem Solving	Empirical	Innovative	Iterative
Key Resource	Money	Data	Values, Agile team
Organization	Rigid and stable	Open to step- by-step change	EXO organization flexible
Innovation Venue	Research & development	Open innovation	Rapid Innovation Unit
Innovation type	Better quality, breakthrough product	More simple, convenient, less costly	Disrupts industry; scales innovation
Authority	Autocratic	Democratic	Participation
Internal channels	Top down one way	Two way communication	Spontaneous radical open participation
Control	Imposed	Transparent	Self-control
Communications	Traditional media	Digital media	Augmented Media, Network
Customer Relationship	Customer satisfaction	Customer experience	Holistic customer integration
Customer Decision	Sales Funnel	Interactive consumer process	Customer Involvement cycle
Impact	Return on Investment (investor driven)	Triple Bottom Line (customer-driven)	Quadruple Bottom Line (stakeholder driven)

Figure 5.1 Leader, Navigator, Catalyzer

Traditional Leaders are threatened and paralyzed by change. They depend on Old Power and outdated methodologies to enable their current business plan and protect them from change. Navigators accept change. They acknowledge the need for it, but are stuck in the old paradigm of assumptions and dated Key Performance Indicators and cost management. They search for confidence and best practices to adjust and become more agile to motivate their team. Catalyzers live change. Adopting a mindset of Transformative Power and Love, the leadership team invests time in building a nourishing and diverse culture. They develop trusting relationships that inspire and empower their team to design new business models that fuel disruption and change. In fixing the broken world and its institutions, executives must redefine their role to become Navigators and Catalyzers of change across generations.

To differentiate the categories, and better understand his or her role, the leader must reflect on the following questions:

» Is it your goal to maintain the status quo, or incremental (evolutionary), or exponential (revolutionary) change?

» When dealing with change, are we resisting, moderately active, or real transformers? Is the focal point of the change on "service," focusing on customers, or on all stakeholders?

» Are new ideas openly and enthusiastically discussed or resisted?

» Is our organization rigid and stable or flexible and dynamic?

» Do we follow the "rules" or strategies of their industry or sector, or challenge them, or change/reinvent them?

» As far as problem solving is concerned, is it empirical, innovative, or visionary?

» Is the key organizational resource money, ideas, or values?

» Is authority based on hierarchy, democratic procedures, or grass roots participation?

» Is control imposed, transparent, or self-controlled?

» Is communication based on traditional media, digital media, or networks?

» Is the customer decision journey based on sales funnel, interactive consumer process, or customer involvement cycle?

» Is performance measurement investor-driven, customer driven, or stakeholders-driven?

In case the presented discussion did not already persuade you, let's contrast a Leader and Catalyzer as two opposing roles. (Figure 5.2)

LEADER	CATALYZER
CEO (Chief Executive Officer)	CEO (Chief Experience Officer)
The Boss	A Peer, Mentor
Old Power	Transformative Power
Love of (financial) Success	Love of Purpose
Rational	Empathetic
Motivate, enable	Inspire, Reinvent (get out of the way)
Direct silos	Collaborate across functions
Order	Ambiguity
Organize people	Connect networks
Strategize	Anticipate
Minimize Risk	Risk taker
Preach beliefs	Challenge beliefs
Hoard knowledge, data	Share learning, insights
Achieve goals	Achieve transformation
Leverage power of position	Earn the right
Fixed on one solution	Open to alternative solutions
Opportunistic	Authentic
Performance	Impact
Shareholder centric	Stakeholder centric

Figure 5.2 Leaders and Catalyzers as Executives

Change or Die

There is no doubt that the current digital technologies powered by emergence of artificial intelligence and blockchain technologies call for Catalyzers of continuous change. They face a world of ambiguity with no time to completely research, test, validate, and then implement. The new environment of speed and turbulence requires executives to rethink corporate culture and structure, reinvent business models, and design sustainable strategies.

Catalyzers crave change to meet current and anticipated challenges, and are continuously innovating and designing superior ways to improve lives of all stakeholders on a local and global level. The focus is not only on what the organization is, but what the organization wants to become. The goal is to generate social change while maintaining sustainable profit and impact.

The evolution from a Leader to a Catalyzer requires an organization to transform its current strategies and operations moving towards a more integrated and digital approach. Leaders progress along the continuum as their goals change to impact their targets on a larger scale. Leaders must adopt a transformative mindset before they can effect change in the business or organization. The organization must become digitally integrated and collaborative before attempting to affect society in any sustainable way. The organizations that take this leap of faith into the unknown are rewarded with customer advocates and loyal employees, as well as a sustainable marketplace.

If the Catalyzer is overwhelmed by the complexity of the problem, he/she rethinks the underlying factors to reshape the challenge. When you redefine the drivers, conditions, and assumptions, you'll see the problem differently and, only then, be able to solve it. However, we are accustomed, educated, mentally programmed, and trained to look at problems pretty much the way everybody else does, based on prevailing paradigms. We enjoy seeing things structured, organized, rational, and predictable. Truth be told, most people resist changes and are afraid of "disruptions."

In his book *Change or Die*, Alan Deutschman presents the results of a medical study. Suppose there are six individuals whose health, even life, depend on "transformation" of their bad habits (alcohol or drug addiction, smoking, bad nutrition, lack of physical activities). The doctor advises them to change or they are most likely dead within a year. How many will succeed in transforming their lifestyle in order to survive? The study proves that only one in six finds strength and determination to change. Two people decide to give it a try but, sooner or later, they give up, and return to the old habits and the suicidal lifestyle. The remaining three never even try to change and thus destine themselves to a deadly outcome. This reality is particularly seen in the results of motivational programs that exhort large numbers of people to develop good habits or see themselves in a more positive light. Only about 2% of people attending these events or following self-help programs actually change their behavior, despite the often large amounts of money people pay for such programs.

As the study mentioned by Deutschman points out, even under the most drastic pressure, only one in six people will voluntarily alter behavior. The other five prefer to resist the change despite the fact that it's, literally, a matter of life and death. That's why we desperately need Catalyzers. They are the force that makes transformation a reality. Similar to chemical processes, transformations occur faster with a catalyst because they require less activation energy.

One of the key premises in *EmPower Us!* is that *Strategic Harmony* calls for *Catalyzers*, with a new set of values and a new organizational culture. This concept is known for centuries. Many traces of our model can be seen in past cultures, from Ancient Greeks to Native Americans.

Let's briefly discuss the culture of Blackfoot native tribes that now reside in Montana, Alberta, and Saskatchewan, as analyzed by Abraham Maslow[67] (altfeldinc.com/pdfs/maslow.pdf). Their culture stood in stark contrast to that of a modern organization. There was an emphasis on generosity as the highest virtue of the tribe. The needs of the tribe as a whole were effortlessly combined with the needs of the individual tribe member. The tribe tended not to have general leaders with general power, but rather they had different leaders for different functions. Each leader was chosen for a particular job based on the needs of that job. Thus, the one best suited to lead the Sun Dance was not expected to lead the representation of the tribe to the government.

Any Blackfoot leader had absolutely no power that wasn't deliberately and voluntarily given to him (or her) ad hoc by the particular people in the particular situation. There was a total trust between the group and the chosen leader because the leader was quite objectively the best one for the job, and the group considered that person to be the Catalyzer. It was assumed that they all had the same purpose, and that the leader was a kind of quarterback who called the signals and coordinated the group toward common ends, rather than one who gave orders, who used power, who tried to influence them, or control them in any way.

The Blackfoot didn't bother with leaders when there was no need to lead, and in some situations, they were simply amorphous, unorganized groups. Although quite unstructured, this worked well. Obviously, they have somehow anticipated parts of our model, namely TEST Values, Transformative Love, Transformative Power and the role of Catalyzers. They lived in harmony with nature and others until their cultures were interrupted and decimated by white European settlers.

Guidepost 6

Catalyzers for Global Change

"Vision without action is merely a dream.
Action without vision just passes the time.
Vision with action can change the world."

Joel A. Barker

Six in ten people around the world think their society is broken! Some are fearful, dissatisfied, and resist changing. Some lack confidence in the institutions, while others are still observing. But there are many already catalyzing the change. In this Guidepost, we will meet the Catalyzers of global change, the three growing global communities striving for change. They know that the world is broken and want it fixed as soon as possible. They are (1) Women, (2) The Next Generation (Millennials and Generation Z), and (3) Historically Marginalized (racial, ethnic, gender minorities, and those below the "poverty line").

We will also discuss two potential contributors to Strategic Transformation, namely the global Muslim community and the Nation of China. For many, these entities are often seen as possible causes of global problems and crises rather than forces for transformation.

Ironically, due to the historical and recent animus between these two communities, the global Muslim community and China might provide opportunities in this conflicted world. As the Chinese pictogram for "crisis" consists of two symbols: "danger" + "opportunity," we decided to look at these two communities from the positive side, to see them as potential forces of change and catalysts for global transformation on the path to Strategic Harmony.

For politicians and media, Women, NextGen, and Marginalized, are just demographic statistics, numbers on a census, or occasional headline-grabbing news. In the context of transformation, they are powerful latent communities connected via global networks that are calling out—EmPower Us!

Each Rising Voice is represented by one of the following globally impactful events:

» *Wonder Woman* goes well beyond its extraordinary worldwide cinematic success to reflect a woman superhero who juxtaposes unmatched strength and strategic acumen with the Power of Love to save the world. This quote exemplifies the empowerment of younger women with a role model of strong values: *"Seven girls playing together during recess said that since they all wanted to be Wonder Woman, they had agreed to be Amazons and not fight but work together to defeat evil."* Self-confident and organized women are an essential driver of global Strategic Harmony.

» #neveragain is a youth movement that began in the U.S. as a response to the mass 2018 shooting at Parkland High School in Florida. This massacre was more than a loss of 17 lives or a news event that captured the media for months. As the surviving youth spoke "Truth To Power," they mobilized the NextGen to raise their voices for change through voter registration and "get out the vote" drives for the U.S. 2018 midterm election. Engaging Millennials and Gen Z with their strong value base and digital connectivity presents a powerful resource on the path to Strategic Harmony.

» *Black Panther* redefined what a global blockbuster superhero movie can accomplish! It allowed us to get real and uncomfortable about our history of slavery and colonialism, and stereotypes about *"Blackness."* It revealed an alternate version of our world with people of color empowered into leadership. In the movie, a secret African nation developed and defended its own advanced technology and culture with real economic, social, and political equality across gender and color lines. It empowered and gave a vast swath of marginalized people of color and immigrants with a vision and hope for a new future. As the demographics of Africa grow exponentially and the migration of the disenfranchised explode, these Rising Voices will transform centers of Power and accelerate the path to Strategic Harmony.

All of the three Rising Voices radiate energy; they gain considerable strength from leveraging Transformative Power (giving voice to their unheard demands and under-represented constituency) and Transformative Love (empowering values and purpose with passion and direction). Their messages address many urgent needs of the exponentially growing connected demographic as they translate this Power into protest, purchasing, and voting actions.

Women exercise their Love through their passion to be heard, involved, engaged, and making decisions about important issues in their personal and family lives such as health, education, reproductive rights, and fair wages. Their decisions reflect a fresh "human-first" approach of compassion, understanding, caring, and concern for others. With many being mothers or mentors of the young, they don't only think of themselves, but channel their energies to support and sustain the Next Generations' wellbeing and opportunities. They express Power through their voices and votes. Witness the record number of 141 women won in the 2020 U.S. Elections including seats in the House of Representatives and the Senate. In addition, there are 9 female governors.

In the case of the Next Generation, our young are passionate and strive for a more sustainable, ethical world that addresses their needs and expectations. They strive for a world that prioritizes correctives for the impending ecological tragedy threatening our planet. They strongly advocate an economic system that is inclusive, that bridges the needs of the poorest in terms of essential services provided. They express Power through protesting across the U.S. and globally for racial justice and police reform, purchasing purposeful, socially responsible products and services, and more actively turning out to vote.

The diverse and historically Marginalized have been forced to live outside the traditional power structures because of their color, religion, ethnicity, and gender preference. Now, they want to be heard, included, and represented at the table. A very large number of them are immigrants, passionate for freedom and opportunity. They left a corrupt, poor, unpromising, often violent and war-torn homeland, and are running to places that will hopefully allow them to live in safety, security, and opportunity.

All these Global Catalyzers are exercising their loud voices and re-inventing a new world order as we watch it play out in real time. They initiate action by distributing content on social media networks, and serve as catalyzing forces in fixing the broken world. They reject the Old Power hierarchies and communications channels. They are in search for the means and the tools to develop Transformative Power to influence institutions and leaders that affect other citizens in their communities and their world. This Power is being generated by adopting and reinforcing the TEST Values, the key to a better world. Communities yearn to trust their leaders' decisions and call for allocation of resources in a just manner. They demand "Radical Empathy" in respecting community members' needs, and in actively involving participants in determining their future. They demand Transparency; their leaders are expected to speak "with one tongue," to unify their messages, to fairly represent the community, and to make their voices heard through the social media.

The reality of these emerging forces of change is that they're not compact and organized. Often, they are merged into one person, for example a marginalized immigrant and a Millennial woman. She gains Transformative Power as she integrates and embodies these three cultures and related agendas. She is positioned to share and scale this experience with other women throughout the world. Most recently, the synergistic Power of these three communities has been realized in the United States political scene as EMILY's List. It supports extremely qualified women from all ethnic, religious, and professional backgrounds to come forward and run for political office. The most inspiring case is Alexandria Ocasio-Cortez, a 30-year-old schoolteacher, waitress, and community worker, born in the Bronx, New York. Working tirelessly door to door, communicating heart-to-heart with citizens in need, she defeated a highly ranking Democrat in her Congressional primary. The powerful long-time Congressman had lost touch, not paying attention to the changing needs of his constituency. She won the primary and then convincingly won an elected seat in the United States Congress. As a woman she is compassionate and fights for equitable services in her community. As a Millennial whose family is of Puerto Rican descent, she envisions a more inclusive economic framework. As far as our Strategic Harmony model is concerned, she is a perfect example of a Catalyzer, able to inspire the new generation of women surfacing in the United States and globally.

As already mentioned, *EmPower Us!* is about the power of multiple generations striving for transformation, demanding inclusive impact and equity with progressive leader's voices of wisdom and expertise to generate a sustainable future. In the rest of this Guidepost, we will take a deep dive into the three catalyzing communities in an effort to understand who they are, what they want and expect, and how they can affect the process of fixing the broken world. We will look at each group through the lens and mindset of how they see the world, their community, and their country.

Women

On the 21st of January 2016, the day following Donald Trump's Presidential inauguration, five million people worldwide gathered for the 2016 Women's March. On that day, resistance became the duty for women around the world!

The massive response of the Women's March demonstrated the power of unity—of shared experiences. This unleashed and assisted women as individuals and as a group to be Catalyzers of change.

Although women's rights have risen, inequalities and discrimination continue to underscore the work that needs to be done. The World Economic Forum projected that it would take at least 100 years to close the equality gap between men and women, with significant disparities in economics and politics. But women's persistence, passion, and love for their inner purpose have sped up change.

Women are and will continue being emerging leaders in society as positive change makers and problem solvers for NextGen, challenging politicians, giving voice to the disenfranchised, mobilizing grassroots citizen groups, and directing major global corporations. Here are five most recent noteworthy wins for gender equality across the globe:

1. Iceland is the first country to make it illegal to pay men more than women.
2. Saudi Arabia allows women to drive for the first time.
3. #MeToo goes global; sexual harassment is challenged.
4. Sex with child brides in India is now accurately called "rape."
5. A record number of women (117) won seats in the U.S. House of Representatives, including 48 women of color.

We are facing a serious long-term question: Is the world ready for Female Leadership? Some historians claim that, in human history, patriarchy alternated with matriarchy, but the present is characterized by a disproportionately small share of women in economic and political power structures. Female representatives play an increasingly important leadership role, but the process is slow and gets a late start. In 1965, the first woman graduated from Harvard Business School. Fifty years later, female students comprise 40% of that population. In the former socialist bloc, women were legally equal to men with regard to possession of property, the right to work, and equal salary. But they rarely occupied leadership positions, even though they were highly represented in expert positions. More than half the doctors, dentists, and pharmacists in Eastern Europe are women.

For the sake of argument, there are many signs of women's' influence. For example, women's impact on consumer spending decisions amounts to 83%. This influence is strongest when buying furniture (94%), choosing a vacation destination (92%), or purchasing a new home (91%), and lowest when purchasing a new car (60%), or purchasing consumer electronics (51%). However, we still live in a male-dominated world, and being a woman leader is challenging.

In this recent decade, women's gain in management jobs has stagnated[68]. Women are just 5% of Fortune 500 CEOs and are only 7 % of top executives in the Fortune 100 companies. They hold just 19% of S&P 1500 board seats.

There are many reasons for the scarcity of women in management positions. They are victims of cultural norms, legal restrictions, and the power balance considering their responsibilities at home. In most cultures, there is a strong division between male and female roles. Traditionally, a woman is too often in a position to be a housewife (home-maker). In selected Arab countries, Latin America, and the Global South, most managers are men with little opportunity for women to develop their careers. Women are expected to be dependent and to serve. Even in developed societies where women enjoy formal equality, cultural stereotypes are not eradicated. Even when women are empowered into the workforce in managerial or professional positions, they are still expected to do the lion's share of household chores and childcare, often leading to burnout. At the same time, the "dads" are exempt from these responsibilities.

These are many reasons for the modest representation of women in power structures. Outdated research suggested that women are perceived as less competent and lack leadership potential. This perception added to the myth of women's lack of managerial capability. Recent research[69] shows that women feel less happy than men when they occupy administrative positions and expect more tradeoffs between life and work.

In considering attitudes in other cultures, male resistance to female executives is stronger in Europe than in North America. Polls in Italy and the U.K. show that almost half of men reject the idea of having a female manager. In the U.S. and Western Europe, only 3% of directors in large corporations are women, and they occupy 12% of middle and lower management positions, although they make up 45% of the employed. In 2012, women accounted for 19% of board seats on U.S. companies, while women in Western Europe held about 15.6% of seats. In 2016, they increased to 20% (U.S.) and 25% (Western Europe.).

But this trend is being challenged. For example, through the efforts of former Unilever CEO Paul Polman, half of the Anglo-Dutch company's 14,000 managers are now female, up from 38% in 2010. That includes 50% of the finance department, an area where women have historically been under-represented. About half of Unilever's board is also female.

Even though the power structures in both politics and corporations are dominated by men, psychological studies indicate that female leaders have many competitive advantages. Experts agree that female bosses are more focused on organizational relationships and not on action, like most men. Female managers prefer to share power and information, and they encourage participation. Other female leadership qualities include a tendency to develop organizational structures resembling family networking. Women tend to be more understanding of people's emotions and problems. They can often avoid conflicts and encourage cooperation; they are known for intuitive and emotional problem-solving approaches, especially for readiness to admit mistakes.

All these traits contribute to Strategic Harmony with less conflict and more personal satisfaction. Women are also emotionally stronger and more resistant to frustration at work; they exhibit greater self-control, patience, and stability in attitudes. Taking all the above into account, female executives are more and more appreciated, both in business and political life, making women the key pool for selecting future leaders. We are entering the era of *femaleadership*.[70]

Next Generation

The term, NextGen, is commonly used to describe Millennials and Gen Z, the people who will have major responsibility for addressing change and fixing the broken world. They have recently been engaged in activities that may transform Power with speaking truth, communicating Love, and living TEST Values.

The first global example was the Arab Spring, a revolutionary wave of demonstrations and protests in the Middle East and North Africa between 2010 and 2012, initiated and supported by social media and networks. It was a great initiative of the Next Generation demonstrating that Arab dictators can be removed through a grassroots popular revolt, rather than a military coup or foreign intervention as was the norm in the past. By the end of 2011, the governments in Tunisia, Egypt, Libya, and Yemen were swept away by popular revolts, in an unprecedented show of people power. Even back in the 1970s with the massive protests against the Vietnam War, such action played a large role in ending the war.

The same year, 2011, millions of students took to the streets of Chile in protests which electrified the country and eventually led to a string of sweeping reforms. Seven years later, these students who managed to overthrow the country's political establishment with street protests and legislative victories, have sent a message of support for the young Florida activists pushing for gun reform in the U.S. The Parkland students movement initiated by survivors of the mass Stoneman Douglas school shooting in February 2018 succeeded in mobilizing 700,000+ people to attend *March for Our Lives* in Washington on the issue gun control.

NextGen seems to be ready and able to engage in changing the world. Globally they are still a Sleeping Power ready to explode. Let's take a look at some facts that define this segment. By 2020, Millennials (born 1981–2000) will comprise 50% of the global workforce. If we add Generation Z (born after 2000) the total will be 70% of the global labor force. By 2025, combined they will comprise 80% of the global workforce.

As an example, let's analyze the USA, since there are enough available data.[21] The first fact is that Generation Z or pre-Millennials are the most radically and ethnically diverse group in U.S. history. Generation Z's values and habits significantly affect family spending. With the NextGen online, shopping malls in the U.S. have been closing at record pace. Also, major apparel retailers are seeing slower growth.

Both Millennials and Generation Z have made a clear challenge when it comes to social responsibility, sustainability, and social impact causes. Sixty percent of Generation Z want to have an impact on the world, compared to just 39% of Millennials. Social entrepreneurship is one of the most popular career choices for this generation. Also, Gen Z pays much more intention to purpose. More than 9 in 10 Millennials tend to switch brands to one associated with a cause. Seventy-six percent of Generation Z is concerned about human impact on the planet, and they believe they can operate as change agents.

According to the Nielsen Global Survey on Corporate Social Responsibility across 60 countries, 55% of global online consumers will pay more for products and services committed to positive social and environmental impact. In Asia-Pacific and Middle East/Africa regions, Millennials are in favor of sustainability actions three times more than older generations. NextGen is also predisposed toward entrepreneurship. In 38 nations, 75% have a positive attitude toward entrepreneurship, and 49% of Millennials hope to start a business within the next three years.

All surveys paint a picture of NextGen as more attracted to become entrepreneurs that generate social impact. They have very positive attitudes to supporting sustainable actions and purchasing and working for social impact-driven businesses. Global Shapers Annual Survey 2017 (25,000 people aged 18-35 from 186 countries) found that more than 40% of NextGen think sense of purpose/impact on society is one of the most important criteria when considering a career opportunity. Moreover, they share a strong propensity for social responsibility and sustainable products.

It is important to note that today's Millennials are better educated then their grandparents (70+ years). Also, 71% of young Millennial women are employed, compared to 66% of Boomer women. For the NextGen, entrepreneurship is the top desired career path.

Millennials and Generation Z are standing behind the global movement toward social responsibility. Rapidly replacing the Baby Boomers and the generation after them, the NextGen, are gaining increasing prevalence and power. Now, they constitute a majority of the marketplace and soon dominate the workforce. They are bringing with them new generation-related mindset, values, and viewpoints reflective of the transforming digital world.

Malala Yousafzai, a 15-year-old Pakistani who spoke out for young girls' education, has earned the distinction of representing three Rising Voices, a female, youth, from a developing country. She was shot in the head by a Taliban gunman; her "crime" was speaking up for the right of girls to be educated. After many surgeries in the UK, she continued her fight for young women's' opportunities to be educated. In "I am Malala" she shared her experience: *"When the whole world is silent, even one voice becomes powerful....If people were silent nothing would change."* Her family founded the Malala Fund to support young women globally to fight discrimination and sex slavery, and to provide young girls with the opportunity to go to school. In 2014, she won the Nobel

Peace Prize as the youngest Nobel Laureate with her inspiring quote, *"One child, one teacher, one book, one pen can change the world."*

Five years later, Malala serves as an inspiration and role model for Greta Thunberg. As a 17-years old, Greta has been chosen as Time Magazine Person of the Year, initiating a global movement to demand immediate action to abate climate change. "She has offered the clarion call to those willing to act and hurled shame on those who are not." At the UN Climate Action Summit 2019, she called out global leaders as failures to concretely address the climate crisis and chastised them with tears in her eyes *"You have stolen my dreams and my childhood with your empty words…how dare you continue to look away and come here saying you're doing enough."*

Greta's talks are transformative, imbuing her message with a deep Love and passion for the planet. It rings a true challenge to the Old Power. She inspired a global movement in just 18 months. In 2019, four million people in 161 countries joined her in the largest climate demonstration in history. In February 2020 the President of the European Commission after meeting with Greta, committed a quarter of the EU budget to mitigate climate change over seven years. She was invited to the European Parliament's Environment Committee's announcement of the proposed EU law for all actions to be climate neutral by 2050 instead of the desired 2030. She commented *"When your house is on fire, you don't wait a few more years to start putting it out. And yet this is what the Commission is proposing today."* She described the proposed climate law as *"surrender, because nature doesn't bargain and you cannot make deals with physics."*

Malala and Greta are just two examples of the power of the Rising Voices for change in our world. They spoke truth to power through their own lives. They skillfully leveraged the social media to deliver their message globally. Now they are recognized by global institutions as spokespersons for their issue. They are models to be replicated and scaled globally.

Here is a personal story from one of our Millennial contributors.

Rising Voice for Change

As a Millennial I feel motivated to contribute to efforts that foster sustainable impact in our world. So, what drives me?

I grew up as a first-generation American Muslim in Shawnee, Kansas, a classic Midwest city where jobs were predominantly labor intensive, an observation which shaped my understanding of what a traditional economy is built on. Joining the World Bank Group in 2016 transformed my perspectives on the economy as I witnessed our society's shift into the digital era. My work was wide-ranging, spanning rigorous economic analysis to digital governance. Yet, there was always the connecting tissue to international development. I quickly developed a passion for development, rooted in my wanting to make a difference in the global economy. Given the emphasis my generation places on social consciousness, I quickly learned that moral and innovative leadership is required to achieve peace and development.

In college, my appetite for entrepreneurship was launched. My peers and I designed a solar powered water heater which cost less than USD 50, and implemented a sustainable business model in rural Guadalajara, Mexico. This was the moment I realized that I want to make values and social empowerment the central theme of my endeavors. Our generation is fueled by purposeful initiatives. Many companies around the world are listening and providing value through their products and services which Millennials crave—"a voice that's heard". It is only a matter of time until the public sector realizes it must respond to the voices of this generation.

According to Shapers Annual Survey 2017, the most important factors that contribute to youth empowerment are entrepreneurship, the internet, and social media. These tools allow us to share innovations, build communities, and streamline processes almost instantly. But their full potential can only become realized when Millennials get involved with public institutions, thereby strengthening them and supporting their legitimacy.

In August 2018, I spoke to 600 youth delegates at the United Nations about the importance of youth involvement with multilateral institutions to solve complex global problems. It was inspiring to see young people respond positively and a sign for the public sector to reciprocate the engagement. Our Rising Voices need the support skills and resources to collaborate on sustainable solutions. In the end having that broad vision and passion is what's most important to create a more sustainable impact in the world.

Osama Al-Saleh, Entrepreneur, Consultant to World Bank

Millennials and Generation Z are very committed to social responsibility and support the TEST Values. They are not easily attracted to social causes, but they are loyal once their trust has been won. With their connections and skills in social media and digital technologies, the NextGen will openly support and advocate companies and products they trust and love, and they will do it for FREE! Additionally, companies that embrace sustainability and value-driven business are more likely to acquire good workers and talent. Just as the marketplace is no longer merely about money, neither is the talent pool. The NextGen wants to work for responsible and ethical companies. It is still about making a buck, but it's also about making a difference.

The rise of these generations proves that organizations (business, politics, and government) that don't transition into value-driven organizations will suffer in more ways than one. This vast emerging consumer and talent base is challenging the tenets of shareholder-driven capitalism! Adherence to old practices and antiquated mindsets is a recipe for disaster and failure.

Marginalized

The international migrant population accounts for 272 million people in 2019, with an increase of 51M since 2010. In 2017, 50 million immigrants resided in the United States, while Germany and Russia each have approximately 10 million immigrants. The nearly 50 million U.S. residents in 2017 who migrated from outside the country's borders constitute more than 15 percent of the U.S. population. The number doubled since 1990 when the U.S. hosted 25 million immigrants, who made up 9% of its population. Germany is the second most popular migration destination globally, with over 10 million people born outside the country in 2017, about 12% of the German population. One of the significant sources of the European immigration wave in recent years is the war in Syria. As of March 2018, UNHCR has counted nearly 5.6 million registered Syrian refugees worldwide.

No wonder immigration is the center of the political debate in the United States, Germany, and the UK. The Marginalized have been unheard, discriminated against, and living in a world of false narratives. They yearn to correct the story and be respected with the facts. *"Decisions about who we commemorate, which events and people are recorded in the history books, and what narratives we tell ourselves about how we got here have real consequences for our societies and the place of marginalized groups within them."*[72]

They want to be included. The mission is not to exclude certain people from the story, but to more accurately remember them, and to rewrite the stories with the actors who have been purposely excluded. This process is transforming and empowering.

Power is shifting. Historically, underserved groups are more visible in today's society, as the new media have allowed a variety of narratives to surface. Organizations and businesses are now held accountable in our transparent world to respect the real stories of their customers and employees and live and communicate the ever-shifting landscape of diversity in their organizational culture, customer experience, and employee relations.

The result is that the Marginalized often see they share a common discrimination and want to be accepted for who they are. They are proud of their beliefs and culture and want others to honor and respect them. They band together, creating a new Transformative Power. When we look at the numbers of Marginalized peoples in the world, it is devastating and threatening to the status quo.

In 2020 the racial inequality of Black Americans has been the focal point of nationwide protests. Although it has been 150+ years since slavery ended in the United States, and more than 50 years since segregation was repealed, the marginalization of Black Americans has manifested across all areas of life.

Here some telling statistics:

» Black people are 2.5-times more likely to be killed by police than white people.

» Between 2008-2018, the imprisonment rate of Black people was six times higher than that of white people.

» Black unemployment rate is double that of the white unemployment rate during the last 50 years.

» During the Covid pandemic, Black Americans' death rate is nearly 2.5 times higher that of White, Latino, and Asian Americans.

» There are 53% White college undergraduates compared to 15% Black graduates.

The LGBTQ+ (rainbow community) is a growing socially Marginalized population, fighting to be recognized and granted equal rights. According to recent studies[23], views toward those who identify as lesbian, gay, bisexual, transgender, or queer have changed substantially, and a majority of U.S. adults now say homosexuality should be accepted by society. In 2016, *The Economist Intelligence Unit Report, Pride and Prejudice: Agents of Change* launched the business and economic case for LGBTQ+ diversity and inclusion. In 2017, it was followed by *Pride and Prejudice Summit: Business as a Catalyst for Change*, with a focus on queer-friendly businesses attracting the best overall talent, winning the loyalty of discerning consumers, and seeking more profitable opportunities. The legal landscape for LGBTQ+ people has also shifted, including a U.S. Supreme Court decision four years ago that legalized same-sex marriage nationwide. Their path to Strategic Harmony is using their positive energy and appetite for change and transformation. In the words of queer authors, John Schneider and David Auten, *"The best way to make these changes is to be change agents… It's enhancing ROI and innovation. It's displaying strength of character and leadership, and, it's challenging business and social norms."*

It's not just groups; there are also whole continents that are Marginalized. Here are some startling facts that reflect the forthcoming shift in Power. Fifty percent of the world's population between now and 2080 will come from Africa. Youth in Africa already comprise 75% of the working age population. By 2030, more than half of new workers entering the global labor force will come from Africa. The average access globally to the internet as of January 2018 was 51%. Access in Africa is among the lowest the world, 49% in Northern Africa, 39% in Western Africa, 12% in Central Africa, and 27% in Eastern Africa. In the next decade, this access will shift significantly upward and serve to transform the continent. *"Users in Africa are up by more than 20 percent, with the reported number of internet users in Mali increasing by almost six times since January 2017. The number of internet users in Benin, Sierra Leone, Niger, and Mozambique has more than doubled over the past year too."*[74] Another area of growth is mobile access. While 68% of the global population has a mobile phone, mobile penetration in Central Africa is below 50%.

The intersection of the growth of youth and technology as well as entrepreneurship in Africa points to a global challenge: to engage these Rising Voices with the TEST Values and develop the mindset. We must fuel Catalyzers with Strategic Transformation strategies to build the New Africa based on Strategic Harmony, instead of Old Power and Old Love models.

Here is an insight of Dr. Joseph Okpaku, CEO of Telecom Africa International Corporation, on the imperative to prepare African youth for their future.

Mentoring the Next Generation – A Tradition and Cultural Obligation

Globally, a new generation is coming of age. The next few years will witness the passing of the torch from our generation to the next one. Our challenge is to enable this transfer of knowledge in our role as elder statesmen. In Africa, it is an age-old tradition that those who come after us must be better than us. If not, we will not have done our job as mentors. That is why in many African communities, parents do not bury their children, because this is not the right order of things. I believe that if we devote much care and attention to bringing up the young generation, they will not only do well, but they will not let us down. They will, in fact, honour and treasure us.

How to vastly improve the quality of life for all, expanding our opportunity and capacity for creative life and the unhampered pursuit of self-actualization, that is our true challenge. Acquiring lessons learnt from careful study of the past infused by the essence of our cultural virtues, that is knowledge. Deploying that knowledge with fairness and honesty through time for sustainable development for all people, that is wisdom. In this context, our knowledge societies of the future would be nothing but the world of a new global renaissance in which we experience an explosion of brilliance, creativity, joy, and equanimity. That, I believe, is the way to create access, empowerment, and appropriate governance in promoting the richness and diversity of global cultures. In so doing, we will eliminate poverty, not manage it, through the creation of genuine and intelligent wealth for the well-being of all, within the constraints of our social and cultural priorities.

Dr. Joseph O. Okpaku, Sr, President and CEO, Telecom Africa International Corporation.

Massive waves of immigration are destabilizing forces in the most developed countries. In the United States, it's coming from the southern border with a threat of gang violence, drugs, and corruption. In Europe, it's coming from North Africa with the threat of spreading terrorism. The answer in many countries (from the U.S. to Hungary, from Austria to Poland) has been closing the borders and sanctifying the local white populations, causing a battle between brown and white.

To a great extent, global migration is a sign of a broken world and its institutions. The lack of a sustainable, values-driven solution continues to encourage populism, Aryanism, white supremacy, and similar manifestations of Old Power. The critical problem is the lack of an integrated global response through the United Nations Refugee program. If we start to look at this problem with Empathy, and through the Transformative Love lenses, we will see human beings running scared for their lives and those of their children. They are looking for equal opportunity and a way to contribute to an open society. They are running away from corruption and Old Power to New Love. The government responses are based on Old Power. In Europe, it protects borders with razor blade wires. In the U.S., it intends to put up walls, close borders, and fire-up the white population with false stories to protect them from the incoming people of color.

Global migration calls for Transformative Power aimed at giving the rights and listening to the needs of the threatened marginalized populations without a home, fearing for their lives and lacking any economic equality.

Migration seems to be a sleeping catalyst/driver for potential change. The energy behind it may be directed toward a "refolutionary" search for Strategic Harmony or may turn into an uncontrollable source of conflicts, and become a force to further break up the world. We need to approach the problem from a holistic, values-driven point of view, adopting a mindset which is global and *empowering all of us.*

Globally, we have faced a long-lasting challenge of sexism, an issue that transcends racial and ethnic divisions. In 2017, the courageous revelations of women abused by an immoral Hollywood producer caused people and institutions worldwide to re-evaluate the "historic normalization of sexual abuse in the workplace." The 2019 study *"Measuring #MeToo: A National Study on Sexual Harassment and Assault"*[75] concluded, *"sexual harassment and assault are widespread problems in the United States, causing pain, limiting people's lives, and negatively affecting communities and society."*

This is an example of the power of values when truly implemented and not just talked about. Namely, a strict and consistent adoption of the TEST Value,

Transparency, has ignited the #MeToo global movement and led to a dramatic change in behavior all over the world.

Muslim Community and China

Another global challenge is the misunderstanding of Islam and discrimination against Muslims. Akbar Ahmed in his current book on how Muslim migration is shaping 21st century Europe[76] suggests that *"there are three overlapping categories within Islam: literalist Islam—those who believe that to be a good Muslim should mean to adhere to the letter and spirit of Islamic law; the mystics—those who believe in a warm, inclusive embrace of humanity which reflects the love of the divine for all creation; and finally the modernists—those who believe in balancing faith with modernity. The latter group believes that democracy and accountability, and Islam are compatible. It is this category that is under threat directly from the literalists."* In addition, the mystical approach reflected in Applied Sufism[77] affirms Islam's progressive essence, illustrating its applicability to modern-day life.

Many European countries have gone down the path of categorizing all Muslims as "literalists," choosing the ways of Old Power trying to control the use of facial covering, a cultural tradition among some Muslims. They suggest that the ban promotes integration and public safety while wearing a veil is inconsistent with national values like gender equality. Quite expectedly, these bans have generated protests of Muslims and even non-Muslims, empowered by love of freedom and cultural identity, causing more fear and separation than was intended.

In contrast, to control discrimination against Muslim immigrants, governments can transform the threat by applying Transformative Power. Many NextGen Muslims, both immigrants, and residents consider themselves the "M Generation," a young, fast-growing, affluent Muslim constituency that is changing the world. Great examples are Dubai and Doha, the high-tech, fast-growing cities with the most modern infrastructure, advanced strategies, grand ambitions, and obvious intentions to significantly change global culture and values. The case of Shamma Al Mazrui, a politician who currently serves as Minister of State for Youth Affairs in the United Arab Emirates, symbolizes such changes. A woman who was then only 22 years old in February 2016 became the world's youngest government minister. Muslims are responding to a changing world!

According to global demographic data, the Muslim population is expected to grow globally by 73% in the next three decades. By 2050, Pew Research Centers project 2.8 billion Muslims globally, more than 25% of the world's population. Of the 11 countries expected to join the world's largest economies this century, six have overwhelmingly Muslim communities, and two have significant Muslim minorities. By 2050, India will have the largest Muslim population globally, an estimated 311 million (11% of the global total), although they will remain a minority in a nation with a projected 1.3B Hindus. Muslim minorities in Great Britain, Europe, and North America are young, affluent, and growing. One-third of all Muslims are under the age of 15, and two-thirds under 30, with the youngest median age (24 years) of all major religions. As the fastest-growing major religion, the Muslim middle class is expected to triple to 900 million by 2030, driving consumption and social and political change. Their spending power is enormous: the most recent *State of the Global Islamic Economy Report*[78] forecasts the halal food and lifestyle industry worth $3 trillion by 2021, and Islamic finance is on a similar trajectory. Finally, countries with a Muslim majority have witnessed a rapid diffusion and adoption of social media platforms. The Arab Region is only second to the USA when it comes to the number of daily YouTube views.

Again, we face a tremendous global challenge. Suppose this newfound economic power and social media access are channeled down the path of greed and Old Power. In that case, it will exacerbate our broken world and generate further division between East and West. Globally, Muslims face the challenge of remembering their roots and integrating the power of their values into their daily actions and purposeful business and government decision-making—commerce, governance, organizational structure, citizen participation, and environmental stewardship. They could engage this Transformative Power to become Catalyzers for global transformation. It is worth mentioning that at the foundation of Islam, there are 99 Names and Attributes of Allah (God) with which our four TEST Values overlap.

Another potential long-term catalyst for global change is China. With a population of nearly 1.4 billion, China is the second-largest economy with a value of $11 trillion, representing 14.8% of global GDP. China has been the largest contributor to world growth since the global financial crisis of 2008 and is the world's largest exporter ($2.2 trillion). Hard to believe, but in terms of Purchasing Power Parity (PPP), a measure which adjusts a country's wealth based on what people can afford to buy, China has already overtaken the United States to claim the top spot.

In 2013, China launched the One Belt, One Road Initiative, the largest global infrastructure project in history. They plan to spend $150 billion a year to link 68 countries along the old Silk Road with Europe. The project aims at building ports, railways, and pipelines, trying to make a China-dominated Eurasia an economic rival to the American-dominated transatlantic trading area.

Chinese online shopping frenzy is more significant than Black Friday and Cyber Monday combined[22]. November 11, Singles' Day is a significant holiday known for online shopping. It started as an anti-Valentine's Day joke in a country with nearly 200 million single people. In 2016, $1 billion-worth of orders was placed in the first five minutes, and the total trade volume of the day was more than $17 billion. China has over 1,000 "Taobao" villages, named after Alibaba's shopping site. Mobile money is pervasive in China, from online shopping to financial services to entrepreneurship. Alibaba defines a Taobao Village as one where over 10% of households run online stores and where e-commerce revenues exceed 10 million RMB (roughly $1.6 million) per year.

China is heavily investing and influencing development in emerging economies. In 2013, China invested $26 billion into Africa, and in 2017, offered a $60 billion loan and aid package to the African continent. According to President Xi, China aims to develop infrastructure, improve agriculture, and reduce poverty in Africa.

Before 2013, the country enjoyed 30 years of double-digit growth, with government spending being the driving force that fueled it. Recently, China has become the only country in the world to slow down its growth deliberately. The government mandated its banks to provide low-interest rates in return for protection of the strategic industry. It created business investment in capital goods but also led to inflation, a real estate asset bubble, growth in public debt, and severe pollution.

Many of China's in-country initiatives reflect its commitment to sustainability. Since the country expects to have 200 cities with more than 1 million people by 2025, authorities are launching ambitious initiatives to improve their residents' quality of life. Beijing is spending $1.3 billion to convert its 70,000-car taxi fleet to electric power. In March 2018 Beijing closed its last coal-fired power station, becoming the first city in China to be coal-free for heating and electricity.

In China you can scan a QR code to rent an umbrella. The sharing economy is a major trend, with the shift to "borrowing/renting" rather than buying, expected to account for 10% of China's economy by 2020. China invests more each year in renewable power than any other country on earth. It's already the world's biggest generator of solar power, doubling its output each year. In 2018, China cancelled plans to build 100 coal-fired power stations and switched on the world's largest floating solar farm near the city of Huainan.

China is on track to become the world's biggest filer of patents. Far from the 'Made in China' cliché, it is a hub of innovation, with explosive intellectual property growth. In 2016, the number of international patent filings rose 45% to 43,000. China's potential role in furthering Strategic Harmony is vast. Its core value is harmony or "balanced coordination between things." It is based on the cultural values of benevolence, righteousness, courtesy, wisdom, honesty, loyalty, and filial piety. However, the Chinese concept is based on yin-yang, the opposing yet necessary forces to maintain order in the universe. It differs from the Western idea of the state lacking conflict.

From the Western perspective, fast-developing China and Muslim countries have not been inclusive of individual rights (although in Islam, these rights are traditional). However, these countries are quickly adapting and turning into strong forces of a global transformation.

Changing the Narrative

The world we are living in is facing challenges and dangers that, at least on the scale we are facing them, are unprecedented. Climate change, poverty, displacement due to war and political instability are being met with fear, ignorance, denial, and anger. Rather than a banding together in solidarity and acknowledgement of our common plight as human beings living on a fragile planet, we find ourselves consumed with fear, anger, and hatred. Trust has fallen to suspicion and outright cynicism, and solidarity has given way to hostility.

Yet, despite the apparent bleakness of the situation we face, we live in an era of unparalleled opportunity. Advancing technology and improved systems for the sharing of ideas, services, and material goods have placed the tools of our own liberation in our hands. Where is the disconnect, therefore, between what is possible and what is actual? Our societies are suffering from a deficit of trust and a paucity of empathy.

Brexit, populism, Islamophobia, antisemitism, racism, bizarre conspiracy theories that posit a faceless "them" as an all-powerful enemy—all of these are diseases of the heart born of a surfeit of fear and a deficit of trust. We have been there before; Auschwitz and Treblinka stand as monuments to the dark places fear and hatred can take us.

In the 1930s the world was similarly shattered, similarly fearful, similarly distrustful. FDR, the U.S. president of the day, challenged that darkness with the slogan "we have nothing to fear but fear itself." This is no less true today. We need systems that challenge fear by fostering the security that builds trust and bring people together in ways that challenge hatred born of fear and misunderstanding.

We already have the tools needed for change; we just have not yet found the narrative that inspires people to seize the opportunity for a society based on empathy, solidarity, and trust rather than egoism, atomization, and cynicism. Finding this narrative of hope is the solemn task of our era.

Shayn McCallum, high school teacher in Australia and Turkey

Martin Luther King once said that *"If you want to change the world, pick up your pen and write."* We followed his advice and wrote *EmPower Us!* By doing that, we managed to change ourselves a bit. Our strong belief is that if there is no transformation within each person, all the technological or organizational change in the world will have no real impact on our institutions and our lives.

In this Guidepost, we have described the potential Catalyzers of global change and offered five pieces of food for thought. We hope to see women, new generations, historically marginalized people, and Muslims and Chinese become Catalyzers of positive change in leading the world on the path to Strategic Harmony.

Guidepost 7

Love Your Purpose

"Two roads diverged in a wood, and I—
I took the one less travelled by, and that has made all the difference."

Robert Frost

Let's start this Guidepost with a story. A farmer found an eagle's egg and put it in his hen nest. In a few days an eaglet hatched with chickens and grew up with them. All his life he behaved as a chicken, believing he was one of them. He would run around the yard, scratch at the soil to search for seeds, worms, and insects. He even learned to crow. Only sometimes, he would wave his wings and fly a meter above the ground. Years passed and the eagle was getting old. One day, he looked in the clear sky, and there he saw a majestic bird that sailed the air currents with graceful dignity, gently flapping the large wings. Eagle stared at the sky, wondering. "Who is it?" he asked. "It's an eagle, the king of birds," said the chicken standing next to him. "He belongs to the sky, and we belong to the ground—we are chickens." So, the eagle lived and died as a chicken, because he believed that he was a chicken.

Are we going to destine ourselves to stay on the ground and accept what is, when we could take off to the heights and catalyze change?

Orienting - Road Not Taken

Strategic Harmony focuses on the way we "think" when faced with diverse roads to our future and the outcomes to our decisions. Picking *"the road less travelled by"* can really make all the difference. It is a metaphor for how we make challenging and life-changing choices and provides an opportunity to self-reflect on our foundational beliefs and assumptions in directing us down the different paths.

But the real work is to truly understand how we got to the choice of the two diverging roads and why we choose one road over another. These questions will provide some direction:

» How can we imagine considering another road or opening the door to a different choice?

» With regard to organizational transformation, what are the choices that a leader considers in making an alternative solution?

» What would it take to change both ourselves and our institutions to generate transformative decisions that reflects the needs of customers, citizens, and employees?

The overarching challenge is: What do we reach for inside ourselves to anchor our decision process? It is our values, mission, vision, and past experiences. We unconsciously aggregate these inputs as our Purpose.

Purpose is the primary driver of organizational transformation. It is why something is done, the aim of the organization, and the feeling to achieve something. It is why the organization's work is essential for transformation or the cause that defines a contribution to society. Purpose defines the priorities of the organization and its culture.

Finding your Purpose

There is a story about Zen master Ryokan walking on the beach. A storm had just blown over and hundreds of starfish washed up by the waves suffered in the sharp sunlight. Ryokan picked up the starfish, one by one, and threw them back into the sea. A fisherman who lived there came up to Ryokan and said: "What's the purpose? It happens every time there's a storm. You can't save them all, so what difference does it make?"

"It makes a difference to this one," replied Ryokan, as he flung yet another starfish into the water.

Taking the moral of the story into account, let's look at the work that goes into finding and developing Purpose. This is a major task that can take six months to a year, depending upon the entrenchment and power centers of the current leadership and management teams and the organizational commitment to change. The commitment to transformation combined with the Purpose are two key building blocks for the future. For example, if we agree with American journalist Sydney Harris[80] that the "*whole purpose of education is to turn mirrors into windows,*" or if we accept his definition that "*democracy is the only system that persists in asking the powers that be whether they are the powers that ought to be,"* we have a very clear view of what to do to transform education and democracy.

There are still many institutions (business, government, or nongovernment) that follow the road taken a long time ago, without ever reflecting, asking, "Why?" It is clear that any road will take you there if you don't know where you are going. In most cases, it's nowhere. Hence, an agreed-upon Purpose serves as a focal point for the application of values and empowering the direction of the organization. Gaining agreement is most crucial; the tensions involved in reflecting, refining, and integrating the Purpose are critical to the company's sustainability. In engaging with Purpose, organizations and teams pass through six stages:

1. Alignment

A board and senior leadership decision is required to gain the team's agreement on organizational Purpose and commitment to transform the OldCo to a NewCo.

2. Intention and Vision

The *"Path to Tomorrow"* is paved by intention and vision. Intention is the internal commitment to anticipated outcomes. It brings energy to your thoughts and a focus to accomplish your goals and Purpose. No wonder it is a core tenet of all major world religions as they suggest that each action begins with the "right intention" to engage in "good deeds." In the Quran, "verily actions are driven by intentions." In the Bible we see "times where good intentions led to bad decisions." Vision is inspirational; it's what we aspire to and want to become.

3. Transformation with Purpose

Gaining agreement on the organization's Purpose is the most difficult challenge facing an organization; therefore, often it is not addressed.

Why are you in your current business? What is your real purpose?

These questions lie at the foundation of the Transformative Why—driving actions, catalyzing change, both internally (individuals) and externally (organization). It is the ground note or essence, the ever-present factor that directs an organization. Clarifying our intention and vision will lead us to our Transformative Why. Thus, when we are aligned with our Purpose, our actions are powered by our intention. In the words of the 5H model, our Hope leads us in such a way that what we think (with Head), what we feel (with Heart), and what we do (with Hands) are all aligned and in Harmony.

The Transformative Why builds on the work of *Simon Sinek*[81]. When asked, most people will know *"What"* they do every day, many people will be able to describe *"How"* they do it, but only a few people will easily answer the question *"Why"* they do it. Sinek suggests that Why (Purpose) is the central core of the Golden Circle. The energy is defined and concentrated in the core and it moves out into concentric circles of How and What. He summarizes the whole process with the following sentence: *"People don't buy what you do, but why you do it."* The Purpose gives the true meaning to all we do in business, politics, life.

Take a look at the following figure:

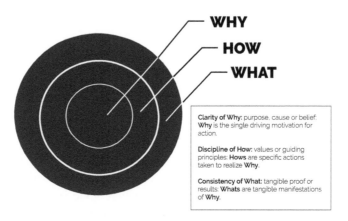

Figure 7.1 Starting with Why

Values define How we interact with others and help us shape our culture. The How defines the specific actions that are taken to realize the Purpose. Values reinforce the vision while directing behavior that members of an organization support and cherish. Mission is a source of motivation addressing What we need to do to accomplish our goals. The What defines the work we are going to do. It defines the tangible outcomes and results necessary to realize our Purpose.

4. Targeting the Purpose

Purpose is not unidimensional. It can be addressed at three different levels:

1. *Personal Purpose*—is the synergy of our inner spiritual calling, values, and vision for the future. It keeps us motivated, focused, and driven.
2. *Organizational Purpose*—is Why an organization exists. It channels the team's efforts to fulfill, activate, and scale Purpose.
3. *Societal Purpose*—is the catalyst for social change. It is Why a constituency aligns to vote out a legislator, or consumers purchase an energy-saving device, or millions attend a gun violence protest.

5. Empowering Your Purpose

An organization without a Purpose just manages people and resources, while an organization with a Purpose transforms and mobilizes people and leverages resources. For example, an active Societal Purpose is essential to propel a sustainable, scalable impact.

According to *Sinek*, the following two guidelines are critical for developing a powerful Purpose:

» Order Matters: Simply having the Purpose buried in the organization handbook is not enough. We must start with Why and then think, act, and communicate from the "inside out" of the Golden Circle.

» Balance: All three levels of the Golden Circle must be in harmony. It means that we must have clarity, discipline, and consistency of message and balance across Why, How, and What.

6. Engaging Stakeholders' Purpose

The Purpose is the starting point for creating value for all stakeholders, thus contributing to Strategic Harmony. There are at least five groups of stakeholders to be considered:

» Consumers (customers, users) are encouraged to be authentic and genuine. Purpose opens the door for consumers to connect with the company or organization and develop loyalty.

> » Employees expect Purpose to be integrated into company culture and employee standards. It gives meaning to the work. Team members feel their contributions are integral to the teams' success. Furthermore, an aligned Purpose attracts the hiring of the right talent.

> » Partners are motivated to generate mutual benefit based on shared Purpose.

> » Investors create shared value, reflecting Purpose and generating sustainable social impact.

> » Community benefits from sustainable strategies pursued with Purpose.

Purpose is the picture we have of ourselves, the kind of people we want to be, the kind of goals we want to pursue, and the kind of life we want to lead. Or, as nicely stressed by Robert Byrne, American Hall of Fame instructor of pool and carom billiards, *"the purpose of (business and private) life is a life of purpose."*

Love the Purpose

For an organization to truly thrive, all its members must Love the Purpose.

Obviously, Love and Power are Drivers that will help us in choosing among alternative paths, because the way we see the world is based on our biases and assumptions. If we see the marketplace through the eyes of Old Power, as competitive companies focus on winning and protecting the turf, we're going to maintain the status quo. If we are open to refocusing the lens on values and a sustainable Purpose, we will listen to diverse perspectives and generational inputs fueling more collaborative, innovative outcomes.

Daily, executives face dramatically transforming environments, exponentially changing technologies and the disruptive marketplace that they are not prepared for intellectually and emotionally. It's no surprise that Jack Ma, former CEO of the Alibaba Group, when confronted with difficult issues, relied on a balance between Intellect (IQ) and Emotions (EQ), paying particular attention to what he calls the Love Quotient (LQ). According to Ma: *No matter how smart machines are becoming, the world's biggest and most pressing problems will be solved by smart humans with the capacity for compassion, understanding, and Love. Love is the human secret weapon that will out-think machines and drive progress.*

Ma suggested the LOVE quotient to be the missing piece in most organizations. *"You have to genuinely love your team and what you're working towards together, because as you grow and the world gets more intense, there needs to be a larger purpose than just what's happening in your office day to day."* This passion and Love must permeate all operations. Love is all encompassing; so must Purpose have that energy and force. As Tom Peters pointed out, *"leadership is all about love: passion, enthusiasm, appetite for life, engagement, great causes, and determination to make a damn difference, commitment to excellence, shared adventures, bizarre failures, growth beyond measure, insatiable appetite for change."*

A purposeful business is based on Love. It could be defined as an enterprise aimed at tackling a problem in the world that benefits both the company and serves as a vehicle for a positive change. In a decade-long study that tracked purposeful and value-driven companies, Kotter and Hesket[82] found that purposeful companies outperformed their counterparts in stock price by a factor of 12. In the absence of Purpose, a company's leadership is likely to have greater difficulty motivating employees and putting the company on course to success.

To illustrate the importance of purposeful businesses, let's look at exemplary brands. One of the pioneers in the field, Anita Roddick, originally founded The Body Shop[83] to help her family survive. However, soon she transformed the company into a tool to make a positive difference in the world. The Body Shop is a cosmetics and skin care company specializing in selling all-natural products. They never use harmful chemicals often found in other cosmetic products. The company's motto is "Enrich, Not Exploit." It is committed to enriching its people, products, and the planet.

From its beginning, Ella's Kitchen[84] has a clear and measurable Purpose: "To develop healthy eating habits that last a lifetime by offering a range of tasty, natural, and healthy 100% organic foods for babies and kids, which are handy for mums and dads and fun for little ones."

Another example is Patagonia, producer of the world's first neoprene, natural rubber wetsuit, while working to combat ocean pollution. They represent a brand engaged in the global conversation on threatening ecological issues and calling upon consumers to help reshape business and society. Recently, they have created DamNation[85], a powerful Netflix documentary that engages in dam removal to help restore river ecosystems. Its founder, Yvon Chouinard, boldly put it: *"If you're not pissing off 50% of the people, you're not trying hard enough."*

Dove[86] Soap is a purposeful brand whose mission is much more than just selling soap and hygiene products. They are using their brand to help improve the self-esteem and body image of girls worldwide.

Love your Purpose is the core strategy that is growing among progressive businesses globally. According to a recent study, 88% of consumers believe companies have the power to influence societal change and should be addressing the challenges of our broken world. Self-centered leadership in business and politics contributed to breaking it. Now it's the time for catalytic leadership to put it back together again.

Purpose as a Differentiator

According to George Bernard Shaw[87], this is the true joy in life, being used for a purpose recognized by yourself as a mighty one. By being consistent and reinforcing the Purpose, leaders can make decisions and propel their actions throughout the entire organization. In fact, the Purpose serves as the North Star directing the organization in terms of the How and What relating to all actions, networks, touchpoints, and relationships. It provides the framework to achieve Strategic Harmony by consistently incorporating Purpose into all operations and actions. You can start by answering the following questions:

» Is your Purpose sustainable? Are you making the world a better place?

» Are your actions based on Transformative Love and Power?

» Are your products or services aligned with the TEST Values?

» Is Purpose integral to current staff evaluation or new staff hire?

» How does Purpose drive your corporate strategies?

» Is your Purpose integrated into the Report to the Shareholders?

» How do you manage customer service and relationships with your supply chain?

Gaining agreement on Purpose is a challenging task. Although Love Your Purpose seems like an easily attainable goal, many companies fall short. This becomes a higher priority as NextGen consumers are demanding a clearer Why. The same is true for politics.

But beyond agreement is the implementation of Purpose across all stakeholders. Loving your Purpose is not binary—on or off. Purpose requires vigilance in the application and living of your values, and the inclusion of all stakeholders in manifesting and building Transformative Power and Transformative Love. In Guidepost 3. we termed this process stakeholder-centric. The objective is to optimize the needs of all stakeholders beginning with integrating values and purpose across all operations; this guides the organization on the path to Strategic Harmony. Values are the foundation; Purpose translates values into action and drives transformation.

Purpose is not static; it must evolve as it lies between your values and the world's needs. It reflects the democratization of the economy based on the transparency in the Information Age.

Purpose is the energy behind catalytic thinking and the differentiator for brands and business models. Aligning the organizational Purpose among all stakeholders generates the Transformative Power necessary for successful Strategic Transformation. In a recent study, 76% of employees (both new hires and current employees) are primary drivers of demand for purpose-driven companies; they are followed by customers (68%), "other stakeholders" (61%); regulators and policymakers (53%), and investors and shareholders (52%).

Suppose all stakeholders are affirming and integrating the same purpose through their decisions, strategies, and actions. In that case, the synergy will generate loyal brand advocates, innovative and highly productive employees, efficiently scaled supply chain partners, generous and profitable investors, and a receptive and supportive community. The Love of Purpose by each stake-holder is synergistic and reciprocal, driving financial impact (revenue, cost savings, profit, community development) at each supply chain level.

This is how Wilson Ferreira Jr., CEO, CPFL Energia, Brazil summarizes stakeholder centricity: *"We believe that the issue of sustainability may have been optional for companies in the past, but today it is a must. ...we have moved from the era of shareholder value to an era of stakeholder value."*

There are many outcomes of not having a Loving Purpose. Your organization fails to attract top talent. It experiences low morale and productivity. It struggles to develop customer satisfaction. Your organization becomes "just another profit-seeking enterprise" without soul and meaning to the customers, employees, partners, or the public. You become just another organization or political party out there to mislead and exploit.

The Business Case

Purpose drives social and financial impact. As Sinek suggests, *"...profit isn't a purpose. It's a result. To have a purpose means the things we do are of real value to others."*

Harvard's study Business Case for Purpose[88] found that *"90% of executives understand the importance of Purpose, but only 46% said it impacted their strategic and operational decision-making. Executives who treat purpose as a core driver of strategy and decision-making reported greater ability to drive successful innovation and transformational change and deliver consistent revenue growth."*

The result was that 58% of those that prioritized Purpose had +10% growth for the past three years. In 2017 this finding was reiterated by the Purposeful Company Taskforce. They concluded that *"the [UK] companies with a declared purpose, adhered to by their leadership teams, and well understood by their stakeholders, perform better on key metrics over time than their less purposeful peers."*

These cases are only the tip of the Purpose Revolution. Innovative companies with strong purpose-driven leadership are leading the revolution and gaining a first mover advantage in gaining stakeholder support and financial rewards. Here are some stories of leaders who translate their purpose into successful outcomes and financial returns.

Starbucks business model was based on its founder, former CEO Howard Schultz's discovery of the "perfect coffee experience" in Italy. He began with developing his baristas' passion and commitment to serve each customer, delivering the "perfect shot" and loving the Starbuck's experience. At the outset the formula worked. Then, with competition and increasing employee turnover, the sales declined. But Howard Schultz pointed out, *"when you are surrounded by people who share a passionate commitment around a common purpose, anything is possible."*

Threatened by plummeting stock prices, tight margins, and a need to retain clients, Schultz went back to his Purpose. He closed 7,100 shops and taught 135,000 baristas how to pour the perfect shot. This is how he explained his decision: *"All I had was my belief that even more that perfecting our coffee, we had to repurpose the passion and commitment that everyone at Starbucks needed to have for our customers."*

This unprecedented action in 2008 transformed the Love and Power of his brand and it never again faulted. *"Starbucks*[89] *purposeful brand is aimed at improving people's lives worldwide. Their corporate responsibility initiative is dedicated to fighting hunger, encouraging service, and helping the environment."* This dedication and courage seemed to be a result of Schultz's own "rags-to-riches" story. Witnessing the struggles his poor father went through while growing up in New York, motivated Schultz to use his business to do something more impactful than just making a profit.

In Nothing We Trust

Trust is an overused, abused cliché in the world of brands. During the last few years, brands have tried valiantly to grab attention and break through clutter. Our latest trick as marketers (that's fooling no one) is waxing eloquent about our brand purpose. Brand purpose is meant to be the company's North Star, asking and answering existential questions about 'why' the brand exists and the meaningful role it plays in making the world a better place. Then by communicating the brand's purpose in clever, creative ways, we hope to create Brand Love and be the brand that consumers prefer and trust.

It's a noble intention but as they say, 'the path to hell is paved with good intentions.' Most often executives treat brand trust as a 'claim' to be hatched in a boardroom and communicated through clever advertising. However, marketers who get it realize that brand trust isn't a claim, it is earned and grows. Consistent customer experience and meaningful involvement evolves loyalty and love transforming the brand into a relationship. This takes a commitment to years of brand building and millions of dollars in marketing spends. But today our shareholders and boards demand instant gratification and often miss the most fundamental step in building a trusted brand.

We focus extraordinary resources in "building trust" through vacuous marketing activities that are meant only for customers who are fickle and not invested. Those who really care about our purpose and advocate its impact are our employees. They are most deeply invested in the company and deliver the experience through which our customers judge us. When those employees don't trust the company and its purpose, no amount of marketing excellence can save the day. Therefore, if you want act and be a trusted brand, start where it matters the most – with the people who

---

> *create the brand experience. Ultimately its company culture that builds brand trust, marketing only shares it .*
>
> *Shagorika Heryani, Regional Head of Strategy, Grey Group AMEA*

Paul Polman[90], former CEO of Unilever, is another leader in pupose-driven business. In his words: *"I discovered that if I focus on doing the right thing for the long term to improve the lives of consumers all over the world, the business results will come."* From 2009-2019 Polman remade this global company (with 300+ factories, 400 brands, touching 2.5 billion customers or one in every three people on the planet) to be a model of corporate responsibility. He cooperated with other companies to implement sustainable and long-term business strategies that increased Unilever's positive social impact and drove systemic change.

Polman was once asked how to distinguish between time spent 'saving the world' and 'building the business'. His answer was, "it's the same!" Sir Richard Branson reiterated the answer. Paul Polman's goal was engaging employees to rally around a higher purpose. Unilever receives an astounding 2 million job applications a year. Why the big draw? Because it tells the story of Purpose that employees want to play a role in telling. As Polman said, *"putting purpose at the center of everything the corporation does is incredibly motivating for its employees."*

Polman lived his Purpose from his first day at Unilever announcing the suspension of quarterly annual reports with short-term earnings affecting stock market value. He said: *"Put your money elsewhere if you don't buy into this long-term value-creation model, which is equitable, which is shared, which is sustainable."* In 2012 the stock was $24 and today in 2020 it's $61. He said, *"if the CEO doesn't focus on customer experience, in no way can you expect the company as a whole to improve customer experience."*

Elon Musk, CEO of Tesla, is one of the most controversial business leaders of our times. His projects like Hyperloop, Tesla car, and SpaceX are visionary attempts to create the future instead of waiting for it to happen. The NextGen love him; the media enjoy focusing on his great moments as well as on his flaws and failures. It is obvious that he challenges traditional values and promotes new directions, in search of the answers. One of his statements reflects his broad vision. *"I came to the conclusion that we should aspire to increase the scope and scale of human consciousness in order to better understand what questions to ask. Really, the only thing that makes sense is to strive for greater collective enlightenment."*

A visionary, Musk believes that his purpose is about setting ambitious deadlines to accelerate movement toward his goal. According to him, people work better when they know what the goal is and why. It is important that people look forward to coming to work in the morning and enjoy working.

Finally, Purpose is integrated into a new socio-economic framework of collaboration to drive our collective goals for a sustainable future.

Collabonomics: A New Socio-Economic Framework

We must collaborate to solve our global challenges. There is no other way.

Competition was hailed as good because it promotes innovation and creativity in creating product and services we want to pay for. But competing only for selfish reasons, disregarding a potential common beneficial interest, becomes a force of a vicious destructive circle in the end.

Trust (or faith) in people and nature is needed more than ever. We are not separate. It is part of every solution.

Slowly but surely even the finance industry is incorporating social and climate risks into their financial analysis when valuing stocks and bonds and other financial instruments. They have already seen the writing on the wall especially in targeting women and millennials as future clients. But are they doing it for the right reasons? Anyway, it is a great trend!

Awareness about external values other than tangible and financial values is on the increase, but awareness alone will not be enough for overcoming our challenges. We need a new socio-economic framework of collaboration for common socio-economic goals and objectives. I call it Collabonomics, "the art of collaborating for collective socio-economic goals". Only then can we achieve and scale the United Nations Sustainable Development Goals (SDG). No company can achieve a single SDG alone without the help of other stakeholders in society. It is as simple as that.

We must learn to listen to each other collaborate; thereby developing a new mindset integrating universal values with business, science, and finance. Faith and secular institutions can exchange learnings on how to incorporate common values necessary for future sustainable growth. Start-ups and multi-internationals can share innovative and creative ideas ensuring financial stability and scalability benefitting both. Gov-

ernments and private capital groups can help catalyze large projects and ensure continuity and achievements of the projects' intent.

Elliot Harris, Assistant Secretary-GeneraL UN Environment Programme, noted at Zug Impact Summit-2017, "be aware of the silent revolution going on in people from all corners of society, whether they work in banks, are farmers, scientists, government officials, CEOs or employees, young or old. They feel that something is not right and that we are steering in a dangerous direction. We must empower and connect them with each other and you will see solutions will emerge at grand scale everywhere."

Klaus-Michael Christensen, Principal, SevenBridge

After many inspiring personal stories, here is a teaching story about a frustrated young man who went to see the wise man in his village.

"I don't know what to do with my life. How do I find my purpose?" the young man asked.

The old man took him to the river where they found dozens of prospectors panning for gold.

"Did all these people find their purpose?" asked the young man. "Only if there is gold in the river," the wise man responded.

"So, how do I find my own purpose?" the young man asked nervously.

"Keep looking. You'll find it tomorrow, next week, next year, or in the years ahead. For now, your purpose is to find your purpose."

Let us conclude the Guidepost with a few insights of global leaders focused on the power of purpose in our lives.

> » John F Kennedy said that *"effort and courage are not enough without purpose and direction."*
>
> » Pablo Picasso maintained that the *"purpose of art is washing the dust of daily life off our souls."*
>
> » For a Nobel Prize winner, Albert Schweitzer, *"the purpose of human life is to serve, and to show compassion and the will to help others."*
>
> » And for the Dalai Lama, *"the purpose of our lives is to be happy".*

Guidepost 7: Love Your Purpose

In following that road less travelled, you must learn how to Love Your Purpose. It lies at the core of transforming yourself and reinventing your institution as one of the cornerstones of Strategic Harmony.

PART III

Build Transformative Business Models

Guidepost 8

Thinking Catalytic

You Can't Turn Back

"The first step is to establish that something is possible; then probability will occur. It is possible for ordinary people to choose to be extraordinary."

Elon Musk

According to Tony Hsieh[21], a recognized, unconventional business strategist and CEO of Zappos, *"There's a transformative shift in business, and what worked before is no longer an option. It's time for evolved entrepreneurs, visionary creators, and change-makers to rewrite the rules of business for the 21st century."*

Reflecting the shifting business conditions, our current leadership community is screaming for new approaches to address the demands of global pandemic and ecological threats. *"Just like the assassination of President John Fitzgerald Kennedy shocked America out of an age of innocence 57 years ago, COVID-19 will be remembered in years to come as the moment the ways of the past no longer ensured the certitude of the future."* Or paraphrased, just as the assassinations of President

JFK, Martin Luther King, and Robert Kennedy shocked the United States' approach to governance, COVID-19 will be a catalyst to completely transform "the certitude" of the way we make decisions in the future.

EmPower Us! is dedicated to do exactly that—to *empower us* all to rewrite the rules of governments, organizations, and businesses for the 21st Century. We propose that generating Strategic Harmony will shift the paradigm, defining a new set of rules that fuel social impact solutions for our broken world. In Part I, we assessed where we are, and in Part II, we aligned leaders' intent with values. In Part III, we are going to transform the business model to achieve Strategic Harmony through purposeful Strategic Transformation. Our goal is for the Catalyzer to experience transformation as holistic by shifting the way you think, embracing the four lenses of the Catalytic Mindset, translating the transformation into the business model, and then executing it.

Let's begin reflecting of how we shift a leader's experience with a mystical story from China.

Facing a final battle after long years of war, a Chinese ruler asked a Wise Man what the outcome would be. General Su was eager to win and ready to die for it, but his army was small in number and unequipped. His enemy, General Li, led an army larger in number, better equipped, well fed, and destined for victory. The Wise Man took the ruler to the lake, picked a flower and tossed it in. They watched the flower for a while, as its whiteness lay calmly on the surface of the water, and then continued to walk. The Wise Man picked another flower and threw it in the stream, which quickly carried it into the distance.

"The stream is small, but it flows and carries away the flowers, which the lake is not capable of doing," stated the Wise Man. "General Li is similar to the lake; large, with many weapons, yet slow and immobile. Sure of his victory, he will stay behind and do nothing. On the other hand, General Su will be in constant motion, leading his men from the front lines of the battlefield. His desire for victory will inspire his whole army. That's why he is going to win."

The present business and political world need an agile approach to leadership, facilitating constant change, and transforming the global economic and political environment. In this story, it is General Su; in our book, we call him/her the Catalyzer. Many descriptive words are associated with the style and essence of catalytic leadership: transformational managers, re-engineers, activators, game-changers, change agents, or paradigm breakers. In this Guidepost, we share our insights on the Catalyzer and Catalytic Thinking in generating Strategic Harmony, social impact, and change. For example, we use the effect of emerging technologies to challenge transformation.

Executives are faced with the challenge of new technologies like artificial intelligence and automation that affect our current and future lifestyles (self-driving cars), jobs (robots), and marketplace (cloud computing). Most are claiming a commitment to digital transformation. But, there is more intention and hype than measurable changes. According to McKinsey, success stories are rare, and some 82% of the U.S. economy has not yet realized the potential of digitalization.

Consistently, global studies confirm that most leaders have neither the understanding nor the skills to operate in the digital world. Some 90% of executives acknowledge the strategic priority of digital transformation, but almost half admit they don't have "the team to deliver and execute the strategy." Can you imagine a professional football coach competing for the World Cup, acknowledging that they need to upgrade their game strategy but don't have players with the skills to execute it? How successful would this team be? That is the reality facing a majority of companies and organizations globally!

The key missing ingredient is the mindset. As suggested by Beth Comstock, former Vice Chair at GE, in *"Emergent Era, digital leadership requires an actual "leap in thinking" and radically new approaches to the flow and processing of information."* Executive teams must adjust to not having all the information and live in perpetual ambiguity. Success in digital transformation requires transforming the OldCo to the NewCo while re-inventing the business model and executing a new sustainable, equitable engine. The same is true for nonprofit, government, and educational institutions. This process is initiated and executed by the Catalyzer, a leader able to initiate and manage transformation.

Catalytic Moment

Realizing the exponential challenges they face, most organizations have embraced transformation as a strategic imperative to become aligned and leverage these rapid changes. But, the successful adoption, implementation, and dissemination of these changes go beyond technology; it requires a shift in mindset. Leaders need to confront their assumptions in the ways they hear and view new data, execute strategies, and evaluate performance. How they translate this mindset into an organizational culture is the critical factor in the generation of new business models. With the digital revolution, this process is loosely-labeled "digital mindset." But as the impact of digital has gone beyond marketing and information technology to encompass the entire organization, a more comprehensive approach to change is required. We call it the Catalytic Mindset.

Technology with Values—a Necessity

New technologies have had a fundamental positive impact on our lives. Nowadays we can do things faster, with less effort, live longer, travel further, and be in touch with practically every corner of the world. All these, let's call them, superpowers bestowed upon us by technology have changed the way we perceive the world and our role in it.

Instant gratification is the new norm. We are constantly bombarded with information. The lives of young people in the developed world are becoming online ads that have only a few things in common with reality. We feel we deserve more, but we are ready to give less. As technology is used to enable us to drive societal changes and battle corrupted governments, it can also be used to proliferate fake news and manipulate the masses.

We are using the powerful tools we've created against us. It seems as if Moore's law has surpassed the society's capacity to adapt to new technologies. Where do we go next? Instead of fearing how our lives will deteriorate in the future, we should look for ways on how to improve them. The goal of any technology development has been to make a better world. Throughout history certain people have tried to use it in the opposite manner. Yet, until now, the good always outwitted the bad. That can give us courage not to despair.

We should use the capabilities that are at our disposal to more efficiently identify these individuals and these movements in order to stop them before they gain momentum. Humanity is more powerful today than it ever was. Let's not get fooled by populists. Let's not abandon our core values, and continue to strive to build a better world with all the amazing opportunities new technologies can offer.

Miha Žerko, CEO, SRC.SI, Slovenia

Catalytic Thinking starts with changing how we see and interpret signs; the questions we ask; the disruptions we anticipate; and our approach to transformation. It's allowing our mind to be free to access a new set of inputs to address a new challenge. It is thinking what you are not thinking about. It's about creating the space to allow a new awareness to emerge. Executives may experience a catalytic moment as they leapfrog into a totally new mindset and new set of behaviors. They must let go of what is and what they anticipate will become. They just need to allow the need to emerge in the environment!

There is a story that reflects on that "moment." A bored King created a contest between a Greek and a Chinese artist. He gave each a wall on either side of the massive great room on the main floor of the castle. The work areas were separated by two heavy drapes. The King challenged each artist to make the most beautiful artistic creation on "their wall" in four weeks. He offered to supply them with anything they needed. The Greek required all kinds of implements for painting and the Chinese asked for implements for scrubbing.

Three weeks went by, and the King was getting anxious to see their creations. The Greek said he would be ready tomorrow and the Chinese said he had another week to complete his work. The next day when the King arrived at the great room, he pulled the Greek's drape aside. He viewed a magnificent and realistic painting of nature. It was breathtaking, and he was overwhelmed with tears. The King decided to declare the Greek the winner, because nothing could surpass the creation. But, upon thinking about it, he decided to give the Chinese artist a chance to show his work. So, the next day he arranged to visit the Chinese artist's wall.

Upon entering the great room, the Chinese artist asked the King to stand by the drape with his back to the Greek's wall. All of a sudden, he pulled the drape, and the King looked up and fainted. When he woke up, he fainted again because what he saw was the most beautiful thing in the world. The Chinese artist had spent weeks polishing the wall, until it became a mirror. His work of art was the Greek's masterpiece, plus the King in the midst of this magnificent artistic creation of nature. In other words, the Chinese artist included the King in the work of art in a fluid and ephemeral way, thus deepening the effect of the Greek artist's work.

The story teaches us that there are two approaches to *"ultimate beauty."* The Greek approached the challenge in a traditional way with paint brushes and paint. His creation was viewed by the King with eyes as magnificent beauty.

The Chinese artist used a disruptive approach and polished a mirror. The King was overwhelmed by the experience of being integrated into the beauty, so much as to lose consciousness. In that catalytic moment he stepped through a doorway into a new consciousness that redefined his experience of Beauty.

This snapshot contrasts Traditional Change with Catalytic Transformation:

TRANSFORMATION	TRADITIONAL CHANGE	CATALYTIC TRANSFORMATION
Tools Used	Paint and Brush	Cleaning materials
Experienced Beauty	Viewed with eyes	Overwhelmed with total experience
What was the outcome	Cried	Lost consciousness, transcendence
What was the change	Magnificent visual Beauty	Redefined experience of Beauty

Figure 8.1 From Change to Catalytic Transformation

Nature gives us many examples of this catalytic moment: the best known is a caterpillar's metamorphosis from a chrysalis to a butterfly. This journey mirrors the transformation from a traditional Bureaucratic Leader to a Digital Transformer and finally to a Catalyzer. Research has shown that within the caterpillar is the beginning growth of wings and feet ready to grow in the transforming chrysalis. So qualified leaders have the capabilities to transform within themselves. As these leaders face unexpected changes in their ecosystem, instead of resisting, they must pause, self-reflect to enthusiastically accept the moment and become part of the change. They need to embrace the drivers of change (technology, habits, client expectations, values, competition) to integrate and synergize as they evolve a new mindset. As leaders transform into Catalyzers, they tap into their future potentialities, skills, and resources required in the organization to transform. This is a space that their organization has never been before. They suddenly understand this reality and, like the butterfly, they cannot turn back.

By analogy, what are the new methodologies and tools required by Catalyzers to address a range of challenges (accelerating at rapid rates): exponentially changing technologies, instant global social communication, Next Generation values shift, viral pandemic, and existential threat of climate change?

Can we expect executives to address these challenges and search for solutions using traditional ways of thinking and strategies?

In building our Strategic Harmony model, we turned back to nature to help us understand and accelerate transformation. We looked at working transformative models in nature that accelerate Harmony in individuals, organizations, and society.

Catalysis is best understood through chemistry. It provides insights into the acceleration of transformation. According to Wikipedia[22], a catalyst is a kind of matchmaker. It is worth noticing that the two Chinese characters that make up the word 'catalyst' are the same as those for 'marriage broker.' In a test tube, a catalyst attracts the desired reaction partners, dissolves their old bonds and quickly brings together the right partners to make a new chemical product. It speeds up reactions without being consumed itself.

A catalyst accelerates the rate of a chemical reaction without undergoing any permanent change. Figure 8.2 illustrates the catalytic process of chemical transformation, which depicts the relationship between the amounts of energy/resources required to achieve an intended chemical reaction. A catalyst is added to speed up the reaction process. It reduces the level of activation energy (or resistance), which is the minimum energy present to result in a chemical reaction. The relationship between reduced activation energy and accelerated reaction time is critical for any system to deliver a more efficient, easy-to-adopt product.

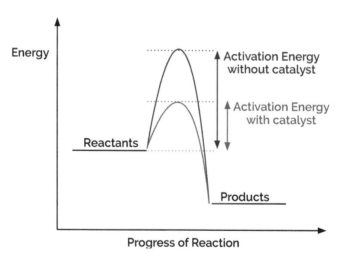

Figure 8.2 Chemical catalytic reaction

In Figure 8.3 we present the concept of Catalytic Transformation by replacing the core variables (reactants, product) of chemical catalysis with values-driven inputs, as in a business model.

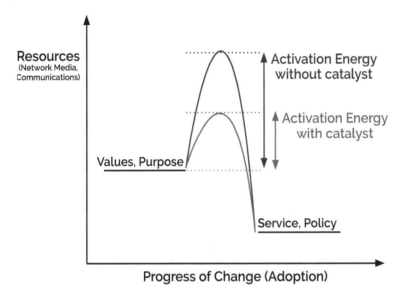

Figure 8.3 Catalytic Transformation

In Catalytic Transformation, the new inputs, catalysts (e.g., values, purpose) become the "reactants" or strategies. They reduce the activation energy required by an organization to adopt new services, policies, or products. Be employing the power of shared values, organizations reduce the forces of resistance, accelerate the reaction/adoption time, and reduce the investment in resources required to be realized in the transformed outcome.

Let's take a look at an outline of strategies to reduce resistance and the activation energy in four business Catalytic Transformation situations:

Cost

» Incentivize trial, early adoption

» Reduce price

Functional

» Increase value (service, usability, convenience)

» Move from reactive to proactive response

Passion (Heart-felt)

- » Incorporate higher purpose/values
- » Address beliefs with tangible benefits

Relationship

- » Increase brand love/trust through authenticity
- » Mobilize community to gain peer support

We can imagine a similar process in personal transformation: the catalyst speeds up chemical reaction in the brain thought process, accelerating the way we understand, integrate, and innovate. The relationship between activation energy and reaction time is critical to understanding the role of the catalyst in both chemical reactions and organization transformation. Activation energy (like organizational inertia or resistance) describes the minimum energy that must be present to result in a chemical reaction.

In an organization sensing the need to digitally transform, the executive team must mobilize the minimum "activation energy" (attitudes, resources) that will address the resistance to change. By adding a catalyst, the activation energy is lowered; thus decreasing the resistance to change and accelerating the formation of "new products." Similarly, by increasing the temperature, the reaction rate increases because of its exponential dependence on temperature. In Catalytic Transformation, we increase the temperature through connectivity and facilitating increased, targeted authentic interactions among stakeholders.

Simply stated, catalysts increase the rate of reaction or change by adding a new factor that requires lower activation energy to create change.

Catalyst Changes the Energy

Analogies between chemistry and business begin with chemical kinetics, which describes what happens when two or more chemicals react to form a product. Sometimes nothing happens, because there isn't enough "activation energy" available to get the reaction going. If we add a catalyst, the energy needed might decrease and the reaction proceeds, perhaps even at an appreciable rate and product is formed.

The catalyst equivalent to business might be a leader, group member, environment, consultant, or any person or thing that promotes the creative process of

---

invention by hosting ideas. As a research scientist, when I had a new project idea, I would present it to a group of 10 fellow scientists. After a maximum of one hour, we would emerge with either a thumbs up or down. In the former, the result was a substantially different idea and an embryo of a research team serving as catalysts. More than once this initial meeting resulted in a patentable idea signed by the attendees.

Temperature, a second feature of chemical kinetics, has direct analogy to business. The speed of a chemical reaction depends exponentially upon temperature. This means that the reaction goes much faster as the environment gets hotter. Let's go back to the idea of a new research project. Instead of meeting as a group, I could have met individually with each person. The result would be different compared to meeting altogether. Here, the meeting room serves as a vessel that contains the group members (reactants) whose ideas collide with each other to form a synergistic result. One idea stimulates other members' ideas, which changes the trajectory of the group input and enhances the ultimate result.

The take-away from the chemistry-business analogy is simple: increase productivity by using a catalyst and increase temperature.

Robert Mahavir Homsy, Ph.D.

Here is an example that contrasts the traditional with catalytic approach to marketing transformation. You are in the market to buy a used car and you are choosing between two dealers to purchase the same model car offered at the same price. Suppose that Dealer #1 advertises a $1,000 discount to attract you and Dealer #2 invites you for coffee with one of your close friends who just bought a car from him and is very satisfied. In addition, Dealer #2 asks other satisfied clients to share their testimonials on Facebook and then he shows them to you.

Both dealers attempt to close the sale using different approaches. Dealer #1 tries to convince you by offering a financial discount. Dealer #2 tries to build Trust by having your friend and former customers share their positive experience. Furthermore, he increases the buzz (temperature) through social media showing support and satisfaction with the dealership. Dealer #2 has thus reduced your resistance to buying a used car and increased the value of their dealership. Basically, he reduced the "activation energy" required to catalyze you to become a buyer.

As an example, let's briefly discuss application of this idea in dealing with a transforming social policy (e.g., climate change). Climate change is a complex issue that crosses borders and demographics and meets resistance among political and business interests. Traditionally, most politicians have a low level of public trust; they frame the intention of the policy in the context of the personal and supporters' interests. They use traditional power relationships to gain adoption. In contrast, a Catalyzer for environmental action will approach the policy strategy by using shared TEST Values as catalysts to appeal to their targeted citizens, businesspeople, unions, etc. They would use transparent data focused on the personal and societal costs of not addressing climate change. The catalyst would reduce the resistance or activation energy (resources needed to drive change) and empower new supporters of the policy to share it on their networks and encourage interaction (increase the temperature).

In Figure 8.4, we contrast the traditional vs catalytic approaches. It can equally be used for climate change, fighting COVID-19, proposing political reforms, or introducing a new product to market.

	TRADITIONAL ORGANIZATION	CATALYTIC ORGANIZATION
Approach	Increase Control	Reduce Resistance
Strategy	Pushing, Convincing "Market AT"	Listening, Adapting, "MARKET TO"
Content	Fueled by Old Power (position, money, relationships)	Fueled by Love (purpose, sustainability, authenticity)
Focus	Customer	Stakeholder
Trust	Not prioritized	Build

Figure 8.4 Traditional vs Catalytic Organization

The analogy in the economic world is the economic catalyst, and it lies at the heart of the shared economy (sharing underutilized assets or services, for a fee, on a peer-to-peer basis). In the new business model, the economic catalyst has two or more clients or networks with underutilized assets that need each other to produce a desired outcome. The demand for one group affects the other since they are interdependent. The two groups rely on the economic catalyst to drive value reactions between them, thus facilitating an easier user experience. This business model is the foundation of the shared economy popularized by companies like Airbnb, eBay, Uber, and Etsy.

To better understand the business model of the shared economy, let's reflect a bit more on the catalytic reaction. In chemistry, a catalyst chemically alters one or more of the materials so that the result readily forms a new product. In the case of Airbnb, there are two interdependent networks: (1) homeowners who have space for rent in their homes, and (2) people traveling and looking for a place to stay overnight. Airbnb built a digital application to serve as an economic catalyst or matchmaker connecting two networks, namely the owners with available rental properties globally and their potential consumers.

The Airbnb digital app creates easy, real time, anywhere, global access, thus reducing the obstacles for consumers interacting and locating potential holiday rentals around the world. As Airbnb further refines the above customer experience, they engender trust and loyalty that further reduces the activation energy (potential blocks to adoption or repeat use). Airbnb catalyzes these two interdependent networks to grow and sustain their business model.

Uber is a similar example of an economic catalyst connecting a network of car owners with a desire to earn money with a network of people who want efficient, affordable local transportation. The business model fulfilled a need with the connected population of users and was then scaled globally. Recently, the Uber model stalled as the customer experience of both drivers and users deteriorated as the executive team's values were challenged by their dissatisfied user network. This caused an increase in the necessary activation energy as an obstacle for repeat purchases that resulted in a drop in business.

Catalytic Thinking

Imagine two shoe salesmen arriving in Africa to test the market. After they have walked around and collected some data, each calls his headquarters. The first complains that his visit was in vain. There is no market for shoes because everyone is barefoot. The second salesman excitedly reports: Wonderful news! Everyone is barefoot; the market is huge and boundless!

If we perceive a situation as "trouble," we wait or hold back. If we see the same situation as an opportunity, we take advantage of the circumstances. The story reminds us of the leadership platitude–*"We need to think differently."* But what does that really mean to be a leader?

Traditionally, the leader's process is:

» Gather and analyze data from the environment

» Choose a direction

» Implement new strategies

But in the Age of New Harmony characterized by constant new inputs, shorter time frames, and permanent change, Catalytic Thinking is required. How do we disrupt the "comfortable" patterns of thought? How do we translate a new way of thinking into a mode of behavior?

The Catalyzer transforms the above process by adding a layer of conscious intention.

> » Analyze data through lens on the intended impact
>
> » Consider the interaction of different future scenarios
>
> » Choose a direction aligned with your values
>
> » Implement new strategies with short-term evaluations
>
> » Be prepared to adjust strategy to feedback and changing data

Let's discuss the development of a purposeful business model. As Figure 8.5 suggests, transformation occurs at three levels: (1) individual/leader, (2) leader/organization, and (3) organization/social impact. The individual/leader transformation relates to the adoption and consistent implementation of TEST Values. The organizational level requires a "change in the mindset," or mental attitude or disposition that predetermines a person's responses to and interpretations of situations. A Catalytic Mindset, rooted in one's core values, is open and agile, serving as a trajectory to propel change and co-create a sustainable future for organizations, communities, or society.

Figure 8.5 Catalytic Transformation Model

Guidepost 8: Thinking Catalytic

Often set-minds are fixed and stable; in contrast a Catalytic Mindset is flexible, and responsive, adapting to new inputs. It is designed to accelerate the 'reaction rate' with which team members anticipate, design, and scale innovative sustainable solutions. It serves as the foundation for an infinite number of platforms that could drive change on an unprecedented scale.

On the social impact level, the organizational transformation is facilitated by the implementation of the L.I.G.H.T. Impacts. The organizational transformation is not sustainable unless it is supported and reinforced by these five impacts. These impacts support and scale the change in the organization as we will discuss in Guidepost 12 L.I.G.H.T. Impacts.

In the words of Jim Collins, the well-recognized author of *Good to Great*[93], "*The catalytic mechanism is a powerful management tool that translates lofty aspirations into concrete reality. It's the crucial link between objectives and performance.*" It is a transformative event, strategy, or policy that is a game changer, empowering the leaders to redirect the direction of the organization. We have expanded on his five characteristics that differentiate a catalytic mechanism:

1. Generates targeted results in unpredictable ways. A catalytic mechanism challenges the assumptions behind a policy or business model. Therefore, the organization, as it approaches transformation with new culture and mindset, will experience unexpected outcomes.
2. Redistributes power for the benefit of the overall system. Catalytic mechanisms facilitate Strategic Transformation even though those in power with vested interests often do not support the change. They subvert the default knee-jerk tendency of bureaucracies to choose status quo over change.
3. Provides a sharp set of teeth to transformation initiatives. Many organizations have good intentions to empower employees and customers but fail. They must go well beyond a statement of values and initiate a catalytic mechanism that all but guarantees that the vision or transformation will be fulfilled.
4. Aligns employees that support an organization's values. Traditional organizations and leadership attract people comfortable with outdated business practices. Catalytic mechanisms are designed to help organizations to attract committed values-driven employees

who don't need to be trained in values, but inherently make decisions that harmonize with company culture.

5. Fuels sustainable outcomes. A catalytic mechanism is not a short-term catalyst for change, but is designed to sustain ongoing transformation and empower a values-driven culture.

The integration of catalytic mechanisms supports the adoption and execution of Catalytic Transformation. They help to reinforce the new global culture of social awareness, advocacy, and transparency. These new relationships have grown into an unofficial digital contract between organizations and their stakeholders. All the stakeholders have to be empowered while being facilitated to become collaborators of the organization's purpose and journey to change. As consumers become more connected, they have a greater opportunity to share their input with the community. Their open customer experience reinforces trust and builds loyalty; some customers evolve into advocates and eventually brand champions. To amplify the customer experience, employees must feel engaged in the purpose and motivated to consistently live their values, providing passionate customer service that delivers purposeful impact.

Let's dissect: how Chobani[24] Greek Yogurt grew as a purposeful brand by implementing Catalytic Transformation; how Hamdi Ulukaya, a Kurdish shepherd immigrant, founded Chobani and became a billionaire CEO and a model for human-centered leadership. Ulukaya believed that business could be a force for good, with the guiding mission "better food for more people." They adopted a passionate Purpose — democratizing good and helping to accelerate universal wellness.

If you take the product (yogurt), and add selected catalysts (values), they transform the generic product into a purposeful brand. As you increase the power of these catalysts, they reduce the resistance to adopt or buy the product. In the case of Chobani, they implemented the four TEST Values:

» Trust—Chobani works closely with dairy farmers, cooperatives, milk processors, and organizations: for more humane treatment of cows to gain their trust. They locally source milk with non-GMO ingredients across all supply chains.

» Empathy—Hamdi Ulukaya, an "empathetic humanitarian," promotes inclusivity with employees from 19 different countries, with 20% (600) being former refugees. He gave 10% of his company profits to the workers. The company is rated as one of the best work environments in the USA.

» Sustainability—Chobani's value for sustainability (e.g., protecting environment, recycled packaging, water conservation, and giving back to community) is integral to all decisions.

» Transparency—Chobani opposes legislation that has a potential to limit the perception of transparency on the farm, including bills against animal welfare.

Reflecting Strategic Harmony, Chobani's transformed yogurt formula, values and strategies garnered 20%+ of the U.S. yogurt market, valued at $8.2B (2019).

How Does a Catalyzer Think?

To achieve Strategic Harmony, we need Catalyzers. Here are eight defining traits:

1. Radically innovative, dedicated to change. One example is Sheikh Mohammed bin Rashid Al Maktoum, Vice President and Prime Minister of the United Arab Emirates (UAE), and ruler of the Emirate of Dubai. Since his accession in 2006, he has undertaken reforms in the UAE's government. In 2010 he launched the vision of making the UAE one of the most innovative countries in the world by 2021. His famous quote is that the word "impossible" does not belong to a dictionary of a leader. The city of Dubai is a good example. Fifty years ago, it was practically nothing but sand and sea. There was hardly any power source and no running water. Today 97% of the city's water supply comes from desalinization, and Dubai has become the second in the world (after Los Angeles) in water consumption per capita. Half a century ago, there was an airport the size of a gas station. Today, Dubai's airport is one of the biggest, busiest, and most beautiful in the world, with energy savings set at 20% per year. A second airport is under construction! Today, the contribution of petroleum production to the GDP of Dubai amounts to less than 5%, while tourism contributes with 30%. As Sheikh Mohammed has been radically innovative with his internal reforms, his regional foreign policies are becoming more inclusive.

2. Future & change-oriented, open to new perspectives, and striving to learn new skills and technologies. We already mentioned the book *Change or Die*, in which Alan Deutschman presents medical study results. There are six individuals whose life depends on a drastic change of habits (alcohol, drug addiction, smoking, bad nutrition, lack of physical activities). The doctor advises them to "change" or die within a year; only one in six finds strength and determination to alter the lifestyle. Two people decide to give it a try, but they give up and return to the old habits sooner or later. The remaining three never try to change and instead pick a deadly outcome. Even under drastic pressure, only one in six will voluntarily alter behavior. The study sheds light on the human capacity to change obstacles to transformation.

The vast majority prefers to resist the needed change even though it's literally a matter of life and death. Typical human behavior is best described by *'I am in favor of changes, but please, change someone else, not me!'* In contrast, Catalyzers are laser-focused on becoming the transformation. There are many examples, from Steve Jobs to Jack Ma, from Elon Musk to Jeff Bezos. These must not be exceptions in the world of Strategic Harmony, but the norm.

3. Open to unpredictable change, disrupting traditions, and risk-taking. Our example is the great maestro, Wolfgang Amadeus Mozart, who attended a concert by a twelve-year-old child prodigy. At the end, Mozart was sure to praise the youth and his superb performance. The proud child responded: I want to become a composer like you. When should I start? Mozart told him to be patient; it would take years of study, a lot of work and many more concerts. Not pleased with the answer, the boy said: But you were already composing at the age of three. Yes, answered Mozart, but I never had to ask anybody when to start. Obviously, Mozart was ready to try and disrupt tradition without asking for permission. Another example is Philip Knight[25], the CEO of Nike Corporation, who used to motivate himself and his employees by saying: *"The only way to avoid mistakes is by never trying! Therefore, we must reward creative mistakes and punish mediocre success!"* Kayak travel website co-founder Paul English's success is defined by his approach to business: *"Fail fast, discover, try... we hire people to be entrepreneurs, to take risks, and try. We give people ridiculous freedom to make decisions and change things."*

4. Passion, intense curiosity, and readiness to experiment. A man visited Baso, the famous teacher of Zen. Baso asked him what he wanted. "Reason and Answer," the man told him. "You've got your own treasure, why are you looking outside of it?" asked Baso. The man became startled "Where is my treasure?" "The fact that you are searching is your treasure," Baso said. The story points out that intense curiosity and yearning for change are the real treasures of a Catalyzer. *"Imagination is more important than knowledge"* is a century-old quote by Albert Einstein. Steve Jobs lived his intense curiosity and obsessive passion for design to make a dent in the world. One of his many brainy quotes may serve as a proof: *"Apple is not about making boxes for people to get their jobs done, although we do that well. Apple is about something more. Its core value is that we believe that people with passion can change the world for the better."* Our society, democracy, market economy, educational system, and all facets of everyday life are still too much tied up with knowledge, and too little with the passion to create and imagine sustainable alternatives.

5. Action-minded, transformation-oriented, and proactive. The Catalyzer is ready to intervene in an expected occurrence; anticipate and initiate change rather than react to events. In the Shogun times, a Japanese warrior, Nobunaga[96], decided to attack a powerful enemy. He believed in his victory, but his soldiers were doubtful. So, before the battle, he took them to a Shinto temple. "After my prayers," he shouted, "I am going to flip a coin. If it's heads, we win. If it's tails, we lose. Destiny holds us in its hand!" Nobunaga prayed in silence and then tossed the coin. It was heads. Seeing this, his warriors eagerly ran into the battlefield and defeated the enemy. "No one can change destiny," said Nobunaga's deputy in the evening while they were celebrating the victory. "It's true," said Nobunaga, showing the coin with heads on both sides. This story points out that Catalyzers are characterized by a deep and profound faith, desire to fight and challenge, and a readiness to attack problems without seeking approval, support, or permission. Martin Luther King Jr was a catalyst for global change with unswerving faith. He approached a new challenge with *"If you can't fly then run, if you can't run then walk, if you can't walk then crawl, but whatever you do, you have to keep moving forward."* Roman emperor and philosopher Marcus Aurelius[27] pointed at three cornerstones of proactive behavior: courage, patience, and wisdom. It takes courage to change the things we can change; it takes patience to accept the things we cannot change; and it takes wisdom to see the difference.

6. Redefine leadership. Take a look at W. L. Gore & Associates[98], one of the largest privately held companies in the United States with more than 50 facilities in East Asia, Australia, Europe, and the Americas. It is best known for its innovative products and a unique organizational culture. Instead of a formal management hierarchy, the company has a flat, lattice-like organizational structure and everyone shares the same title of associate. There are neither chains of command nor predetermined channels of communication. Associates choose to follow leaders rather than have bosses assigned to them. They are encouraged to communicate directly with each other and are accountable to fellow members of their teams. Such teams are typically organized around opportunities, new product concepts, or businesses. As teams evolve, leaders emerge as they gain followers. The unusual organizational structure and culture contribute to the company's overall success and associate satisfaction and retention. It has inspired the new management style called open allocation; the employees are given a high degree of freedom in choosing what projects to work on, and how to allocate their time. And, of course, it augments their creativity and innovation.

7. Systemic, holistic thinking. Catalyzers must have a holistic view, ability to see the total entity and the interdependence of the diverse parts. They must be able to integrate the connected chain of factors at their roots (human, economic, technological) that are critical in devising sustainable solutions. However, it is not simple. Remember the story about four blind men who were asked what an elephant looks like? The first crawls under the stomach and describes the elephant as a big balloon. The second takes hold of the tail and says: "An elephant resembles a snake." The third guy, holding a long tusk in his hands says: "An elephant is like a twisted spear. Leaning back on the animal's leg, the fourth disagrees: "An elephant is like a trunk of a tree." A Catalyzer must always try to see the whole picture. His/her task is to address everyone's interests (all stakeholders) creatively, not just for some. His/her goal is to harmonize the system and not the subsystems. The Catalyzer knows that every whole is more than the sum of its parts. The interaction of the parts should be aimed at achieving the goals of the whole. Whatever happens in an organization should be seen from the point of view of the whole, considering its vision, mission, goals, projects, and programs. Only then can the system be organized, the tasks delegated to subsystems, and finally completed.

8. Striving for the stars. It is that "ignitable energy within you waiting to be touched upon and utilized."[99] But where does that unadulterated striving come from? It grows out of curiosity, passion, fear, competition, caring, purpose, and success. When Ira's daughter was four years old, she would sit on his shoulders and look up to the stars wanting to touch them. He said to her "Reach out with your hands and fingers to the stars." She responded, "I did not touch them." Ira responded, "Stretch with all your might." That is the striving to reach your goal.

Catalyzers strive to fulfill a passion and purpose for sustainable change. Their ambition is not self-centered but focused on success for the community, country, and world. Only Catalyzers, powered by great dreams and able to fantasize huge innovative projects, will eventually become ready to make those dreams come true. Most people are doomed to stay forever locked in the constrained world of the status quo. It is mostly because they lack imagination; they are grounded by the absence of courage, fear of taking chances, and inability to think catalytic.

So, how do you rate yourself as a Catalyzer? Can you *empower us?* What are the areas that you need to strengthen to catalyze and sustain your purpose?

The most important decision, the one that will affect every other decision you make, is the commitment to improve yourself. It directly affects the quality of your relationships, your work, and your future. Always keep in mind that tomorrow is the beginning of the rest of your life. Whatever you have been doing that is missdirected can be changed, if you only believe that the world of Strategic Harmony is around the corner.

Guidepost 9

Catalytic Mindset

Reinventing

If you start with the mindset that you know nothing,
you will learn a lot that nobody knew before.

David Maraniss

In Japanese, the phrase *shoshin* means "beginner's mind." Any Zen teacher would ask his students to keep such a mind, always ready and open to everything. In the beginner's mind, there are many possibilities; in the expert's mind, there are only a few. The creative and open mindset is the key source to transformation and change.

Often, we don't accomplish our goals and don't get what we want or deserve because of our mindset. Like a voice in our heads, it tells us what we can do and what is impossible, what is worth doing and what isn't. Henry Ford's brainy quote, *"whether you believe you can do a thing, or not, you're right"*[100] comes to mind. To review, mindset is based on beliefs and values, those inner touchpoints that determine our decisions and the way we live and work. If we want to support behavior leading to sustainable outcomes, we need to make sure that we have the mindset aligned with those values that drive the behavior. Therefore, after the individual and team gain a consistent approach to their values, they must turn to integrating these values within the organizational culture.

In our model, we call this values-driven culture the *Catalytic Mindset*. This mindset takes a deep dive into the critical elements developed in earlier Guideposts. This Guidepost provides a path to adopting this mindset by asking a series of questions which require readers to reflect on where they are and where they want to go!

On its path to Strategic Harmony, an organization must align with four interconnected lenses to drive its organizational culture. At the core of each lens is one of the TEST Values. The value anchors and "governs" the direction of the Think lenses. The lenses are interdependent and woven together by the Catalyzer to form the Catalytic Mindset as the foundation of the organization's culture:

1. Think Quantum
2. Think Circular
3. Think Connective
4. Think Intelligence

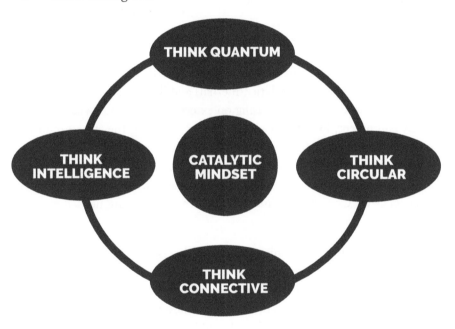

Figure 9.1 Catalytic Mindset

The following table in Figure 9.2 provides a snapshot of the four think lenses – the TEST Values, major actions they drive, and their solutions. Detailed analysis of all the four lenses can be found in the Guideposts to follow.

LENSES	VALUES	MAJOR ACTIONS	SOLUTION
Think Quantum	Trust	Adjust assumptions; disrupt old patterns	Openness to change challenges old beliefs, redefines risk, stimulates divergent solutions, and expands intended impact
Think Circular	Sustainability	Reinvent business model	Readiness to adopt sustainable and circular-economy-based approaches
Think Connective	Empathy	Leverage networks and digital assets	Connective mindset and networking
Think Intelligence	Transparency	Optimize data points and analytics	Data turned into collaborative tool to evaluate impact and guide sustainable decision-making

Figure 9.2 Four Catalytic Mindset Think Lenses

Why these four lenses? They reflect the fact that there are two forces transforming an organization: catalytic (internal) and digital (external). Most organizations are accustomed to focusing on external components when investing in new equipment, hiring new employees, or changing the structure or location of a company. But organizations have difficulty with the internal changes required for successful transformation. Two lenses (Think Quantum and Think Circular) are focused on the internal changes, while the two external lenses focus on Connectivity and Intelligence. All four are needed for transformation.

Each of these lenses is a mini-mindset that is essential to develop Strategic Harmony and the supporting organizational culture. This is not a linear process; all modules are active, learning, and expanding. Each is being cultivated as they reflect new ways of thinking, innovating, and executing. As our model suggests, each team member should look through these lenses as he or she assesses, design new business models, and execute strategies. Moving from one lens to another, we discover diverse perspectives and the weaknesses and strengths of our strategies.

The new mindset changes the approach to decision-making. As a manager evolves into a Catalytic Mindset, these lenses become woven as a transparent fabric that all challenges and decisions pass through. The new mindset challenges the re-invention and "confronts" traditional business operations. It is no surprise that, if the mindset is not adopted and committed to, the rest of the transformation will fail.

As you reflect on each of these lenses, we suggest that you challenge yourself and mentally rate how agile you are and how prepared is your organization for Catalytic Thinking.

Think Quantum

Quantum thinking is best defined as the ability to see an issue from all sides and dimensions. It shifts the paradigm by "removing fixed mental constructs" that resist change. It breaks down the "everyday patterns" of analysis and replaces our anchored assumptions with a new flexibility and agility to respond differently to changing inputs. It requires a high level of Trust in the leader in his or her vision for change, the team, and the process of transformation. This Trust fuels the personal courage and confidence to question business norms and confront their own criteria and past decisions. Finally, a leader must Trust the intended impact to reinvent solutions that address the real needs for all stakeholders.

The term is also associated with Quantum Leap, a dramatic advance in knowledge or method, an idea that can be traced back to the mid-twentieth-century physics. It denotes a sudden change from one energy state to another within an atom. Quantum thinking provides leaders with new insights and power to propel change, but at the same time guides them to be humble as a "small piece" of the vast intelligent universe.

Think Quantum challenges organizations' blindly accepted traditional beliefs. These beliefs frame the mindset and form the foundation for the culture. Our broken world is based on many false perspectives, out-of-date practices, and biased assumptions. These closed paradigms block innovation and transformation. It is important to use divergent thinking to disrupt the status quo and propel creativity.

Furthermore, Think Quantum is driven by the impact intended. In the volatile and unpredictable world of digital ecosystems and networks, the exponential impact turns into great expectation combined with big ambition. It challenges the leader, change agent, and entrepreneur to redefine risk and failure and what the expanded intended impact is. In the transformation process, the Catalyzer is faced with the question: What is your expected impact? Salim Ismail[101] from Singularity University explains it like this: *"If I say go impact 100 people, you'll use your traditional thinking to operate that way. When we say go impact a billion people, you're forced to think exponentially."*

These new perspectives drive leaders to understand the threat of survival if they do not adapt and adopt a path to integration and change.

Think Quantum provides the foundation to integrate the four shifts in thinking required to achieve Strategic Harmony. The first three set the context, while the fourth shift provides a new methodology.

First, the Catalyzer starts with a laser focused Purpose. *Loving your Purpose* drives the expected impact by increasing the motivation and loyalty of all stakeholders. It is associated with the following question:

How clearly is your Purpose defined and integrated throughout your operations?

Second, the Catalyzer's *intention* sets the direction and scale to impact the change exponentially. Catalyzers must Love the Problem and the path to its Solution. Their mindset is based on self-directed risk-taking, readiness to improvise and learn from failure, and the ability to turn the unexpected into a positive result. With the organization's support, the Catalyzer transforms expectations from generating incremental (10% increase) to an exponential (10X increase) gain. Catalytic leaders without an exponential intention are similar to people ready to use a car and not a jet plane to get to a distant destination. It is associated with the following question:

Is your business model defined for today (10% growth) or for the future (10X growth)?

Third, *design thinking* drives innovation and engagement. By integrating values, we get purposeful design thinking. Catalyzers adopt it as a creative and flexible solution-based approach to solving problems. In dealing with complex issues that are siloed or partially-defined, it focuses on addressing human needs, considering the Web of Life. The problem is defined with a human-centric orientation, and the solutions are generated by creating ideas in brainstorming sessions, and by adopting a hands-on approach in prototyping and testing. It is associated with the following question:

Is purposeful design thinking integrated into your innovation model?

Fourth, *Lean methodologies reflect the process, speed, and time frame expected for innovation and respect for people.* At its core is the Minimum Viable Product (MVP), a startup mentality focusing on just enough features to satisfy early adopting customers. MVP contrasts the traditional product development approach (costly, long research/testing with no guaranteed success) with the *Lean Startup Method* designed by Eric Ries. It's a three-step iterative process that allows businesses to adjust their course based on real-time consumer feedback and demand. The steps are:

1. *Build* – Create a minimum viable product (MVP) based on a set of assumptions
2. *Measure* – Launch MVP and measure your hypothesis based on your assumptions
3. *Learn* – Accept or reject your initial hypothesis and iterate on the MVP

MVP is based on quick interactions, like those with a 3D printer. You can make changes in real time, test them, and re-evaluate the results. It allows the innovation to gain traction as it gets developed in contrast to waiting for the product to be perfect. It encourages continuous innovation while keeping the risk and costs low. With the scaling of digital technologies, organizations garner "real-time" feedback and address innovation iteratively. Small changes or iterations of a product or service save time and resources. Teams don't have to start from scratch, and the timeline for a traditional innovation process can be reduced from 18 months to 3-6 months.

This Lean process can be applied to change initiatives throughout the organization. It helps (1) initiate and encourage innovation initiatives; (2) increase their effectiveness and efficiency; (3) decrease time to implement/market by reducing the lead time between idea and launch; (4) decrease operational costs focusing on one feature with significantly reduced R&D, thus cutting back operational costs; and (5) provide better customer/stakeholder experience because design is refined by real-time customer feedback.

Here is the associated question:

Is your innovation strategy MVP-based or a traditional R&D process?

The Transformative Power of MVP is demonstrated by Tessemae' s best-selling brand of salad dressings and condiments. CEO Greg Vetter was struggling for months to launch his natural salad dressing. He didn't have packaging, labeling, bottling, or manufacturing set up. But he did have an appointment with the buyer for Whole Foods Supermarkets. So, he courageously put together his MVP, a container of his mother's homemade Lemon Garlic salad dressing. The audition got Vetter his salad dressing launch at an opening of a Whole Foods store, where he sold 55 cases. Nine years later, Tessemae is the leading organic salad dressing in the U.S. with annual sales in excess of $25 Million.

In sum, Think Quantum is the foundation of Catalytic Mindset. Some call it a new mental superpower[102] as it's both empowering and humbling. Transformative Power and humility are most welcome traits of a successful and admired Catalyzer. The result is that the team embraces contradictions and avoid judgments. They empathize with diverse perspectives seeing things from various sides. Quantum means a shift from linear thinking to constantly innovating, holistic thinking. Think Quantum allows the Catalyzer to anticipate and envision the future with the next generation business models and related products and services.

Let's illustrate the comprehensive effect of Quantum Thinking using IKEA as a case study. The company's vision and thinking goes beyond home furnishing products. They want *"to create harmony for all people impacted by their business."* The drive and focus of the company is to offer inspirational, functional, affordable, and sustainable products to as wide a range of consumers as possible. In 2019 the company had 211,000 employees (they call them co-workers) in 433 stores in 53 countries across the world. They are connected with a well-designed global network that distributes its products in a most efficient way. They print their catalog in more than 200 million copies; only the Bible, the Koran, and Harry Potter had more copies in print in 2018.

IKEA's business strategy is to listen to their consumers, employees, and supply chain. The company's vision is *"to offer a wide range of well-designed, functional home furnishing products at prices so low that as many people as possible will be able to afford them."* They have recently adapted the customer experience to respond to customer expectations with click-and-collect sites in some city centers, home delivery, and a new augmented-reality app for smartphones to help customers visualize furniture in their homes. IKEA is driven to reinvent an immersive experience As Fortune[103] writes, *"Witness the full-size sample rooms that IKEA sets up in stores and where customers will sometimes be caught napping. The rooms play an essential, if secret role, showing consumers how to fit IKEA pieces into their lives."*

Think Circular

As William McDonough, the father of circular economy suggested, circular thinking is rooted design. It is systems thinking to explore nature's rules and apply them in the design of the new. Air, water, and temperature do not interact in a linear mode but are interconnected. Think Circular is intended to replace the current linear economy with circular model "where waste is designed out right from the start." It transforms the design criteria from "take, make, dispose" to "reduce, reuse, and recycle." Resource use is minimized while reuse of products and parts is maximized.

Circular thinking is based on Sustainability, the key goal being to meet the needs of the present without compromising the future generations in meeting their needs. It integrates the equitable impact on all stakeholders in the context of a Quadruple Bottom Line (QBL-people, planet, profit, prosperity).

Think Circular is a powerful internal criterion and lens of the Catalytic Mindset. It requires us to think differently about how products, policy, and even organizations are designed; how the economy works to meet human needs; how to build business models to reflect circular thinking; and how to effectively access the sustainable impact on QBL.

For example Think Circular demands that the business model achieve circularity through the value:

» offered in your business through new combinations of products and services to fulfill your current or future stakeholders' needs;

» created by exploring how to change your operational processes, improve resources sourcing, and develop new collaborative partnerships to close your value chain;

» delivered by changing the means of interacting and reaching your customers and stakeholders;

> » captured and transformed in business results (social, environmental, and economic);

> » transformed over time, since a good idea not feasible today could be feasible in the future.

Here is the associated question:

Does your business model achieve circularity?

Think Circular is a holistic solution that benefits the planet. The 2019 ING Group's report "Opportunity and Disruption: How Circular Thinking Could Change U.S. Business Models," reports *"U.S. companies could unlock $4.5 trillion of additional economic output, in just 11 years, if they institute a circular economic model — one that reduces waste, relies less on raw materials, and increasingly uses recycled materials."*

Sixty-two percent of executives plan to move their companies toward a circular economic framework, while 16% have accomplished the transition[104]. Heineken's adoption of the Think Circular model has been exemplary - achieving zero waste at several of its breweries; reusing plastic, glass, and metal, and also eliminating organic waste from its manufacturing process; as well as generating revenue actually selling its organic waste, spent grains and barley husks, for processing into animal feed. The report's author concluded *"Circular models have the potential to redefine businesses by creating new revenue growth opportunities."*

Think Connective

Traditional organizations are based on hierarchy. Strategic Harmony calls for *Wirearchy!* The value and strength of connections are no longer based solely on position and rank but on ability to actively participate in a network of "wired" people, organizations, and institutions. Think Connective expands, scales, and leverages all relationships through instant communications via global networks. Joshua Cooper Ramo[105] defined *The Seventh Sense* as the age of constant connection. It is built upon the networks that we access daily for information, activities, and identity. Old business models are focused on a product or service and based upon one-to-one relationships. Mass media reflects one-to-many connections. The digital world is built on many-to-many network connections. They change power relationships in economic, political, and security aspects of our lives and businesses.

Think Connective means transforming from "inner thinking" about connections between yourself, your product, or your company, to "outer thinking" of the needs of your targets and the network—how to appeal to your network with the objective of creating mutual benefit. It is based on the Value of Empathy, understanding and sharing the feelings of another. Connectivity is built on "obsessively" understanding the individuals of the network and responding to and engaging their needs.

Think Connective means digital relationships. Digital leaders must refine and develop "connected and information-rich assets" that pervades the entire organization. It begins with a commitment to developing interactive digital dialogues that generate trusting and sustainable relationships, leading to action (sale, commitment), ongoing feedback, and engagement (sharing) of the brand. In contrast, there is social (media) advertising, which is similar to broadcast advertising but replacing traditional with social media. It loses the interactivity and involvement of a genuine digital relationship. A Weebly survey reported that 89% of small businesses use Facebook to promote their business, but 62% suggested these ads missed the target and provided poor-quality leads or low conversion.

Why? Because Facebook advertising uses the broadcast model to reach their Facebook friends. Most often the campaign is not designed to engage their friends in an interactive relationship that they will in turn share with their network.

The process of transforming an organization to a digital orientation requires a customer-first mentality, a networking mindset, and a deep understanding of all the digital and non-digital relationships. Media becomes "digital" when the organization is connected interactively with people and generates rich sources of data and information on those that they connect.

Think Connective shifts the value from a product/service to a network—the people who are sharing the product or the interconnected networks of people engaged with the product/service. It also refers to ecosystems whose channels are connected, and the processes by which those channels are developed and maintained. By thinking through the lens of your networks, your organization generates value through its "network" rather than its products and services.

Take the example of a global nonprofit that has more than 10,000 alumni from their 30+ years of programs. Each year, the organization spends a lot of time and resources applying for grants for new programs to graduate new alumni. However, the nonprofit has infrequently interacted with the alumni base garnered during three decades to develop and expand its database into a powerful network providing services and related partnerships. The network can empower the organization, because each node can interact, inspire, and grow connections through its involvement and interactions. Instead of focusing all their resources on getting grants for new programs, they built a new business model. They challenged their team to listen to their alumni, develop these relationships, and link them as resources. Now the network has become a potential revenue generator with the power to distribute their services in real time to potential users.

The mastery of network thinking can be applied to promote a commercial message, influence target markets on local, national, or global levels, and affect the citizens' opinions in an election. The network mentality uses all the individuals, organizations, and "crowds" that are available. It benefits from the aggregation of the nodes in the network. An engaging message, customer experience, and interaction of the nodes amplify the energy and the Transformative Power of the network. Messages travel faster and gain value as influence is generated. As people share and collaborate in the network, there's an energy exchange based on Trust and Transparency.

Once an organization has adopted the Catalytic Mindset, it must integrate the values and strategies to reflect the new culture. The focus begins to shift from individual relationships to community and then to network. Catalyzers listen more attentively to the buzz of the global marketplace as an aggregation of communities. They discover new approaches to interact with their digital assets and leverage their network to create new value for their organization.

We are living in a world of organized crowds; success is determined by leveraging networks and crowds. Therefore, we are talking about Crowdsourcing, Crowdfunding, Crowdsharing and Crowdlearning. Fifty years ago, "Think global, act local" was the maxim promoting the emerging process of globalization. Since then, most organizations think and act like islands. Today the wisdom says: *Network globally, connect locally, impact globally*, or you will disappear! To survive, not to mention grow and develop, all organizations must cherish a fully global and connective mindset. Traditionally, one could succeed by climbing the local hierarchy. Today, the only way to achieving your purpose is to be integrated into a network, amplifying connections with as many nodes as possible.

Social Network… Agent of change

The expression "Social Networks" refers today to online communities. However, they have been always there. They are the expression of inter-actions between humans. Internet helps materialize networks into data on connections: number, type, frequency, density… But, beyond data, a social network shows the distribution of trust within and between com-munities. The connections a person has are a consequence of the number of persons trusting him or her. Social Networks are built upon a val-ues-trust cement. If nonexistent, the social network dissolves. If strong enough, it is a powerful system that influences peoples' beliefs, decisions, and behaviors. It gives access to information, resources, and markets.

From an economic perspective, networks reinforce institutions that set up the rules of the game. Networks generate social capital created by con-nections around common values and facilitating collective action. For instance, in the Medina of Tunis (Tunisia), Souks are the place where artisans and shopkeepers locate, mingle, and share values, in the same market alley, one next to the other. This might seem counterintuitive, as close distance enforces fierce competition. However, the collaboration gains exceed competition threats. Artisans meet and interact for friendly talks and unstructured information exchange. This leads to knowledge spillovers, recruitment opportunities, and collaboration to gain markets or mutualize costs.

From an organizational perspective, a network is an asset. It is the es-sence of individual being as a social agent of organizations, societies, and civilizations. Data availability provided by current online tools gives to humanity an unprecedented potential to understand these organisms. Government, companies, and NGOs should develop strategic thinking to build their networks and leverage on them to diffuse information, pro-mote innovation, and create value. Organizations should rethink and reframe the architecture of their internal networks (employees) and ex-ternal networks (partners, suppliers, clients…) to reach their goals.

Noômen Lahimer, Founder, Evey Technologies

Network Orchestration

For the first time in human history we have an opportunity to build "ideal markets" in which any "supply" is directly connected to any "demand" without intermediaries. We can cut all the middlemen out. The new style of doing business is called the "network orchestration" model, and we have already talked about popular shared-economy examples and business-model disruptors like TripAdvisor, Alibaba, Red Hat, Airbnb, and Uber.

We live in the world of digital gatekeepers with direct communication to millions of people. Access to these networks gives individuals and organizations control of the messaging and avoiding middleman/press/surrogates of the traditional marketing channel. The world is moving from consumer economy to shared economy, the key word being "shared" instead of being "consumer." That's a great mindset transformation. Network-first thinking is critical to understanding and mobilizing the most valuable asset in transmitting our message and service to the target markets. Just like in the political arena, who controls the Twitter and social media platforms controls access to strategic influencers.

The network grows and becomes sustainable as members become engaged and "in love" with the product/brand, passionately distributing the message as "Brand Champions" through their networks. The formula fits every organization wanting to change their brand through unique messaging. Warby Parker has a very successful online prescription glasses retail model that donates one pair of glasses for each pair sold. Understanding the millennials' attraction to buying from socially responsible companies, the company has donated more than three million pairs as the retail model grows. Furthermore, Warby Parker[106] disrupted the retail eyeglass giants by focusing on the total customer experience. They sold their frames and lenses at one-fourth the competitors' price. Furthermore, they included a virtual reality feature where you upload your picture, select your frames, and ask people to vote for your best look on social media sites.

Another example is Philips Healthcare practice[107] teaming up with Salesforce to build a platform that they believe will reshape and optimize the way healthcare is delivered. The envisioned platform will create an ecosystem of developers building healthcare applications to enable collaboration and workflow between doctors and patients across the entire spectrum of care, from self-care and prevention, to diagnosis and treatment, through recovery and wellness.

Think Connective methodologies include: accessing, building, sustaining, and leveraging networks. We invite you to check the boxes that relate to your organization's application of these methodologies.

☐ Acknowledge the network exists (either latent, active, or database driven)

☐ Transform a product /service to a network orientation

☐ Determine access to the network

☐ Design value-added proposition to enrich relationships and develop trust

☐ Prepare user-friendly messaging to engage and delight the network

☐ Encourage ongoing and regular network members' interaction and reward involvement

☐ Generate loyalty by creating levels of network commitment

☐ Build advocacy for members' willingness to use their reputation to build the network's value

☐ Leverage champions who reflect the passion for the network and take the initiative to grow and expand it

Today, connectivity is experiencing an interesting twist, the development and use of blockchain technology. In principle, it addresses the issues of transparency and trust, and at the same time, symbolizes a shift in power from the centers to the edges of the networks. As pointed out by Olaf Carlsson-Wee[108], we are about to experience the new phase of Internet: a world with many blockchains and hundreds of tradable tokens built on top of them; entire industries are automated through software; venture capital and stock markets are circumvented; entrepreneurship is streamlined; and networks gain sovereignty through their own digital currency. Think Connective is a powerful means to achieve and scale Strategic Harmony.

Think Intelligence

The key issue is how we can become intelligent about the people and organizations in our networks. For Tim Berners-Lee, the inventor of the World Wide Web, *"Data are a precious asset and will last longer than the systems themselves."*[109] As we open any business publication, we are inundated with references to the power of big data, analytics, and data mining; this is changing the landscape of business operations. It means to dig deep into our data to drive both creative and critical insights and directions that the team might realize from the analytics.

Think Intelligence is a game-changing lens that impacts the revenue and costs sides of the balance sheet[110] in the following ways:

» Revenue Growth. Predictive analytics allow more precise targeting of customers, with quicker reaction to market changes.

» Deepened Customer Loyalty. Obsessively listening and gathering data on customer experience uncovers needs and changing expectations to proactively customize marketing and products.

» Greater Efficiency. Real-time digital analysis of supply chains uncovers efficiency drains, realizing time and cost efficiencies.

» Reduced Risk and Operational Losses. Comprehensive analytics signal changing market conditions and anticipate customer dissatisfaction with time to respond and adapt.

At the foundation of Think Intelligence is the value of Transparency, knowing and trusting the source and relying on its authenticity. It effects the power of the data, their reliability and impact on both the organization and its targets.

The challenges of Think Intelligence are fourfold:

» Align data-driven organization;

» Access to data;

» Quality of data; and

» Manage Intelligence.

The first issue is organizational alignment. It is predicated on a culture of collaboration among diverse silos, and it requires communication built on trust, accountability, and transparency of data. Many organizations struggle with legacy thinking, systems, and structures. They lack the courage, trust, and confidence to invest in data-gathering systems and teams with the skill-sets to effectively execute them.

Second, every organization needs access to the rich data. No wonder that 76% of executives[111] from top-performing organizations cited data collection as essential, compared with only 42% from companies that fall behind their peers in performance.

Often, teams have access to rich data but don't have the mindset or the tools to understand how to leverage or use the data to help transform their organization. There are many important questions for your reflection. You can start by checking the boxes below and providing answers:

☐ What is your organization's approach to data?

☐ Are data passively or actively collected, alive or static? Is everything digitized?

☐ Are traditional and digital sources integrated?

☐ Is your data collection and analysis linked to your strategic goals?

☐ How are data collected, analyzed, disseminated and processed?

The third issue is quality of the collected data and how you are measuring the data. Measurement is an issue as traditional Key Performance Indicators (KPIs) do not really measure the factors that distinguish a purposeful brand. As Luis Di Como, Unilever's Executive Vice President, Global Media, comments: *"There is an obsession that the only KPIs out there are 'reach' or 'number of followers'. We need to talk about what the real impact is on brand equity—the real impact on the values of the brand."*

The final issue is how to manage intelligence. Data-driven organizations are seeing upwards of 20% to 30% improvements in their bottom line due to unlocked efficiencies and more granular financial insight. The key questions to address are:

» How to use data for decision-making?

» How to incorporate data in Digital Marketing Strategy?

» How to incorporate intelligence to anticipate disruption?

» How to manage data security?

» How to manage the exponential expanding data sources (internal and external, structured and unstructured, subjective and objective)? Is it interaction by interaction, activity by activity, or minute by minute?

The best Think Intelligence cases can be found in e-commerce. Whenever you shop at Amazon[112], you receive a product recommendation while visiting their website or through email. It's an example of data-driven decision-making. Amazon's recommendations are based on what the customer has bought in the past, the items in his/her virtual shopping cart, what items the customer has ranked or reviewed after purchase, and what products the customer has viewed when visiting the site. Also, Amazon uses artificial intelligence and key engagement metrics such as click-through rates, open rates, and opt-out rates to further decide what recommendations to suggest to which customers. By integrating recommendations into nearly every aspect of Amazon's purchasing process, from product browsing to checkout, the company has found that product recommendations drive sales and increase the bottom line.

A major executive priority is cyber security and protection. Data have become a source for global political and economic power. The recent U.S. and European elections were influenced by data mining, hacking into databases, and spamming digital media campaigns. As data are power, so is the protection and security of the data.

Data-driven marketing is shifting from passive data capture of Customer Relationship Management (CRM) to action-oriented real-time personalization. Various predictive actions generated by Artificial Intelligence open new trends in Martech (marketing technology).

Social Listening - an early warning system

Our world is transforming radically. With 4.2B people on social media, there are few strangers left. Network connectivity and social media have fundamentally changed the way people: Learn About Brands, Form Opinions, Buy Products, Seek Support, Look for a Job, Give Feedback, Invest in Stocks, and Engage Governments. Consumers have power like never before, and they are changing the rules of engagement. In fact, Comcast became America's most hated company, based on a social media attack from a site called Reddit.

Now, Chief Marketing Officers are using data structuring platforms to develop real-time insights into their stakeholder behaviors, preferences, and perspectives. For example, a global laptop vendor is using social listening as an early warning system that provides them the ability to detect laptop issues 3-5 weeks before a single phone call hits the call center— saving them significant costs and reducing costly staff escalations.

In order to understand the rapidly changing voices of their citizens, to serve their people more effectively, and to refine relevant policies, governments, NGOs, and Civil Society must also embrace social listening

---

and digital citizen engagement For example, Barbara Han and John Drake call for the creation of a global early warning system for infectious diseases. "We are at an exciting point in time where technology and Big Data present us with an anticipatory option, which has real potential to improve global health security."

Innovative Governments are adapting and transforming using social listening. Smart Dubai, the technology service provider to the Dubai government, has recently implemented the Social Happiness Index that measures insights and happiness, mining social media data. The data is parsed, structured, and scored using an AI-powered sentiment engine, developing insights into the seven pillars of the Dubai City Happiness Index. Here are the populations' ratings on The Big Seven: Economy (79%), Environment (79%), Living (70%), Digital Services (64%, Governance (57%), People (57%), and Mobility (50%). Having a real-time view of the global sentiment for each of the Happiness pillars, Smart Dubai is now able to provide insights to the respective departments and ministries to maximize citizen happiness.

The path to Strategic Harmony lies in the ability of organizations to listen to their digitally engaged communities and serve them, in real time, at their moment of need.

Irfan Verjee, VP Digital Business Solutions Group, Sprinklr

Reliable access to real-time data and analytics, as well as an open flow of data drives the resiliency and innovation necessary for the transformation to a catalytic organization. The idea pointed out by Napoleon Bonaparte that "War is ninety percent information" is still true, only now we are talking Big Data, Data Farming, Dark Data, Open Data, Database, Data Warehouse, Data Mining, Data Governance, Data Modelling, Data Protection, and Data Integrity. All these issues should be considered in developing and maintaining Data, one of the cornerstones of Catalytic Leadership.

RESET the Mindset

In order to achieve the Catalytic Mindset we need to go beyond thinking of these four lenses as independent silos. According to Catherine Roome, President of BC Safety Authority[113], *"There is nothing more critical to the success of an organization's strategy than the quality of the people who lead that strategy.*

And while most of our past education and on-the-job experience has built up our management skills, what the world needs today is a new way of thinking. This is different than acquiring a new set of skills. It's a mindset switch: to come at complexity from a place of curiosity; to achieve breakthroughs using systems thinking; and, to push down our egos, in order to increase our adaptability as change accelerates."

Catalyzers require two mitigating processes that influence and direct the input of the four lenses. The first, Self-Reflection, is an internal process that allows one to be more receptive to change. The second is Integration, an alchemic process of entwining multiple external inputs to generate new outcomes.

Self-Reflection

Aware people know that we can rise above our fears, weaknesses, and assumptions by observing and reflecting on them. Self-Reflection means confronting our judgment and bias; nurturing change; growing patient in our relationships; and harnessing the wisdom from our inner development. Psychologists, mystics, spiritual teachers, leaders, and visionaries have written thousands of volumes on the topic, describing different tools like meditation, personal reflection, purification, mindfulness, and contemplation. The Catalytic Mindset begins with Self-Reflection on Purpose and incorporates the core values in all decisions and actions.

Self-Reflection requires Catalyzers to reserve some time each day to pause and reflect on their choices and behavior, addressing issues such as:

> » Do we approach planning with a clear intention on sustainable impact?
> » Why and how are our decisions made?
> » What assumptions are they based upon?
> » Do decisions consistently incorporate our values?
> » Do we consider and are we open to alternative scenarios?
> » Do we incorporate alternative perspectives in our decisions?
> » Are our strategies consistently driven by our purpose?

For example, an organization that wants to launch a new global initiative will outline the vision, mission, goals, services, and expected value generated. However, it will rarely reflect on the real purpose, how to accomplish it, how to integrate the values in all decisions and actions, and what is the intended sustainable impact of the new initiative.

Thus, Self-Reflection can be applied in a form of a mental accountability matrix. If you're implementing a new policy you have to evaluate (1) if it reflects your core values, (2) if and how it accomplishes your goals, intentions, and values, and (3) how it affects each one of the stakeholders in your constituency. Obviously, Self-Reflection begins with asking rather deep questions about personal values. For example:

» Do we live all our values in terms of interactions with all stakeholders?

» Are our values lived with regard to the products and services that we offer?

» Are our values lived with regard to how we treat our employees?

» Are all our values lived with the arrangements that we have with our partners?

» Are our values lived with regard to our investors?

» Are our values consistent with our community and the impact that our products and services have on our community?

Let's take a look at Uber. The business disruption pioneer exemplifies a disconnect between its innovative digital organization and its traditional leadership style. First case is the former CEO Kalanick's choice to allow Uber drivers to cross the picket line of the New York City taxi services boycott to protest the U.S. travel ban. Second case is his humiliating critique of 103 Uber drivers being accused of sexual harassment of passengers. Both cases are seemingly at odds with the values of their target market. It is not the first time that Uber has come under fire under Kalanick's leadership. Many customers were willing to turn to Uber's competitors because they publicly support different core values. Kalanick has responded to the criticisms by saying that he realized the significance of the changing marketplace and admitted his need for "leadership training" to improve his organization. However, the buzz became so negative that the CEO was forced to resign.

Uber Board decided to prioritize a change in culture[114]. They hired Dara Khosrowshahi, former head of Expedia, with the task to create a diverse and inclusive workplace for everyone. He incorporated humility and integrity as new tools in approaching conflict. He employed transparency in a nationwide U.S. infomercial. When authorities in London decided to ban Uber, he promptly issued an open letter stressing that *"While Uber has revolutionized the way people move in cities around the world, it's equally true that we've got things wrong along the way.*" On behalf of everyone at Uber globally, he apologized for the mistakes they've made. He promised to be long-term partners with the cities they serve; and to run the business with "humility, integrity, and passion." Obviously, a dichotomy of values can cause ethical conflicts. The best way to resolve them is to Self-Reflect on the values and bring them into alignment. In this particular case, one of our TEST Values, Empathy, would be applicable.

The next step for the organization committed to transformation is to Self-Reflect by asking these challenging questions:

» How do you design a business model and strategic plan to reflect the intention for transformation and sustainable impact?

» How do you create the company culture that reflects your values in the intention for change?

» How do you provide the ongoing skills training necessary for the continuing education of employees?

» How do you involve employees and stakeholders in the design of the transformation plan and implementation?

» How do you maintain transformation and innovation in responding to the changes in your environment?

» How do you evaluate the plan?

The Catalyzer must thrive on Self-Reflection (inner) and continuous change (outer) to support the organization's culture and stimulate innovation. The Catalyzers are vital to integrate these required changes and strategies. The inability to change the "Leaders" mindset and the related organizational culture are the major obstacles to organizational transformation.

It is essential that Catalyzers in the global marketplace align their values with those of their diverse workforce and changing customer base consisting of Millennials and Generation Z. This calls for a mindset shift, and not simply a change in tactics. This alignment is a potential source of greater efficiency, productivity, and innovation. Self-Reflection will help them to think people/stakeholders first as they strive to generate sustainable impact for their organizations.

Integration

Integration is the second "process" necessary to develop a Catalytic Mindset. In order to realize breakthrough business models[115] and generate sustainable growth, Catalyzers must manage disruption and guide the integration of diverse networks. It is a process in which the organization synergizes purpose, values, and assets both within and outside of the organization. Integration begins by changing the organizational culture from a rigid system consisting of siloed staff, departments, budgets, fixed jobs, and strategies to a collaborative alignment of talent, resources, and innovation.

Based on our experience, there are several components that must be integrated within the business model. For each, we have prepared a list of questions that need to be addressed. Reflect upon each question, and benchmark the level of integration practiced by your organization by rating your organization 1-5 (with 5 the highest).

Values

» __ Are your organization's core values clearly defined?

» __ Are they consistently integrated into operations and across organizational boundaries?

Generations

» __ Are representatives of different generations (Millennials, Gen X and Z, Baby Boomers) "included" in all teams, leadership, strategic planning, and innovation?

» __ Are diverse generational concerns, insights, and abilities considered in development of transformative business models?

Functions

» __ Are department functions retained as distinct entities or broken down to facilitate diverse perspectives and experiences?

» __ Are department functions sharing information, data, and insights or coveting them?

Media

» __ Are campaigns driven by product or media or values in the message?

» __ Are diverse media channels converged with consistent messaging across all outlets?

Impact

» __ Is performance evaluated solely by economic dimensions (profit) or inclusive of social impacts?

» __ Is a Quadruple Bottom Line framework (people, planet, profit, and prosperity) applied to determine sustainable outcomes for all stakeholders?

Ecosystems

» __ Does your digital ecosystem enable customers, employees, suppliers, and networks to share and scale resources to pursue challenging objectives and common interests?

» __ Do you provide platforms for accessing shared assets (e.g., software, data, and computer resources)?

How well did you do? If your total was 36 or more, your rating is better than average. The described culture shift necessitates a change in the business structure. Departmental silos must become more open as executives work collaboratively with their employees rather than isolating themselves. Once the internal organizational culture is transformed, the executive team must implement their mindset externally with new customer experience strategies. Organizations must place a high value on listening to what their consumers want as a part of their experience, and not simply regurgitate old models.

Swedish company IKEA is an exemplary case[116] of integration on all levels, from determining company values to taking care of the ecosystem. IKEA's values are based on the belief that every individual has something valuable to offer. Its culture is based on a 'spirit of togetherness, enthusiasm, and fun.' One of the ways IKEA finds out about the needs of its customers is by undertaking home visits. Every year, thousands of homes globally are visited to gain feedback and ideas on what sort of products the customers are looking for. These ideas are then used as the starting point of the design process. Home visits are not only important for developing IKEA products. They also help create solutions that are relevant on a local level. The managers in IKEA believe that by working together, all employees have the power to solve seemingly "unsolvable problems." Therefore, from the early stages of the design phase, IKEA product developers and designers work with a diverse team of technicians, manufacturers, and specialists. This partnership helps to keep product prices low and to find the latest techniques to create products the 'IKEA way.'

IKEA's mission focuses on sustainable long-term growth by investing in the future, which benefits its employees, customers, and suppliers. It invests most of its profits back into the business—existing and new stores, lowering customer prices, product development, and sustainable solutions. IKEA's mission is based on a belief that furniture should not be a luxury good but affordable for most.

Finally, in transitioning to the Catalytic Mindset, leaders will need to transform and develop a combination of several critical skills. All these skills help Catalyzers to integrate values, embrace contradictions and divergent beliefs, empathize with arguments, and retain objectivity while searching for Strategic Harmony.

By checking the boxes that apply, you can self-evaluate your abilities and become aware of the gaps:

- ☐ Humanistic—you have a strong concern for human welfare, values, and dignity characterized by compassionate, sympathetic, and generous behavior, and the ability to see the universe and its inhabitants connected and related to each other.

- ☐ Futuristic—you are able to inspire with visions of the future; ready to explore beliefs, concepts, and courses of action beyond present reality and context.

- ☐ Intuitive—you are able to understand or operate without explicit instructions; capable of grasping higher-order concepts and ideas.

- ☐ Divergent—you are able to generate creative ideas by exploring many solutions; capable of envisioning alternative directions and strategies with limited data in an ambiguous environment.

☐ Synthesizer—you are able to incorporate diverse inputs; capable of integrating and transforming information and data from different contexts into a new model or approach.

☐ Accelerator—you are able to catalyze processes and accelerate change; capable of processing data and information at hyper speeds.

In this Guidepost, we have discussed four lenses of the Catalytic Mindset that operate interdependently. As pointed out throughout the book, changes in World 4.0 are not isolated to one sector. It is the synergistic combination of internal and external factors that drive exponential disruptions to the marketplace and stimulate life-changing innovations. Both Catalyzers and their organizations must harmonize with these interconnected factors to anticipate the ever-shifting changes. The linkage between these factors provides the foundation for an organization to adopt Systemic Decision-Making. This approach to strategic planning allows leaders to more effectively control task prioritization to overcome obstacles and achieve optimum results more efficiently.

Data Alignment in companies, organizations, and society rarely happens by itself. It requires a Catalyzer to bring forth the data necessary to drive positive change, inspiring others to choose the paths less travelled by. Strategic Harmony heavily depends on a critical mass of Catalyzers to reinvent our broken world.

As you reflect on the Guidepost and the many questions, we have one final question: *How many boxes did you check and how much work do you have left?*

Guidepost 10

Strategic Transformation

"The only way you survive is you continuously transform into something else. It's this idea of continuous transformation that makes you an innovation company."

Ginni Rometty, former CEO IBM

For more than a decade, our institutions have faced unprecedented changes ranging from exponential digital technologies, immigration, COVID-19 pandemic, to climate change. How do we respond, adjust, and transform?

Let's look at our challenges through a short story by Franz Kafka[117]. A man named Gregor wakes up one morning only to find he's been transformed into a giant insect. Laying on his hard, armor-plated back, he is astonished to see his domelike brown belly divided into stiff arched segments, and numerous legs, pitifully thin compared to the rest of his bulk, waving helplessly from the bed. Even though confused by the drastic new circumstances in his life, Gregor must get up, get dressed, talk to his parents and even meet his boss who comes knocking on his door on the way to the office. After experiencing this impossible change, the life of Gregor is supposed to proceed quite normally.

To go on is necessary, but is it possible?

Who's Knocking?

Every morning we wake up to 10+ notifications sharing the next disruptive technology, health issues, political events, shocking climate trends, volatile money markets, devastating hunger, and radical new business models. They are knocking on our doors with posts and videos introducing trends and tools on innovation, leadership, healthy living, technology, and transformation. "Unprecedented" has become the New Normal.

With all these overwhelming changes, is it even possible to proceed normally?

If it is possible, what is the New Harmony?

Futurists say the world has changed forever; what is the basis of this change?

How do we determine what is normal? Have all our stakeholders' needs and expectations changed? What factors determine how your company or organization interfaces with the changing business ecosystem?

Obviously, most leaders have not fully decided on how to respond and leverage disruption. Our professional lives require an approach to process and manage these exponential changes. Strategic Transformation provides a values-based roadmap to design sustainable initiatives integral to transforming organizations and fixing our broken world.

A peek into the world of business transformation gives some vital insights. The best lessons can be learned from unsuccessful outcomes of digital transformation efforts, as explained in previous Guideposts. In the last five years, the strategic imperative for digital transformation increased in the global business community from 50% to 90%. Still, the surprising transformation projects' failure rate[118] of 84% is directly related to management's approach to strategic planning and change focusing on technology, not mindset changes.

Intuitively, executives realize that a mindset change is necessary for successful digital transformation, but it's "hard" and complex, as it confronts old assumptions and confirmation bias and requires an internal commitment to change by each individual and the organization as a whole. Most executives indicate[119] that culture and organizational changes are the hardest (74%), while only 26% consider technology changes to be the most challenging. But when it comes to investment, many executives are ready to invest in digital (technology), and only a few in organizational transformation.

The source of most digital transformation failures lies with traditional management. This is the overarching mental construct of hierarchical, profit-centered approaches that have been nurtured in executives since childhood and reinforced in business schools. It's no surprise that "leaders" respond to disruption from this foundation.

Our business marketplace has dramatically changed from industrial to consumer-driven, and then to information-orientated. The command-and-control economy is evolving toward a shared economy. Hierarchical management structures are dismantled resulting in flexible units and open communication channels. Transformative Power in the marketplace shifts from seller to buyer as consumers and other stakeholders are demanding real choices and a "voice'" for change is growing. A mindset of incremental improvements to the status quo will not address the expectations and speed required to address the Post-COVID-19 world.

Furthermore, the demographics are quickly shifting. Generation Z at 26% of the population is now the largest consumer segment, globally connected, sharing the same widespread digital culture. According to World Economic Forum predictions[120], 65% of today's children will end up in careers that do not even exist yet. They demand an exponential response!

Faced with drastically changed marketplaces, most executives try to hold on to the model of traditional management to drive incremental change. But those from the hierarchical corporate setting rarely succeed. Traditional leaders and organizations are no longer trusted.

Analyzing the last 18 years of transition, the Edelman Trust Barometer[121] offered a shattering snapshot of the deterioration of trust among our leaders and institutions.

Here are the titles of their annual reports:

- » 2002 – Fall of the Celebrity CEO
- » 2007 – Business More Trusted Than Government and Media
- » 2010 – Trust is Now an Essential Line of Business
- » 2013 – Crisis of Leadership
- » 2016 – Growing Inequality of Trust
- » 2017 – Trust in Crisis
- » 2018 – The Battle for Truth
- » 2019 – Trust at Work
- » 2020 – Trust and the COVID-19 Pandemic

What do these titles tell us? They demonstrate that leaders have lost touch with their constituencies, undermining the very foundation of leadership. There is constantly diminishing trust among all stakeholders: targets, employees, partners, investors, and community. During this global leadership crisis, executive teams across all institutions must rebuild this trust and navigate through the maze of digital transformation.

In the Global CEO survey, PWC reported that 55% of CEOs think that a lack of trust is a threat to their organization's growth. Few organizations have focused on increasing trust, as they were unclear as to an effective strategy. Trust has escalated from a soft corporate issue to a critical component of business strategy, as Michael Lyman, Senior Managing Director, Accenture Strategy, North American suggests *"U.S. companies must adopt a top-down culture that fully bakes trust into the company's strategy, operations, and broader DNA. Those who don't are putting their future revenues at risk."*

Most executives, leaders, and entrepreneurs face these burning questions:

» Do they have the courage to face change?

» What happens when an organization realizes that the world has changed so that their old business model will not function in the current disruptive environment?

To address these questions, management must fundamentally re-shape how they think, recalibrate, and execute change strategies. Initially, they must acknowledge that transformation is a continuous state in World 4.0. "Leaders" must redefine who they are as "management" in the new environment. In order to accomplish this tall order, they must challenge where they are and where they are going. Executives must turn to transformation strategists and coaches to guide their transition from OldCo to NewCo. Their team must strive to transform all operations integrating sustainability as a critical filter in all decision-making.

Here is a brief journey of the transition from traditional management to values-based, impact-driven Strategic Transformation.

Shift to New Story of Business

During the past 40 years, there have been major changes in the practices and expectations of business and the expectations of a Capitalistic economic system. The broken world has challenged the basic tenets of Capitalism, the sole shareholder focus now being questioned in progressive boardrooms around the world. CEO of Salesforce, Marc Benioff, called for an 'inclusive capitalism' *"that serves the causes of human equality and diversity and cherishes the ecology of the planet, alongside driving returns to shareholders."* This strategic approach of taking a longer-term view than quarterly shareholder reports reaps rewards. McKinsey found that such progressive companies outperform their peers, with 47% higher average revenue growth and 36% better earnings growth.

Ed Freeman[122] expanded the approach to stakeholder centricity, suggesting there is a shift to a more Responsible Capitalism from the Old Story of Business. The latter was built on hierarchy, power, and control, while the New Story of Business requires collaboration among key stakeholders. But the story is much deeper (see Figure 10.1).

The traditional company (OldCo) was based solely on profits and maximizing shareholder value; its leadership was motivated by Old Power (self-interest and greed); business ethics was a contradiction. The new company (NewCo) is based on abundance instead of scarcity (and its manifestations like fear and rigid control of resources). It is fueled by Transformative Power (human interest, generosity) to drive decisions; stakeholder interests are interdependent and outcomes mutually beneficial; tradeoff thinking is unacceptable; circular thinking is demanded; and sustainable strategies require collaborative, innovative solutions. While the OldCo cherished Win-Lose thinking, the NewCo is dedicated to the harmonic search for Win-Win solutions.

OldCo	NewCo
Old Power (currency)	Transformative Power (current)
Old Love (me, personal)	Transformative Love (purpose, humanity)
Scarcity (Fear, not enough)	Abundance (secure, enough)
Hierarchy and control	Collaboration with all stakeholders
Win-Lose	Win-Win

Figure 10.1 Shift from OldCo to NewCo (Based on Ed Freeman)

The following story highlights the shift in mindset and the increase in necessity. A large chemical company decided to commit to being more sustainable and cleaner. The CEO announced a 'massive' and lofty sustainability goal and proceeded to tell the divisions and plant sites that he was very serious about this. The engineers came up to him and said: "Sorry but we can't do it. This process is too dirty, this equipment is too old, and we can't meet the target." The CEO said that the environment was a serious issue, and he was willing to make it a winner. So, he told the engineers to prepare to close the plant. A few weeks later the engineers came back and said that a miracle had occurred. They figured out how to do it. When the CEO asked what it would cost, the engineers were embarrassed to say that the new method would actually save money.

This story demonstrates that a company guided by clear purpose and recognizing a "threat to one's survival/self-interest" can resolve a conflict among stakeholders. By challenging assumptions (quantum thinking) and re-imagining the conflict, they created more value.

Shift to Enlightened Management

The idea that business must transform and shift to be values-based is not a new concept. In the past, transformation was a choice if it was in concert with the organization's purpose. But today, it is a necessity for survival of current business and growth of entrepreneurial ventures. Let's look at the work of Abraham Maslow, designer of the Hierarchy of Needs, as a foundation for Strategic Transformation. Let's see how it applies to our Catalytic Mindset.

In 1998, Maslow challenged contemporary business leaders with a notion of Enlightenment[123]. *"The old-style management is steadily becoming obsolete. The more psychologically healthy people get, the more will enlightened management be necessary in order to survive in competition, and the more handicapped will be any enterprise with an authoritarian policy."*

Maslow's" Enlightened Management" is realized when a company, its leaders, employees, and consumers all converge in their interests. It is based on the following assumptions that resonate with demands of the broken world that needs to be fixed. Please check the boxes of the statements that really reflect your current organizational culture.

- ☐ Everyone is trusted.
- ☐ Everyone is informed as completely as possible.
- ☐ Team strives to achieve quality, workmanship, and efficiency.
- ☐ No authoritarian leadership or subordination hierarchy governance is accepted.
- ☐ Team shares ultimate managerial objectives across functions and operations.
- ☐ Goodwill rather than rivalry or jealousy reigns.
- ☐ Management is objective about other's capacities and skills and one's own.
- ☐ Team strives toward self-actualization – innovate and experiment, learn from mistakes.

☐ Team strives for group harmony, enjoys good teamwork, collaboration, and love.

☐ Everyone prefers to be a prime mover than a passive helper.

☐ Business and community are tightly aligned, almost impossible to separate.

☐ Vision and values are balanced with measuring profit, shareholder value.

Reflecting on these guidelines, how many boxes did you check? How does your organization rate as being "enlightened?" What shifts do you need to consider?

Shift to Radicalization of Management

During the last decade, the shift in management thinking has gained steam, but most practitioners did not heed the warnings. The visionaries shared a road map, but the leaders did not divert from their comfort zone.

We share these insights not to overload you with management theory, but to point out that the necessity for change in the rules of business is crystal clear, but many business leaders defaulted to their old assumptions. In World 4.0, rewriting the rules for transformation is a necessity for survival!

Steve Denning[124], a visionary management thought leader, states that the golden age of management will surface, undergoing a paradigm shift based on new sets of values. Don Tapscott, a strategist and author of *Macrowikinomics: New Solutions for a Connected Planet*[125], concurs: "*This is a time of fundamental change. If you look around the world today, you see a whole set of institutions that are stalled or in a state of atrophy or even failing. This is in contrast to the contours of a set of sparkling new initiatives that show how these institutions create value very differently around new communications media and a new set of principles.*"

Tapscott supports the concept of "Strategic Harmony" in addressing the broken and failing institutions. In contrast to proposing "new principles," he focuses on collaborative innovation to transform the economy and social institutions. For him it's a challenge to lead the transformation in our households, communities, and workplaces. Innovation and collaboration must fuel transformation!

Denning came to the same conclusion after researching various management books. He distilled 10 shifts in management thinking, which he termed Radical Management[126]. Its aim is to be "financially and spiritually profitable."

We suggest generating Transformative Love: operationalizing customer delight and employee happiness. It aspires to uplift the human spirit by driving Transformative Power, unleashing creativity in every human being, while also achieving more disciplined execution than traditional management. It is as passionately romantic as it is relentlessly operational, specific, and practical.

He contrasts Traditional and Radical Management for each of the 10 shifts:

SHIFTS	TRADITIONAL MANAGEMENT	RADICAL MANAGEMENT
Objective	Maximizing shareholder	Profitable customer delight
Strategy	Sustainable competitive advantage	Continuous strategic adaption
Value generation	Preoccupation with efficiency	Creating value with stakeholders
Networks	Uni-directional value chains	Multi-directional value networks
Task allocation	Steep heirarchies	Shared responsibilities
Innovation	Control and bureaucracy	Disciplined innovation
Values	Economic value	Values that grow firm
Communication	Command	Conversation
Focus	Managing the machine	Stewardship of stakeholders
Transformation	Episodic improvements	Paradigm shift in management

Figure 10.2 Denning's Shift from Traditional to Radical Management

In his later work[127], Denning suggests that the search for the holy grail of "sustainable competitive advantage" is futile, and maximizing shareholder value is "the dumbest idea in the world!" It should be replaced by "profitable customer delight," a cornerstone of digital marketing.

We suggest that you use this table to Self-Reflect on your organization! Analyzing the ten shifts, you will be able to rate your organization's transition from Traditional to Radical Management.

Shift to Transformation

The transition and disruption in business is mirrored in politics. When Donald Trump won the 2016 U.S. presidential election, many pundits shifted from predicting his demise to exploring why their predictions failed. How did the best political analysts and pollsters with quality data miss the outcome so dramatically?

Pundits and experts will discuss their errors for years to come, but the political landscape just reflected what has been happening in the business world for many years. Politicians did not listen to or respond to the needs of the "citizen marketplace." The voters challenged political brands because they were disgusted with lack of "citizen services." Pollsters read the signs from their "old political mindset." This underestimated need for citizens to participate can also backfire if citizens end up not being heard, resulting in feeling betrayed or even worse, being made to feel they were merely manipulated.

As noted by Allen Murray[128], the same condition is relevant to the commercial marketplace. Firms practicing traditional management missed game-changing transformations in industry after industry, e.g., computers (mainframes to PCs), telephony (landline to mobile), stock markets (floor to online). Their failure was not because of 'bad' management, but because they followed the dictates of what they considered 'good' management.

Disruption is unpredictable, inescapable, and constantly knocking at our door! We must adopt, embrace, and leverage it, and not try to "defend" against it. Whether we're looking at election surprises, climate change, Airbnb, Thumbtack, or pop-up restaurants (linking star chefs to foodies), we see that there is no one-size fits-all transformation. These breakthrough enterprises move beyond the traditional product and service-centered business model to leverage the exponential opportunities of a collaborative network driven model.

How does this disruption create opportunities for innovation, growth, social impact, new products and services, and rapidly changing communications? When we hear disruption knocking, we must be resilient, ready to move mentally and migrate our organization through the process of Strategic Transformation.

Strategic Transformation

Let's discuss the four modules of Strategic Transformation.

Figure 10.3 Strategic Transformation

The "leadership" must start with the intention for Organizational Change, incorporating values and a culture of rapid innovation, experimentation, and risk-taking. We must create a vision of the idealized organization and articulate how team members can share thinking and collaborate productively as a core competency to support the organizational structure. The clarity of an open organizational culture generates Power to attract talent and reset the organization for change. As innovation and productivity decline, and workers are more disengaged, we advocate a laser focus on constant innovation through experiments, playfulness, and creativity. Adobe has created a great internal culture for change. They offer huge company perks, such as onsite yoga and cafes, paid family vacations and health care. Their Kickbox program gives any staff member who requests it, a red cardboard box filled with stationary, snacks, and a $1,000 pre-paid credit card to explore their idea, no questions asked! We need to reinvent our organizational environments in World 4.0 as "playful corporations" encouraging improvisation and imagination as playful strategies to spur new possibilities in uncertain environments. We must engage in disruptive play.

Purposeful Design inspires teams to integrate the organization's purpose and values across all operations to generate innovative business models. The design process incorporates both Quantum Thinking and Circular Thinking to radically challenge assumptions, deconstruct the fixed mindset, and supplant it with a holistic interconnected approach to design. If your team is empathetic and obsessively listening to its stakeholders and diverse touch points, you are hearing the needs and integrating the feedback into your business model. Finally, you collect and interpret insights to design transformative business models.

Tesla reveals the practice of Purposeful Design. Why does Tesla exist? Why are they making electric cars? Why does it matter? The answer is quite simple. In mid-2016, under Elon Musk's leadership, the company changed the corporate mission to *"accelerate the world's transition to sustainable energy."* This Purpose drives every design decision. It can expand or contract depending on desired outcome. For Tesla, everything from how to install charging stations worldwide to the interface design of the digital dashboard is guided by their purpose. The final design aggregates all these purpose-driven tasks, as Tesla engages in accelerating the global transition to sustainable energy.

Digital transformation is aimed at developing an integrated strategy that is focused on leveraging digital connectivity, incorporating data to augment 'values-driven' decision-making, collaborating among inter-generational teams, and driving a superior stakeholder experience and brand loyalty. Digital transformation translates values and mindset consistently into a transformation of the organization's structures, operations, and strategies.

» Connective Thinking is the lens that transforms products/services into networks and platforms. Networks scale the personalization and distribution of messages and physical products, while technological innovations transform the business ecosystem. Aligned, they drive organizational change.

» Digital transformation reinforces and scales the changes initiated. The Think Intelligence lens guides teams to transform information and actions to user-friendly analytics. These analytics drive decision-making and help anticipate the future. It allows organizations to rethink their bottom line and redefine how they measure their impact on all the stakeholders, instead of just the investors.

Social Impact Analysis requires organizations to replace the traditional Key Performance Indicators (profit, revenue) with Sustainable Impact Indicators (SII) considering interests of all stakeholders. The goal of each organization is to focus Quadruple Bottom Line or the balance of 4Ps: People (customer, citizen, employee), Planet (environment), Profit (value generated), and Prosperity (community).

For the most part, organizations (for-profit, nonprofit, or government) do not have the intention to create sustainable change, social impact or a Win-Win situation. Most often, they focus only on short-term goals of event turnout, brand awareness, or profit. So the journey to change begins with re-discovering their Purpose and aligning their intention and values. They must be crystal clear to inspire stakeholder loyalty, fuel sustainable impact, and catalyze change. All stakeholders must be united by loving their purpose so that it becomes like a Love Affair between two people or an employee and their job. Passionate teams in love with the purpose and values generate Transformative Power, a key ingredient in building and scaling exponential impact.

Let's take a look at applications of the Strategic Transformation model.

In the U.S., the diverse response to the COVID-19 pandemic reflected the difference between a political self-interest, inconsistent policy vs a holistic Strategic Transformation strategy. In 2020, Business Insider Intelligence reported executives' response to the impact of COVID-19 on their companies and the economy. Considering supply chain issues and limited travel, 78% thought it would likely trigger a recession. These "traditional leaders" did not look holistically at the effects of COVID-19 on the mindset of all the stakeholders and the effect on their consumption patterns.

In contrast, Deloitte's recent global survey[129] of leaders provided practical insights for leadership teams to take appropriate action to the COVID-19 crisis. They suggested five qualities of resilient leaders or Catalyzers that support the Strategic Transformation model, providing a comprehensive response:

1. *Design from the heart ... and the head.* In disruptive situations and crisis, Catalyzers must integrate soft skills (TEST Values) of Trust and Empathy with stakeholders with the rationality of Sustainability and Transparency. *"Leaders must simultaneously take a hard, rational line to protect financial performance from the invariable softness that accompanies such disruptions."*

2.   *Put the mission first.* Catalyzers are laser-focused on Purpose to anchor and direct their organizations to address the crisis while leveraging opportunities.

3.   *Aim for speed over elegance.* Catalyzers use available though imperfect data to take decisive action. They are ready to quickly adjust their actions based on feedback.

4.   *Own the narrative.* Catalyzers embrace the disruption and threats, being Transparent about current realities. They gain Trust by balancing challenges with the future that inspires their team and stakeholders to persevere.

5.   *Embrace the long view.* Catalyzers balance the short term with long-term impact. They build transformative business models that spark innovations that will define a sustainable future.

Many U.S. Governors (e.g., New York, Maryland, California, Michigan, and Washington) applied the above strategies to address the COVID-19 crises in their States; 70%+ of people polled believed they were doing a good job.

Many corporations globally have approached crisis and change from diverse perspectives Here are two corporations that strived to apply the Strategic Transformation model with success

First is 3M, a Fortune 100 company; its values converge with purpose-driven design and investments to fuel innovation. According to Inge Thulin[130], then President and CEO, *"diversity and inclusion, in addition to sustainability, are her personal values, and they are key to making 3M an even more competitive enterprise."* Its "Pollution Prevention *Pays*" program redesigns products to meet environmental standards or social needs, generating new business opportunities. Their company-wide commitment to sustainability laser focuses on product reformulation to proactively minimize waste and avoid pollution. 3M's Novec Fire suppression fluids are the first viable, sustainable alternative to hydrofluorocarbons. Their proprietary technology flips the approach to extinguishing fires. They remove heat from the fire—safely, cleanly, and without harming the environment! That means no water damage to sensitive electronics or precious artifacts, no long-term damage to the environment.

The 3M Quadruple Bottom Line approach translated into sustainable outcomes. In 2017 under CEO Thulin, 3M revenue grew by 5%, and it posted an impressive total return to shareholders of 34% including dividends.

With regard to its response to the needs of the global pandemic, 3M has been consistent in its approach. CEO Mike Roman said in January 2020 that 3M answered the global demand by ramping up production of N95 masks and doubled its global output to 1.1 billion per year, including 35 million a month in the United States. It has already made additional investments to enable it to double its capacity again to 2 billion globally within 12 months, and will certainly be prepared if there is another pandemic.

A second example is Nike focusing on the Purpose to unite the world through sport – to create a healthy planet, active communities, and an equal playing field for all. Seventy-five percent of its products (shoes and apparel) contain recycled material. For 30 years, the company is committed to *"holistic sustainability"* or striving to live the values of sustainability and transparency through the entire supply chain. This effort was a response to activists' feedback regarding the negative impacts to contract workers and the environment in the developing world. Nike collaborated with MIT, sparking more holistic efforts that go "beyond just monitoring impact," including factory redesign and managerial training, improvement of product design processes that affect manufacturing, and strengthening of labor and government institutions in developing countries. Their commitment to sustainability resulted in innovation processes that created the $1 billion-plus Flyknit line, which uses a specialized yarn system, requiring minimal labor and generating large profit margins. It reduces waste by 80% compared with regular cut and sew footwear. Since its launch in 2012, Flyknit has reduced 3.5 million pounds of waste and fully transitioned from yarn to recycled polyester, diverting 182 million bottles from landfills.

Recently, its innovation team created Flyleather, a material that looks, feels, and smells like natural leather. It is made by binding at least 50% reclaimed leather fibers together in an innovative, environmentally sustainable water-powered process. It reclaims leather otherwise lost in the manufacturing process to create a material that is 40% lighter and 5x more abrasion-resistant than full grain leather, while reducing water used in production.

In 2017, Nike's sustainable practices grew its position as the world's largest supplier of athletic apparel while generating increases of 6% in revenue with 12.8% in profits. The Quadruple Bottom Line approach is becoming acknowledged as it generates sustainable products and profitable outcomes!

In 2020, Nike's leaders, foundation, and the company continued their intention to give back to its local communities committing more than $17.5 million to COVID-19 response efforts worldwide. Nike's innovation, manufacturing, and product teams came together to provide for an urgent need: Personal Protective Equipment (PPE) in the form of full-face shields and powered, air-purifying respirator (PAPR) lenses to protect against the coronavirus.

Process

Strategic Transformation is associated with five challenges: (1) develop organizational resilience; (2) replace "Leaders" with Catalyzers; (3) bridge the gap between values and action; (4) address needs of all stakeholders; and (5) focus not only on profit, but also on sustainable outcomes.

Today, the major organizational challenge is resilience, or the ability to be prepared for unforeseen change. Most organizations have a "fixed mindset" and they resist the challenge to adapt. Research proves that the majority of employees feel their companies are not prepared to deal with the present challenges. They don't have the skillsets or the talent to execute a transformation strategy; 60% of business leaders[131] are not aware of the possibilities associated with using NextGen technology. This poses massive opportunities for the few firms that pride themselves on their ability to create and "own" digital disruption, but it threatens thousands of jobs in companies not ready to transform.

The key to managing disruption is harnessing the organization's capacity to remake its business in the sustainability-digital era. As suggested by Gary Hamel[132], a new organization is emerging, capable of achieving both continuous innovation and transformation along with disciplined execution, while also delighting those for whom the work is done and inspiring those doing the work. These organizations have moved the production frontier to what is possible. The first step is developing organization-wide capabilities to transform.

Resilience requires leadership! The second great transitional challenge is to replace traditional Leaders with Catalyzers. Catalyzers are resilient leaders who guide organizations to anticipate, respond quickly, decisively, and adapt to change and sudden disruptions in order to survive and sustain. As we pointed out, there are old-fashioned leaders and there are Catalyzers. The former manage the existing system in a traditional (bureaucratic) way; the latter innovate and catalyze change. To better understand the shift from traditional leading to catalyzing, let's take a look at the following story.

Once upon a time there lived a peasant in China. He had a son who worked on the farm with the help of a horse. One day the horse ran away, and the local farmers said, "Bad luck." The peasant frowned and replied, "Perhaps." Next morning, the horse came back, followed by a whole herd. When the local farmers saw them, they said, "Great luck." Again, the peasant replied, "Perhaps." After a couple of days, the peasant's son broke his leg while riding one of the new horses. The local farmers again commented, "Bad luck," and the peasant repeated, "Perhaps." The next week, a war broke out and the emperor's army did not conscript the peasant's son because of his broken leg. The local farmers said, "Great luck," but the peasant just whispered, "Perhaps."

The story actually talks about the union and harmony of opposites. As they bounce around, and cycle back and forth, a state of imbalance leads to harmony, and then the state of harmony soon gives way to imbalance. We will always need bureaucrats, but the real change will only come from Catalyzers.

The third challenge is to bridge the gap between values and action. Traditional management is about following the "road taken;" Strategic Transformation is responding consistently to changing directions. Traditional management is about financial results, while Strategic Transformation is about sustainable impact for all stakeholders. Hence, Strategic Harmony is the capability to influence that Gap or bridge the discrepancy between what the organization promises and what they deliver. Authentic behavior fuels Trust.

The fourth challenge is actively listening and responding to the needs of all stakeholders. NextGen consumers are digital natives, more socially responsible, expecting purposeful communications, and a rich, engaging, genuine customer experience. They see the world as interconnected, not as separate silos of self-interest. Their reality is transparent. NextGen must be engaged through 'their lenses," living values of purposeful organizations. These behaviors will gain their Trust as consumers or voters and loyalty as employees.

Finally, the last challenge is to replace the traditional business goal of maximizing profits for the shareholders with optimizing sustainable outcomes for all stakeholders. We call it Purposeful Strategic Transformation. Using words of Paul Polman[133], former CEO of Unilever, "*We need a new economic model, a different business model. Not one based on being "less bad" or on occasional acts of benevolence, but one where business has a positive impact on society in all it does.*"

For the same reason, Maslow wraps up his discussion on new management with a teaching from Pope John Paul II [134]: "...*The purpose of a business firm is not simply to make a profit, but to be found in its very existence as a community of persons who in various ways are endeavoring to satisfy their basic needs, and who form a particular group at the service of the whole of society. Profit is a regulator of the life of a business, but other human and moral factors must also be considered which, in the long term, are at least equally important for the life of a business.*"

The path to Strategic Transformation is a clarion call to leaders and managers to anticipate and navigate the forces of disruption, positioning their organization for the inevitable changes and piloting their business on the path to sustainable outcomes. Its framework is two dimensional, values-based and impact-driven. Built upon the four lenses of the Catalytic Mindset, the approach integrates Purpose into all operations and transforms each management function, aligning them with the goals of a Quadruple Bottom Line and the requirements of the changing world. Integration is essential to realize social impacts.

Transformation Calls for Proactivity

Let's quit the business jargon and wrap this Guidepost up with a variation of the ancient fable, "The Ant and Grasshopper Story."

There was once a grasshopper who loved life. He spent his time lazing in the sun, eating when he wanted to, sleeping when he wanted to, generally enjoying himself all the time. He lived like he did not have a care in the world.

One day as he was sun-bathing, he saw an ant pushing a bread crumb across the ground. The grasshopper asked, "Hey brother! What are you doing?" The ant replied, "I am gathering food for the winter while the weather is still warm. Once winter sets in, I am going to stay home and just eat from my stock of food." The grasshopper made fun of the ant's dull life and went on sun bathing saying, "There's enough time for such boring work. You should take time to have fun like me." Soon the summer passed and the winter started to set in.

As the weather became colder, it became harder for the grasshopper to get out. However, he soon started to feel hungry. He decided to brave the weather and find himself some food.

When he stepped out, everything was covered with snow and he could not find anything to eat. He continued to search for food everyday. He did not find anything. Finally, he grew weak and died of hunger.

What are lessons of the story? The ant is proactive, strategic and goal directed. The grasshopper is passive, judgmental, and short-sighted.

They have different mindsets and their behavior differs accordingly. The ant is team player, investing time and effort with other ants to sustain themselves. The grasshopper is a loner, care free, and having fun in the moment. When the seasons changed and faced with hunger, the grasshopper was forced to transform into a survival mindset searching everywhere for food. By not responding to the signs and anticipating the future, he finally turned into a loser.

The Strategic Transformation roadmap begins with the shift in thinking from passive to proactive, from a transactional to a catalytic mode. The key is the change in focus from maintaining the status quo to managing and sustaining transformation across the organization. As Vivian Greene suggests[135], *"Life isn't about waiting for the storm to pass. It's about learning to dance in the rain."*

Any transition means that you start in one place and expect to end up in another. It is important to stay focused on the progress. The Guidepost that follows will provide a Roadmap to Transformation.

PART IV

CATALYZE STAKEHOLDER IMPACT

Guidepost 11
Transformation Roadmap

"In many spheres of human endeavor, from science to business to education to economic policy, good decisions depend on good measurement."

Ben Bernanke

A soldier entered a monastery and asked a monk: "Is there really a heaven and a hell?" "Who are you?" asked the monk. "I am a warrior," the soldier replied. "Impossible!" exclaimed the monk. "Who would send you to war with your face of a thief?"

The soldier, red with anger, began to draw his sword, but the monk continued: "So you have a sword! It's rusty and blunt." As the soldier raised the sword to strike him, the monk remarked: "Here the gates of hell open!" At these words, the soldier sheathed his sword and bowed. "Here open the gates of heaven," said the monk.

The difference between the road to heaven and hell is a matter of perspective, but it's the transformative journey that really counts. And the destination depends on the values we live along the way.

Following the path of Strategic Transformation, it is important to be aware of the progress we are making. To track the progress, we have developed a system to benchmark each of the ten building blocks, presented in Figure 11.1. Each building block includes best practices and is benchmarked with a required *executive action*.

The Roadmap's best practices are:

1. Drive leaders to adapt not only what they do, but how they think.
2. Rivet TEST Values across all operations.
3. Adopt a Catalytic Mindset, not just a mindset driven by new technologies.
4. Transform communications and governance from Old Power to Transformative Power.
5. Demand co-creation with stakeholders to generate collaborative advantage.
6. Drive continuous innovation and change at every level of the organization.
7. Purposely design business models by radically challenging assumptions and methodologies.
8. Leverage "digital" to power a superior stakeholder experience and brand advocacy.
9. Incorporate Sustainable Impact Indicators in decision-making.
10. Maximize all stakeholders' value based on a Quadruple Bottom Line.

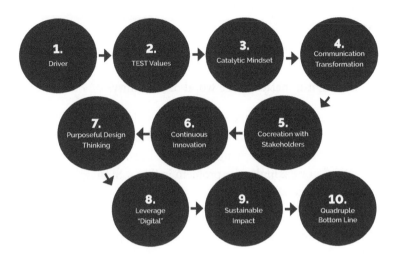

Figure 11.1 Strategic Transformation Roadmap

In previous Guideposts, we have introduced each of the ten human-centered practices. Each practice is transformative for the leader and organization. But when the practices are integrated as a holistic strategy, Strategic Transformation becomes a powerful solution to reinvent the organization. Our objective is to demonstrate how these practices synergize to contribute to Strategic Transformation and generate Strategic Harmony.

1. Driver

Practice #1 asks leaders to adapt not only what they do, but also how they think. The key to Strategic Transformation is the leader's transformation to a Catalyzer. They can be a member of a leadership team or distributed leadership (team of leaders). Is he or she empowering us to transform? They must act quickly and proactively based on trust, responsibility, and shared value. Their goal is to drive the direction of the venture. But what drives transformation?

Transformation can be initiated externally from the competitive marketplace, disruptive innovation, or the environment, or internally from the team or the Catalyzer. The initiator of the change is crucial, but more important is how the new inputs are addressed. The leadership team can approach the challenge with a reactive approach "want to solve it," or "how do we fix it." Alternatively, the team can approach it by asking "why did this occur?" Such a challenge is best addressed with the "Three Whys:"

1. Why might this (topic, challenge) matter to me?
2. Why might it matter to people around me (company, team, city, nation)?
3. Why might it matter to the world or humanity?

Another approach to better understand the challenges is the application of "Five Whys." It is a probing technique based on five iterations of "Why" used to determine the root cause underlying a problem. Each answer forms the basis for the next "Why." For example, the problem is that a Strategic Transformation strategy was not successful:

1. Why was Strategic Transformation a failure? (First Why)
2. Why Strategic Transformation Strategy was poorly communicated? (Second Why)
3. Why Strategic Transformation Strategy has been delayed? (Third Why)
4. Why Strategic Transformation Strategy has been understaffed? (Fourth Why)
5. Why top management support for Strategic Transformation was lacking? (Fifth Why, the root cause)

Still another method is "Question Behind the Question"[136], a series of open-ended questions used to find the real challenge. The questions focus on personal responsibility and action, beginning with why and how. How are you being asked to solve the problem? What is the causing concern on the management team? Here is an example. Your major competitor just launched a new digital service. The management team asks for a response.

1. What are your concerns about this new service?
2. How does it affect our business?
3. What do you think about those changes?
4. How does it affect our employees?
5. What are your plans for a similar service?
6. What new expertise is required to launch a new service?
7. What is the rationale behind your decisions?
8. What are your assumptions?
9. How does it affect your bottom line?
10. What is your next action?

Digital disruption addresses us daily; it's here to stay. Each organization's success depends on its leadership's willingness to self-reflect and nurture a culture that embraces and owns change at all levels. The key issue facing each executive is to determine the real Drivers of change.

Executive Action: As far as the Drivers phase is concerned, there is a needed executive action. Take the time to contemplate: Are you driving change or are you driven by it?

2. TEST Values

Practice #2 rivets on TEST Values (Trust, Empathy, Sustainability, and Transparency). Values that matter! They define a leader, a brand, a strategy, an action. Organizations are defined by how they use Power and Love, flexibility, openness to change, and ability to initiate transformation.

In this Guidepost, we will expand upon the definitions of TEST Values to view how these values *"live"* in a strategically transformed organization and serve as the baseline for all team actions.

Trust is, as already pointed out, the fulcrum, the first and necessary ingredient in personal, business and political relationships. According to Stephen Covey, "Trust is the glue of life." It defines a customer's relationship with a brand; a citizen's vote for a candidate; students' relations with a teacher; and employees' motivation to work. The balance between trust and mistrust[137] is based on four experiences: sense of injustice; lack of hope; lack of confidence; and desire for change. When that trust is breached, an organization, industry. or society as a whole suffers. Trust is built on integrity, engagement, and participation of people. Edelman Trust Barometer 2018[138] defines Trust as essential to rebuilding the shattered political, financial, media, and business institutions. The Accenture study defines Trust as a critical factor in a business strategy affecting each stakeholder.

Empathy is the ability to connect with and relate to others. It is considered the most critical value by executives in a University of California Annenberg School study[139]. It is an essential tool at every workplace in designing (internal and external) communications. As a powerful emotional skill, it allows us to understand what varied constituencies are experiencing and respond in a meaningful, caring way.

It challenges the concept of a traditional workplace which is competitive and cutthroat, and it enables leaders to experience success in the changing marketplace by listening "obsessively" to the buzz around them, in order to relate to the people they serve. Empathy is essential in refining and maximizing the stakeholder experience and developing consumer advocacy relationships. Also, it is currently integrated in the development of experiences in museums, hospitals, political campaigns, classrooms, workplaces, as well as consumer brands.

Most managers talk at each other, instead of making a concerted effort to listen and discover opportunities for compassion and collaboration. The catalyst for transformation must be open and supportive of two-way communication. Once people can step out of their "fixed mindsets" and experience vulnerability, they truly begin to feel what those around them are feeling. Empathy forces executives and politicians to go beyond their self-interest and biased perspectives to focus on others and develop better collaboration.

Sustainability used to be a choice, but now it is a necessity if an organization wants to succeed. In the past, sustainability denoted business decisions that protected and supported the environment. It has expanded to include socially responsible and ethical decisions that affect all stakeholders, internal and external to the organization through the Web of Life. Sustainability drives performance, thus impacting the Quadruple Bottom Line. In the last twenty years, *"high-sustainability"* companies dramatically outperformed the *"low-sustainability"* ones in terms of both stock market and accounting measures.[140]

Transparency is the driver for open and honest communications and real time information. GlobalScan[141] acknowledges the crucial importance of transparency in developing reputation, acquiring quality and sustainability performance. Howard Schultz, CEO of Starbucks, upped the bar in stating *"The currency of leadership is truth and transparency"*. It demands two-sided accountability. With the quick global spread of COVID-19 that we have experienced in 2020, the necessity of transparent and consistent messaging was critical to the safety and survival of millions of people.

With the pervasiveness of digital media, every communication is verifiable, so trust and confidence in brands, customer relationships, and environmental responsibility footprint are all built on transparency. As pointed out by the CEO from Siegel+Gale[142], *"Young people nowadays see through nonsense, so in this increasingly digital world, transparency will become more and more the norm for brands. Since modern society is driven by rampant individualism, there is a growing demand for unlimited transparency.*"

In principle, any values-driven management team reflects the TEST Values across all operations.

1. Managers are held accountable to incorporate trust, empathy, sustainability, and transparency in all decisions.
2. Design teams integrate values for the benefit of all stakeholders.
3. Values are used as a catalyst to reduce resistance to change.
4. Marketing weaves a values-based message into a strategy to drive authentic communications.
5. Leadership is committed to ethical and inclusive community culture.

Executive Action: As far as TEST Values phase is concerned, there is a needed executive action: Determine the agreement or Gap between consistency of living company values and organizational actions.

3. Catalytic Mindset

Practice #3 advocates the Catalytic Mindset, expanding transformation beyond being driven by new technologies. Values and purpose translate into organizational culture. As discussed in Guidepost 9, there are four lenses that challenge long-standing assumptions of the broken world. They transform a fixed mindset into one that builds a collaborative culture, propels a new business model, facilitates digital transformation, and generates sustainable impacts. These lenses are, as you probably still remember:

1. Think Quantum—challenges the leader to redefine risk and failure and expanded intended impact
2. Think Circular—redesigns stakeholders' value, delivering restorative and regenerative products and services
3. Think Connective—drives networks and next generation business models
4. Think Intelligence—expands data-based decision-making

Going back to our initial conundrum: why aren't more businesses reporting success with digital transformation efforts? The thorny challenge is that they view problems through the wrong lens. It is either organizational, technological, or data-driven. Instead, they need to adapt to a more unfamiliar mindset that starts with empathy for the user and combines those insights with what's technologically feasible and economically viable, as suggested by David Glenn[143], Director of KPMG Digital.

Each lens incorporates methodologies that expose the team to divergent and often challenging approaches. For example, quantum thinking involves evaluating multiple perspectives, then 'seeing' them through someone else's eyes. Such empathy gained from *"perspective-taking"* is a precursor to nuanced thinking, communicating effectively, and taking positive action in the real world. As the Catalyzer and culture evolves, the four lenses fuse together to form a holistic interconnected mindset.

Executive Action: As far as the Catalytic Mindset phase is concerned, there is a needed executive action: Adopt the four lenses and reflect on using them to drive action and impact by:

1. Redefining what outcomes are considered successful, driving sustainable impact.
2. Challenging and leveraging all disruption and transformation from a holistic perspective.
3. Connecting your team's systemic efforts by scaling networks.
4. Viewing opportunities through advancing approaches to collecting and analyzing data.

4. Communication Transformation

Practice #4 is dedicated to transforming communications and governance from Old Power to Transformative Power. The transformed organization is driven by passionate Catalyzers who open communications and drive participation based on Purpose. They foster a culture based on listening that builds trust and mutual respect among consumers and employees. Carol Potter[144], Edelman Group President and Chief Executive Officer in Europe, suggests *"People want brands to have an impact upon society, compensating for what they perceive as the lack of government effectiveness. In contrast, they believe that brands can make a difference for good....brands are held to account on what they stand for, and people will vote with their voices and their wallets. It truly does seem that brands are the new democracy."*

Furthermore, Catalyzers' authentic communication among employees facilitates transformation, including flattening organizational hierarchy, breaking down siloes, and collaboration among inter-generational teams.

Executive Action: The needed executive action is focused on open communication between functions and generations. To measure employee communications, we propose the following four questions:

1. Reach: How many employees are you reaching? Representing which functions and generations?
2. Engagement: How are employees (different segments) engaging with purpose-driven content?
3. Behavior: What are employees (different functions) doing differently related to the communication?
4. Purposeful Impact: What is the impact on performance, productivity, employee engagement, retention?

5. Co-creation with Stakeholders

Practice #5 asks an organization to co-create with all stakeholders in order to generate collaborative advantage by pooling of knowledge, ideas, and resources. Co-creation among the team, partners, and even competitors define a new age of collaboration. Organizations' future performance is dependent on their ability to find the right partners to thrive in a digitally disrupted world.

Organizations must prepare for a reset to implement stockholder-centric changes in business operations, communications, and decision-making.

Executive action: In this phase, the required executive action is leverage cooperation among all stakeholders. The measure of Organization Trust (Figure 11.2) is a precursor for collaboration, as it reflects how workers feel, think, and behave. An example is seen in the table below:

Mark the box for each of the following behaviors regarding how you feel, think, or intend to behave.	Scale: 1 = "Strongly Disagree" to 7 = "Strongly Agree"
I care about the people I work with.	1 2 3 4 5 6 7
I demonstrate respect and concern for everyone I interact with.	1 2 3 4 5 6 7
I possess the knowledge needed to succeed in my work.	1 2 3 4 5 6 7
I make everyone around me better.	1 2 3 4 5 6 7
I am a "go-to" person on our team.	1 2 3 4 5 6 7
I am an honest person.	1 2 3 4 5 6 7
I want the people I work with to win, not just myself.	1 2 3 4 5 6 7

Figure 11.2 Organizational Trust

6. Continuous Innovation

Practice #6 drives continuous innovation and change at every level of the organization. Continuous innovation is an imperative for transformation. An outdated solution is to integrate a traditional R&D unit into the organizational structure. It absorbs the assumptions and bias of the organization that inhibits transformation. In contrast, the rapid innovation engine is designed to accelerate and sustain innovation. It is outside the organization, with a separate budget reporting directly to the CEO or Board. It includes members from different functional areas and generations.

Executive Action: As far as Continuous Innovation is concerned, a required executive action is: Establish a rapid innovation engine and make the necessary adjustments to fit the company culture.

Work on the system, not things

For most companies, innovation is a shiny facade, a box to be ticked, or, at best, a way to attract and manage 'talent.' Their innovation labs are overflowing with young aspiring professionals, 'twenty-somethings' for whom participation is an opportunity to be seen and heard. Like Silicon

---

Valley, they want to 'move fast and break things' without understanding their company's 'past and present.'

But there are fatal flaws in this approach. First, the lack of cognitive diversity within the innovation labs, and second, the missing link between 'the old' and 'the new'—between the side of the business where the money is actually still made, and the isolated lab where a handful of hopefuls are trying to 'reinvent the future,' any future.

The number of innovation labs and accelerators is nevertheless growing although the value they create is minimal. It's mostly 'new things.' We used to call this 'product development' but the term 'innovation' has taken over and also therein lies a problem. By naming the creation of new things 'innovation,' we are missing something fundamental. First, that most value is created through improving the 'existing' and seldom by big breakthrough innovation. Second, that real innovation isn't something that can easily be designed on a canvas with a few colorful Post-it notes. It more or less happens, often for unexpected and undesigned reasons.

Take Apple's iPod, certainly a new 'thing,' and so was its business model. But the real 'innovation' was the change in people's behavior towards music—a change that reached far beyond the actual 'thing' and its business model.

Sure, you can design new 'things' and business models but you can't design behavioral change. Context is crucial. If companies were to better understand this broader, contextual view, they would shift their thinking from 'innovation' as a potential outcome to 'experimentation' as a way of working with a highly unpredictable outcome. They should move towards transforming 'the system'—how people work, learn, and create value together. Not just in isolated pockets, such as innovation labs, but right across the entire organization.

We must stop copying Silicon Valley and start working on the 'thing' that really matters: changing the system. It is hard work and it may take a lifetime but it will have a far bigger impact than any accidental innovation lab or accelerator can ever have.

Mark Storm, a catalyst for change and renewal

7. Purposeful Design Thinking

Practice #7 uses Purposeful Design Thinking as a tool to drive Purpose across NewCo business models. Design thinking, as a methodology, does not immediately consider an upfront solution; it examines both present and future conditions and parameters of the problem, exploring alternative solutions. As such, it serves to create purposeful business models.

For the past century, analytical thinking has helped solve the complicated problems that were predictable, linear, and well defined. In contrast, in the constantly changing world, the challenges are undefined and ambiguous. Design Thinking[145] surfaced with a people-centric approach—exploring customers and employees' pain points and interactions with the organization. The research focus has shifted from "how" to "why" in order to pinpoint the actual customer experience. Design Thinking helps to discover unarticulated user needs and align these to future business goals. It has been adopted by Fortune 100 and SMEs globally, and is spread almost as by a magic wand.

Purposeful Design Thinking lies at the center of transforming your business model while incorporating value, purpose, and sustainable impact to all stakeholders. It challenges traditional beliefs and assumptions about the "right way to do something"; it poses the uncomfortable questions; it uses Radical Empathy to fuel new sources of data and more refined insights; it encourages experimentation and risk-taking to disrupt the status quo and deliver new sources of value; and it fuses divergent platforms to realize innovative solutions.

Designing with a Greater Purpose

"Design is problem solving." This was the mantra that made me a designer. The idea that if you could identify problems—real problems for real people—design was how you solve them. It sounds good, and is true to a certain extent. But the reality of today's digital designer is that the problems we solve are not the problems our world needs solved... The problems that seven billion people need solved.

Human-centered design attracts people from a variety of backgrounds, united by a desire to impact the world around them through design. The reality of it is far more mundane. The day to day of this work is often fighting uphill battles within organizations, leaving ideas of changing

---

the world too far to touch. The problems of the world are left for another day.

Resources put behind large-scale human problems aren't enough to make a difference. It's not a failing of design, but a failing of every industry and sector that impacts society. If design is different than those other industries, shouldn't designers be able to rise above and dig into these problems?

There's no easy answer for how to employ designers to solve big problems. What designers can do—and are great at—is asking hard questions that shed light on known problems, unveiling their nuances and complexities. Our ability to combat hunger, poverty, violence, racism, or addiction, lies in finding a common purpose and plan to get there. But as long as our institutions cannot compete with high-growth technology companies for talent, how can we expect a sea-change? The onus falls on our institutions to invest in problem-solvers.

There must be a new world model where designers can be personally and professionally fulfilled in mission-driven organizations. Without it, the ideas of Strategic Harmony and purposeful design won't reach their potential.

Craig Phillips, User Experience Strategist, Senior Product Designer, Utmost

Application of design thinking provides business models that leverage connectivity and data, transforming the traditional product or service into the "network" as the core offering of the organization (e.g., Alibaba, Airbnb, Amazon). This requires the 'shifts' in thinking and operations discussed above.

Despite the many successes, there have been problems in design thinking causing many digital transformation efforts to fail. David Glenn, in reflecting on the failures, suggested that various parts of an organization are often not working together cohesively. It takes open collaboration to identify the cause of a problem and develop a successful solution. In response, Transformative Business bridges new technologies and emerging market needs by focusing on designing for the needs of all stakeholders:

1. Infusing purpose and values to ignite value (stakeholder experience)
2. Propelling collaborative advantage (stakeholder-centric culture)
3. Efficiently distributing and scaling value (supply chain structure)
4. Producing value (shareholder impact)

Executive Action: As far as this set of best practices is concerned, the required executive action is: Build a collaborative, purpose-driven team to anticipate and "own" disruption and develop Transformative Business Models.

8. Leveraging Digital Transformation

Practice #8 focuses on leveraging "digital" to power a superior stakeholder experience and brand advocacy. Digital transformation powers "digital" as a "connected," "information-rich," and "pervasive" resource. Digital serves as a catalyst to disrupt and, if properly leveraged, transform the organization; it requires integration across functions and generations to sustain innovation.

Digitizing an organization transforms the traditional marketing functions. For most companies the transformation is focused on adopting emerging technologies and not integrating digital across the entire operations. Digital transformation requires changes in leadership's mindset and business model including:

1. Integrate active listening with a Social Customer Relationship Management system
2. Design a purposeful brand

   - adopt a strategic purpose that creates Shared Value

   - engage customers through living shared values in their brand experiences

   - power brand from the "inside-out" through culture, capabilities, and engagement

3. Converge traditional and digital media
4. Refocus customer decision process from sales to post-purchase behavior
5. Mobilize advocacy through brand champions as integral to marketing strategy

The power of this Strategic Transformation process is the integration of human-centered practices. Aaron Hurst, author of *The Purpose Economy* noted, *"CEOs expect to see the demand for purpose in the consumer marketplace increase by nearly 300% by 2020. This demand means consumers putting less emphasis on cost, convenience, and function, and increasingly make decisions based on their need to increase meaning in their lives and buying products and services that fulfill that need."* According to Laurence Fink, CEO, BlackRock Investment Group ($4.6 trillion in assets), there is a necessity to integrate across functions because *"quarterly earnings don't articulate management's vision for the future. Investing in customer experience requires a view into the future."*

A good example of leveraging digital transformation to create a powerful experience is Richard Branson's global Virgin business empire in retail, music, and transport with interests in land, air, sea, and space travel. His business philosophy is simple: *"Treat customers as you would like to be treated (or even better) and solve problems in ways that exceed expectations."* His focus is on people: *"Business isn't about making money, it's about people. A business is about making connections. A business is about finding solutions. A business is about creating opportunities. A business is about making things happen. A business is about going the extra mile. A business is about love."* And technology is there to make sure that it all happens.

Executive Action: In this phase, the required executive action is: Use purposeful branding and connectivity to redefine and scale the stakeholder experience.

9. Sustainable Impact

Practice #9 incorporates Sustainable Impact Indicators (SIIs) in decision-making as emphasized by Peter Drucker: *"You can't manage what you can't measure."* SIIs match the organizational values, ensuring that your goals remain realistic to achieve a sustainable ROI. The modern digital platform generates information-rich data to redefine monitoring, measurement, and evaluation. The tasks on our Roadmap concerning this phase boil down to the following actions:

1. Refine marketing analytics to monitor, evaluate and adapt.
2. Integrate customer intelligence to target segments.
3. Mine and analyze data to personalize communications and offerings.

4. Redefine metrics from "performance" to 'impact" for all stake-holders (e.g., replace Key Performance Indicators (KPIs) with Sustainable Impact Indicators (SIIs)).
5. Incorporate SIIs in data-driven decision-making.

In PWC's Ninth Annual Global CEO Survey, CEOs said that success is more than just financial profit. To support this behavior, 86% changed their method of measuring success and held themselves accountable. Denise Morrison President and CEO of the Campbell Soup Company is exemplary: *"Our success metrics include "Are we living our purpose? We believe that doing so will make us a better company for all of our stakeholders… that you not only can make a profit, but you can make a difference."*

Executive Action: As far as sustainable impact is concerned, the suggested executive action is: Use digital assets to augment end-to-end customer experience evaluating with Sustainable Impact Indicators.

10. Quadruple Bottom Line

Practice #10 maximizes all shareholders' value and Quadruple Bottom Line (QBL). In 2018, Larry Fink[146] issued a Manifesto for a new model of corporate governance. His investment group requires that each company investment prepares a long-term growth strategy which reflects the following benchmarks: *"Society is demanding that companies, both public and private, serve a social purpose. To prosper over time, each and every company must not only deliver financial performance, but also show how it makes a positive contribution to society. Companies must benefit all of their stakeholders, including shareholders, employees, customers, and the communities in which they operate."*

Black Rock's position adds power and immediacy to the corporations transforming their purpose and impact. This policy was supported by 181 CEOs at Business Roundtable in 2019 in redefining the purpose of a corporation: *"Each of our stakeholders is essential: customers, employees, suppliers, communities, and shareholders. We commit to deliver value to all of them, for the future success of our companies, our communities, and our country."* The translation of this proclamation into corporate action will necessitate executives to rethink their business.

The QBL refines the goals of the organization to reflect the mutual benefit and shared interest of all stakeholders. If all the stakeholders are "on the same team," conflicts and tradeoffs will be converted into creative solutions. The evaluation of the bottom line is measured by SIIs. Creating Shared Value[147] generates collaborative advantage while delivering tangible social benefits to all stakeholders.

Two Fortune 2019 studies documented this shift to purpose-driven business: 64% of Americans say that a company's "primary purpose" should be "making the world better," and 41% of Fortune 500 CEOs say solving social problems should be "part of their (core) business strategy."

Executive Action: In this phase, the required executive action is: Benchmark your digital transformation progress and Social Return on Investment.

Road Map is Mindset

This Guidepost shares a journey through the ten practices of Strategic Transformation. By outlining each practice and how they can be applied, you will increase your readiness and capability to generate transformation. Since many research studies show that only a few executives effectively apply change management techniques, this is your chance to change the score!

However, this is a transformation journey through the unknown, requiring a creative and flexible mindset to successfully reach the destination.

Using the Unknown as a Creative Resource

Cultivating creativity and next level notions is developing a generative relationship with "the unknown"—one of consciously engaging it rather than avoiding it. We can't discover what we already know; discovery is essential to novel ideas and solutions. It requires that we embrace a state of ambiguity, uncertainty, and the unknown as we explore the creative process. We have to keep the divergent discovery space open long enough to play around for next level ideas to emerge before we converge them into actionable steps.

One way to consciously engage the unknown is setting up new foundational principles of creative engagement—to bring out new ways of thinking, being, and interacting.

Here's a case study of a corporate advertising team facing major challenges. They discovered by implementing one small foundational shift, they achieved new results. The team had a lot of creative ideas, but their

---

meetings were unproductive and contentious because it was *"like herding cats."* Their meetings were spent competing to see whose idea was best, constantly judging and criticizing each other, and only reluctantly giving in when they had reached a deadline. They would often leave their meetings feeling compromised or deflated.

In a creative thinking workshop, they were guided to set principles of engagement from improvisational theater (where you are constantly immersed in the unknown). These included *"Yes-And"* (accept and idea and build on it, which leads to generating new ideas) and *"Defer Judgment"* (suspend judgment temporarily during the ideation process). These divergent principles used during brainstorming expand beyond analysis into creative thinking and create more space for exploration and discovery. And then, after diverging, take the new ideas and converge them with your goals, let go of those that do not harmonize with your strategic goals, and modify others to make them workable. We combined new principles of engagement with experiential learning to drive new actions.

As a result, the team came up with the idea to change their meetings to *"Discovery Sessions."* One simple tweak opened up the space for the norm to engage the unknown: diverge first into discovery, exploration, and expand upon each idea to mine new territory before converging the ideas into actionable items. The mindset was lighter and more experimental. It became fun, more collaborative, and less competitive. They left the sessions with novel actionable ideas. By turning ambiguity and uncertainty into discovery, their meetings became more enjoyable, productive, and every voice felt heard and contributed to the outcome—a true co-creation.

Michelle James, CEO, Center for Creative Emergence

Instead of concluding remarks, here's another story.

A man goes to a Zen master[148] and says, "I would like to move to your city. What do you think of the people here?" And the Zen master says, "What are the people like in your old city?" And the man says, "They are awful, mean, spiteful." The Zen master says, "They are the same here. You shouldn't move."

The next day another man goes to the Zen master and says, "I'd like to move to your city. What do you think of the people here?" And the Zen master says, "What are the people like in your old city?" And the man says, "They are very nice, interesting and smart. I enjoy living there." And the Zen master says, "They are the same here. You will enjoy moving in."

Empower us to drive *Strategic Transformation* signals a big move is needed. But, as we already pointed out, it's really the mindset that matters, not location. Also, it helps to know that the old cities are crumbling, and the new cities are being built by Catalyzers.

Guidepost 12

L.I.G.H.T. Impacts

Accelerating Strategic Harmony

"One does not become enlightened by imagining figures of light, but by making the darkness conscious."

Carl Jung

A blind man went to visit a friend. It was night when he could return and the friend offered a lighted lamp. "I don't need this lamp, dear," replied the blind man. "Nights and days are similar to me. I will use my stick to find the way." His friend said, "You better keep it. It is for others to see you in the dark."

Let there be *LIGHT*! As we move through the modules of Strategic Harmony, we are focused on the impact on the marketplace, community, and society. This process illuminates institutions and organizations as their purposeful solutions help to realign our world. We call it the principle of L.I.G.H.T. (Lifelong Learning, Innovation Engine, Good Governance, Holistic Living, Transformative Economics). If you place LIGHT on darkened institutions or degenerated values, they are re-energized and focused on their purpose.

There are five L.I.G.H.T. Impacts accelerating harmony for any organization or business. They re-write the rules for organizations to sustain impact and ongoing transformation. For each Impact, leadership must design an action plan to generate a sustainable effect on its journey to become a catalytic organization.

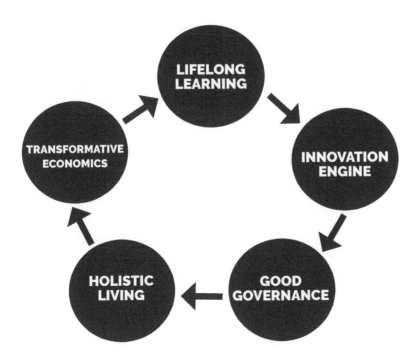

Figure 12.1 L.I.G.H.T. Impacts

The application of L.I.G.H.T principles is a set of tools used to transform an Old-Power-based organization to a flexible Transformative Power-and-Love-aligned environment.

Let's dive into the five L.I.G.H.T Impacts, and briefly describe the impact of each component.

Lifelong Learning

Lifelong Learning is the individual's ongoing, self-motivated quest for knowledge and inner growth. It serves as the foundation for individual transformation, resulting in expanded creativity and innovation, active citizenship, self-sustainability, and employability. Lifelong Learning is an economic imperative in the world of exponential technologies, changing jobs, and constant transformation.

It goes beyond new technological and management skills; it focuses on ongoing self-improvement of communication, interactive soft skills, time management, decision-making, leadership, and relationship-building. As discussed earlier, less than 30% of team members across roles and generations feel adequately prepared for the skills needed to execute transformation in the 21st century. The speed and necessity of change require the entire team to learn reflective, values-based skills, collaboration/teamwork, digital marketing analytics, and emerging technologies. Integrating Lifelong Learning is a requirement to prepare teams to navigate the path for Strategic Harmony.

Lifelong Learning reflects ongoing, self-initiated "education" that is flexible, diverse, and available at different times and in different places. For example, Islam attaches great importance to knowledge in this recognized statement: "Seek knowledge from the cradle to the grave."

Learning throughout life is propelled by integrating personal development (transformative learning) and professional development (strategic learning). The organization must design an action plan that encourages and supports this self-reflection and learning.

In a decade, future leaders will operate in a world driven by artificial intelligence, robots, and machine learning. As MGI partner Susan Lund[142] maintained, *"The idea that you get an education when you're young and then you stop and you go and work for 40 or 50 years with that educational training and that's it - that's over. All of us are going to have to continue to adapt, get new skills, and possibly go back for different types of training and credentials."* Acquiring talent is a key resource for competitive advantage in the modern world.

Educational Leadership Practices For 21st Century School: An Imperative for Developing Nations

Global trends, technological evolution, and exponential increase in knowledge and information have greatly altered today's educational landscape. The demands of the 21st century have challenged the very essence of leadership — past, present, and future and have led to an imperative for the renovation of educational systems, particularly, in Developing Nations.

These sweeping changes require changes in our education systems, as well as educational leaders who can navigate the challenges of the 21st century, creating a learning environment that effectively meets the learning needs of all learners. Therefore, change initiatives should emphasize the

---

training of school leaders in the use of current and best practices. Consideration must also be given to policy review and development, curriculum review, development, and implementation in order that learning institutions remain relevant.

Research has shown that education systems that fail to innovate simply repeat yesterday's educational programs and strategies tomorrow, which further jeopardize education's reputation as a contribution to development efforts. Pedagogy in the 21st century has shifted from transmissive to participatory pedagogies; therefore, today's learning environment should identify creative and innovative ways to successfully address the learning needs of 21st century learners.

21st century learning environments should reflect the demands of today's digital's era and as such should promote digital literacy and the 4 Cs: Critical thinking and problem solving, Communication, Collaboration, and Creativity and innovation. Failure to adequately meet the diverse needs of today's learners would result in an injustice to the holistic development of our nation's children and their ability to effectively find their places on this global stage.

Sharon McDonald. EdD., Transformative Leadership, St Lucia

Why is Lifelong Learning critical to the catalytic organization? The new working environment requires agile mindsets and evolving skills; it calls for decision-makers to challenge their long-held assumptions and to bring new light and insights to accepted business indicators (e.g., price, profit, distribution). Therefore, "education programs" in an environment that is ambiguous and disrupted must be continuous in responding to these needs. We must re-invent the rules of continuous improvement and education. It's no longer important to focus the learning process around just what we do and how to do it, but also why we do it and how to transform what and how we do it.

Transformative learning is driven by an inner quest to transform perspectives and realize growth and innovation. Individuals must develop their capacity to self-reflect as well as develop the soft skills that prepare them to anticipate and initiate change, and clarify their values and purpose (rather than acting on those of other people) to become independent thinkers.

Take a look at a simple example. Imagine we ask people who need to get from point A to point B to describe the "vehicle." They will come up with the dictionary definition: a road vehicle with four wheels, powered by an internal combustion engine. In a traditional education process, we are supposed to learn and apply that definition whenever needed. In a transformative learning environment, we must guide people to question and rethink. For example, are there cars with three wheels? If yes, could there be cars without wheels, floating on air like hovercrafts, flying, or on rails, or endless metal chains like tanks, or...? Are there other engines, like electric, hydrogen, anti-gravity-based, using magnetic levitation...? After such speculating, we could end up with a much broader definition of a vehicle. It does not just exist to have wheels and an engine but to carry a small number of people to short distances safely, efficiently, sustainably, and comfortably. If we now start discussing how a car is doing what it is supposed to do, we may quickly develop a set of "transformative ideas." How safe is the car, as there are more people killed in car accidents than in wars? How efficient is the car, since most of the time, it carries only one person, at an average speed of a bicycle, consuming (non-renewable) resources, and causing vast levels of pollution? After such a transformative learning process, we will question the purpose and conclude that whoever made us use cars in everyday life may as well be our worst enemy. Hence, we will rethink and uncover a new, revolutionized, transformative solution to the need for short-distance transportation.

The described Strategic Learning is a continuous search for knowledge and ideas to augment the purpose, retrain for new job requirements, and leverage future opportunities. This approach uses timely data to help organizations quickly learn from their work and adapt their strategies. It means integrating evaluation and catalytic thinking into strategic decision-making for reflection and innovation. In our world of exponentially changing technologies and redefining of requirements for future jobs, this integration of virtual and in-person learning becomes a necessity to deliver a relevant experience.

Lifelong Learning, the North Star of our Future

Even before birth, we listen. Melodies our parents played or sang during the months of our pre-natal womb residency can be remembered and recognized by the infant, often with emotional associations. So we arrive already learning, and continue as "preschoolers" in the first sixty months to observe and decode sounds, light patterns, movements, and changes of sensation until we can begin to identify a jigsaw puzzle of a trillion pieces called "reality." We learn to talk before knowing about dictionaries or rules of grammar. Isn't that amazing?

But then most of us who go to school have to start all over again. We were told what to learn, and then tested to see if we had paid attention. Our natural awareness is forced to confront a maze designed for us by people who don't know us. Our personal fascinations are interrupted and linked to a locomotive called "get good grades, or else!" Our unique curiosities is restrained and retrained, and we have to stay on track and get educated, or become a failure.

To educate comes from Latin "to lead (ducare) out (ex)." It is the opposite of indoctrinate, which means to put beliefs (doctrines) into us for the convenience of society, as if we were all just parts of a machine.

Turning into the new Millennium, we find ourselves in such acceleration that new knowledge is coming faster than anyone can process it. We fashion multiple lenses to anticipate disruptions and opportunities as well as to challenge limiting assumptions. We now must transform competition into collaboration if we want to fly in this vortex of progress. The call is out for us to adapt, and those who are not ready will be carried along by the faster traffic. Leaders at all levels need to step beyond their professional degrees and develop social, emotional, and technological intelligence necessary to navigate the unknown roads ahead.

Lifelong Learning is our calling, our direction, and our ongoing metamorphosis. The sooner we realize that the true university is the Universe, the more agile we will be in expressing our intrinsic talent in articulating this wondrous, unifying, Second Millennium human and scientific renaissance.

Fredric Lehrman, Director, Nomad University

Lifelong Learning is an imperative for businesses and organizations striving to be sustainable in our global business environment and our individual societies as well. These learning experiences help to prime Catalyzers to respond to the unknown challenges they will face for change and increase their commitment to Lifelong Learning.

Innovation Engine

Innovation Engine is the venue for managing and facilitating continuous innovation: adopting exponential technologies to meet new requirements, responding to unarticulated needs, or mobilizing teams to address unexpected disruptions in the ecosystem. The Engine reflects the organization's innovation strategy. It could be one or a combination of best practices: decentralized autonomous teams, internal entrepreneurial ventures, corporate venture-capital initiatives, outsourcing alliances, open innovation, crowdsourcing, and rapid prototyping. The Innovation Engine must be harmonious with the business model; it must be continuously engaged in searching for fresh or disruptive solutions that are synthesized into the transformative business model design and tested. Constant innovation is realized by unbridling the thinking process, expanding technologies, reinventing business models that breakthrough, disrupt, and make a sustainable impact in the market or society. It is best accomplished through a Catalytic Mindset that breaks down antiquated organizational structures (siloes) that inhibit creativity and innovation. The best examples of the Innovation Engine principle are *Change the World* companies listed by Fortune[150]. They fuel high-impact innovation and investment programs that benefit both the company and society. A good example is BYD, the Chinese electric vehicle maker, changing the world by speeding up the shift to electric vehicles to reduce pollution. Unlike expensive Tesla, BYD makes electric cars and buses with starting prices as low as $8,500. Such companies retain top talent, navigate new markets, form new partnerships, and enhance their brand. Communities benefit through access to technology, capital, skills, supply chains, and partnerships, as well as reducing pollution.

Traditionally, the future of any organization was coined in special innovation-oriented research and development units. Not anymore! In the contemporary environment, Innovation Engine (IE) becomes the focal point for transformation both within and external to the organization. IE differs from the traditional R&D unit using elaborate field testing and prototyping but which doesn't allow for real-time adjustments and quick turnaround time.

Why is this critical to the catalytic organization? Virtually every organization, small or global, is facing the challenges of disruption and necessity to innovate. Many organizations paste on innovation as a window dressing to show they are active in response to changes in the marketplace. This has been labeled "Innovation Theater" but will not realize the long-term organizational transformation necessary to design and implement breakthrough sustainable concepts.

In contrast, Innovation Engine is a low cost, low risk, agile venue to generate, evaluate, and disseminate innovation and sustain change both internal and external to the organization. It is the hub for channeling efforts to ignite and evaluate changes in business models, structure, strategy, and impact. It generates Transformative Power and is often one of the first changes initiated by organizations undergoing Strategic Transformation.

IE is a dedicated and autonomous unit that reports directly to the CEO, senior leadership, or Board with a separate budget and review process. Although a separate unit, it is not designed as a silo for innovation. It involves and cooperates with functional units rather than competing with them. Its goal is to fuel a mindset and culture of innovation throughout the organization. It facilitates quick response and unbiased evaluation of new ideas; consults with the organization's functional units on breakthrough solutions; tests and evaluates new business models and distribution channels; and provides a holistic, integrated approach to problem-solving and digital strategy. The innovation must generate value for the organization within a targeted time frame.

Open Innovation and Organizational Culture

Open Innovation implies the use of internal as well as external sources of knowledge (universities, institutes etc.), confronting the principles of a closed model that is oriented only to internal sources. As a consequence, Open Innovation causes a huge shift in paradigms considering the approach to innovation in companies. Henry Chesbrough's book on the topic introduces the term "open innovation" and provides the first sustained analysis of the new innovation approach. Adopting such a complex model implies two different processes: (1) the process that leads to open innovation and opens up practices that have formerly been closed, the adoption process, and (2) the process corresponding to practicing open innovation, the open innovation practices.

What does an organization's culture have to do with it?

Organizational culture is an abstraction; yet the forces that derive out of it are powerful, and if we do not know how they operate, we can easily become their victim. For that reason, if new managerial practices such as the open innovation practices are brought to the organization without aligning them to the organization's basic assumptions, they will not be

---

sustained, and the created situation can even be harmful in the long run. Furthermore, organizational culture can foster or hamper the adoption process depending on how well it is addressed by the management.

Through changing and managing culture, a company's management at the same time affects the perception of the employees, helping them to shift the mindset toward more productive open innovation behavior. During the adoption process, the cultural change mechanisms are applied to align culture and strategy while later the cultural management mechanism takes over and ensures sustainability of the open innovation practices.

These mechanisms differ in purpose rather than in means. In other words, when organizational culture changes, the emphasis is on changing the basic organization's assumptions, while when organizational culture is managed, the emphasis is on maintaining and preserving those assumptions and values.

Emir Dzanic PhD, Director, Cambridge Innovative System Solutions

How to create a team responsible for innovation? IE usually has a consistent core membership (8-12 members) that is diverse by design. It includes well-experienced executives from different functional groups within the organization, as well as millennials/Gen Z staff. It chooses expert leaders from outside the organization to provide a fresh perspective, challenging the team's old patterns and providing responsive feedback to leadership. This diversity instills creative tension which encourages breakthrough innovation.

How to create an innovative culture? As we all know, the key issue is not only how to get new, innovative ideas, but how to challenge and replace outdated approaches that don't work anymore. Hence, IE must be driven by the company's values and newly adopted Catalytic Mindset which integrates the formerly described four lenses (Quantum, Circular, Connective, Intelligence). Members must learn to listen "obsessively" to the customers', employees', and partners' voices as a foundation of the new company culture. IE facilitates organizational change (e.g., integration of "siloed" functions, strategies, and analysis) to enhance innovation and sustainable outcomes.

IE fosters an entrepreneurial 'start-up atmosphere' to encourage breakthrough innovation. It serves as an employee's training ground for a collaborative approach to innovation. Members of the IE become advocates for change within their functional groups (e.g., Finance, HR, IT), and help to support the new organizational culture.

What are the methodologies? Similar to transformative learning, it is important to apply trial-and-error thinking. If a strategy doesn't fail every now and then, it's a sure sign that it's not innovative. The IE's responsibility is to apply foresight, data analysis, and creativity to anticipate and get ahead of the change. Its actions can range from initiating organization-wide transformation or fueling the customer experience to proving an innovation concept. The objective is to integrate the IE's approach as innovative culture that permeates the organization. The cornerstones of such a culture include:

» Purposeful design thinking - integrates core values with design thinking process

» Catalytic thinking - increases adoption by decreasing resistance (activation energy) required for change (following a line of least resistance)

» Disruptive innovation - challenges old beliefs and gaps in the market to re-invent business models

» Lean methodologies - incorporates Minimum Viable Product and business canvas to accelerate innovation

» Customer insights – refines data collection and analysis to better define customer needs

» Learn from the best - leverages success in different verticals and markets to jumpstart innovation and decrease uncertainties

Innovation Engine (symbolically represented in Figure 12.2 as Digital Innovation Unit) is particularly important in implementing digital transformation strategies.

Innovation must include artificial intelligence and machine learning in the new model-building. Here is an example how using innovation to mitigate infectious disease outbreaks and improve maternal and child health was proven impactful. The action took the shape of CAMTech[151] hackathons, 48-hour events in which a group of curated individuals from different backgrounds come together to drive innovation in healthcare. Such an approach has allowed clinicians, public health professionals, engineers and entrepreneurs to act as first responders to infectious disease outbreaks, like Ebola and Zika. Several hackathons, bootcamps, and innovation awards have also focused on improving maternal and child health and closing the gender gap in Medtech (medical technology).

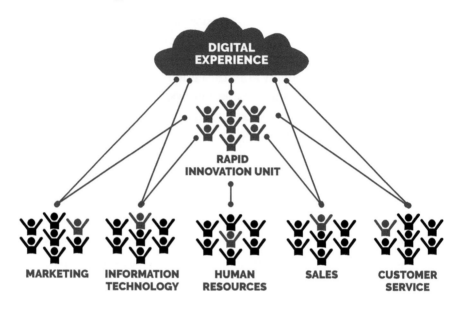

Figure 12.2 Digital Innovation Unit

According to Innovators Magazine[152], applying CAMTech's co-creation model, which assembles multidisciplinary teams of clinicians, public health professionals, engineers, and entrepreneurs to biotech would accelerate the industry's technology production. By fostering innovation focused on infectious disease outbreaks and maternal and child health, the biotech industry will make significant strides in ending extreme poverty, inequality, and climate change by 2030.

Good Governance

Good Governance reflects the structure and lines of communication among and between the stakeholders of an organization. It embodies an active voice in decision-making, representing the diverse interests of all stakeholders. It encourages broad participation and depends on radical empathy or getting to the "roots" of what employees or citizens want and need. It must discover the citizens' and employees' real voice. Good Governance must be equitable in structure, transparent in communications, and encourage feedback. A good example is Principles of Good Governance[153] by the Ministers of the Council of Europe. They reflect a high standard in addressing issues such as ethical conduct, rule of law, efficiency and effectiveness, transparency, sound financial management, and accountability.

Good Governance refers to effective and ethical ways of directing and controlling organizations in the best interest of all stakeholders. It fuels Transformative Power in any organization, especially if combined with integrity, dedication, and passion for change. It is the overarching approach to conduct public affairs, manage resources, make and implement decisions, and manage interactions between sectors.

Why is this critical to the catalytic organization? As such an organization has venues for constant education and innovation, it must responsibly govern its stakeholders and constituency, meeting their needs in a responsive and empathic manner. Good or effective governance ensures that the organization benefits and is accountable to its intended beneficiaries in contrast to "bad" governance which is insensitive to these inclusive needs with a focus on self-interest.

During the last decade, there has been a call for an inclusive organizational structure. One example is Holacracy, which was developed as a method of decentralized management and organizational governance. In this model, authority and decision-making are distributed throughout a "holarchy" of self-organizing teams and roles rather than being vested in a traditional management top-down hierarchy. Employees are motivated and encouraged to go beyond their "rigid job description" to foster leadership and new responsibilities. Holacracy shifts the power dynamics from people to organizational purpose. Zappos has successfully employed it, while Twitter and Medium have tried it and adapted the methodology.

During the COVID-19 crisis, Good Governance at all levels is stress-tested in full view of the media and their citizenry. People are questioning the transparency of the facts, accountability of the institutions, response time, and efficiency in addressing vital needs of distressed stakeholders. Governments need to step-up in this crisis. Leaders are held closely to task as lives are at stake. Innovative solutions are being tested. *"Governments will need to draw on deep wells of expertise and tap new, innovative ideas. They will need to be nimble and steadfast, with one eye on the near term and the other on the medium- to long-term horizons."*[154]

Smart cities grew focused on the use of technology to make them more effi-cient in regulation and control. The pandemic stimulated these cities to collec-tivize intelligence to consider collaborative solutions to COVID-19.

In late February 2020, South Korea had the second-highest COVID-19 infection rate of any country. They immediately implemented a 7-step plan exemplary of Good Governance that resulted in curbing the spread and mini-mizing the deaths. The plan was compassionate and responsive in addressing the needs of all the stakeholders (patients, physicians, medical staff, citizens); leaders developed trust and common purpose among citizens and used digital technology to spread the message, and IT to control the spread.

> » Protect first responders (physicians and medical staff)
> » Prevent further infection to citizens at hospitals
> » Cover all citizens' COVID-19 medical expenses
> » Implement IT infrastructure for expanding testing and tracing
> » Use media to develop protective culture of wearing facemasks
> » Provide public with real-time transparent information on virus spread
> » Consistent leadership support for all country effort

What are the cornerstones of Good Governance? In 1997 the United Nations Development Program agreed on a set of principles that are reflected in the five elements[155] that define Good Governance:

1. Engagement - is listening and applying the voice of all in decision-making and constructive participation to represent their interests (e.g., consumers, patients, students, and citizens). Good Governance mediates differing interests to reach a broad consensus on what is in the best interest of the group.
2. Direction - reflects those that are chosen to govern will carry out just, righteous, honest, and ethical activities that fulfill the constit-uency's purpose. Leaders have a long-term strategic vision on Good Governance and sustainable human development.
3. Impact - mirrors the responsiveness of institutions to serve all stakeholders while balancing competing interests. The results must reflect the appropriate, effective, and efficient use of available resources.
4. Accountability - is the moral and legal obligation to transparently account for, accept responsibility, and disclose its activities and

transactions. This is built upon the open and free flow of information up and down the organizational hierarchy and understanding the decision-making process.

5. Fairness - considers community's wellbeing to be equitable and inclusive of all interests particularly the most vulnerable. The Rule of Law should be consistent and enforced impartially, within the powers of the organization or institution.

Take a look at the #NeverAgain Gun Control Movement, initiated in February 2018 by GenZ students. In order to become sustainable and successful in the long run, #NeverAgain must emulate this good governance model to manage operations, relate to its base, and operate. Thus, it must succeed in mediating differing interests to reach a broad consensus across all ages. Also, the movement leaders must be able to carry out just, righteous, honest, and ethical activities that fulfill the constituency's purpose. Furthermore, the movement will have to deal with the difficult task to serve all stakeholders while balancing competing interests, providing free flow of information up and down the organizational hierarchy. Finally, the movement must prove equitable and inclusive of all interests, particularly of the most vulnerable groups. Since its founding, 67 pieces of legislation have been passed in 26 U.S. States.

Good Governance is not just a nice way to solve complex problems calling for a balance of interests in a complicated and volatile world. It is a part of a broader trend. Every now and then we witness inspiring scenes of people taking the future of their companies or countries into their hands. Such processes will ignite demand for Good Governance and political reform everywhere, starting with some of the most progressive companies and ending some of the least responsive governments.

Winning Elections: The Science of Trust

There is a false narrative that politicians' strategy must be eye-for-an-eye in our resistance to the opposition. However, if politics is about relationships and relationships are built on trust, then why else would we be asking any other question than: Are we building trust?

We should ask how our purpose and strategies are building trust. The neuroscience of trust shows us that it is not WHAT issues we stand for, but rather HOW we stand for them as an expression of our values that builds trust. Let's take a look at the elements of trust:

FIGHT LIKE HELL FOR WHAT WE BELIEVE IN–Fight for the progressive values and issues we stand for and play to win. We must fight for our issues, not against the person.

BUILD UNITY ON VALUES, NOT IDENTITY POLITICS–Trust is built in HOW we fight. Let's define our values and have the discipline to live them "beyond a reasonable doubt." We must leave identity politics behind and rally around our common values.

BE REAL ABOUT THE MIRROR, FORGET THE WINDOW– Most successful leaders had the uncanny ability to look in the mirror in times of failure, not out the window (Jim Collins). We should focus on how we can grow from lessons learned.

EVERY CORNER STRATEGY–In the information age, campaign dollars have a sharp diminishing return. We can get more utility by investing in our message, and organizing in every community. Then our message will spread.

EMBRACE PROGRESSIVE POPULISM–People want fundamental change with real ethics reform, eliminating big money influence. We must be sincere about ceding power to the people as these steps are essential to rebuilding trust.

RADICALLY EMPATHIZE–Empathizing does not mean we must agree; some may be racist or bigoted; aggressively condemn their actions, but listen to the concerns of all people. Empathy is tough.

STOP NEGATIVE POLITICS–We are disrespecting voters when we try to scare them into voting our way. These tactics erode trust. Respect the voter enough to come to her/his own conclusion.

With trust as the basis of our engagement, we can nurture political brand champions, help us turn out the vote, and win elections.

Sam Rasoul, Delegate, Commonwealth of Virginia

Holistic Living

Creating L.I.G.H.T. Impact goes beyond innovation strategy and good governance. Holistic Lifestyle is concerned with the interaction of individuals and organizations with the community and society. A vibrant and engaged organization will be aligned with its Purpose and strive to fulfill its goals. It's the set of tasks and techniques used to maintain health, work balance, as well as fulfillment of purpose for individuals and organizations. It reflects the natural, environmental, and allopathic treatments to heal the mind, body, and heart of an organization. Health starts with the individual as a holistic system—emotional, financial, cultural, and physical. It can be translated to the organization or social institution. All stakeholders should understand the culture, structure, policies, and operations of the organization in order to fully participate. They must be empowered to recommend solutions that enable the organization to achieve sustainable outcomes in the community or society. As an organization adopts transformation, it experiences a "lifestyle challenge." It must champion its purpose transitioning to the new adopted culture.

Good examples are corporate wellness and fitness programs as the center of work-life balance from FitBit, Google, Houston Methodist, Motley Fool, and Zappos. They are giving employees the tools and opportunities to live a healthier, fulfilling lifestyle. They provide challenges that drive collaboration and improve health. BP, for example, has run a one million step challenge where employees who hit the mark over the course of a year are eligible for a more deductible health plan. In one year, 23,000 employees took more than 23 billion steps.

According to Virgil, an ancient Roman poet[156], the greatest wealth is health. It is no surprise that living a holistic lifestyle has recently become a global trend. In essence, it means to choose to live our life and heal our body in a natural way while creating work-life balance. Conceptually, we observe everything as a whole. For example, any sickness is not just physical. It can also be an outcome of emotional, social, and other issues.

Holistic Living is intended to make us more prepared for challenges in life as we are motivated to observe the signs and effects of our surroundings. Simply stated, Holistic Living is concerned with the interaction of the individual, and organization with the community and society. It reflects the health of emotional, financial, cultural, and physical systems. Thus, whatever imbalance manifests within an individual, often it is projected to their organization, community, and or country.

Why is this critical to the catalytic organization? In the world of high velocity change, on demand agility, disruption of norms and comfort zones, and stress to perform at a high bar, individuals' and organizations' health are required to adopt transformation and design and implement vibrant, innovative solutions. The catalytic organization must set its standards high to maintain health and work balance, as well as fulfillment of purpose. The leadership must model and champion this challenge and advocate the holistic lifestyle. The community/ team should be open to self-organize around these "healthy living systems" to determine its wellbeing, performance, and survival/growth.

Every transformation should start from within

Today, we are experiencing big paradigm shifts at all levels due to an ecosystem hyper-connected, globalization, entrepreneurial revolution, emergence of horizontal enterprises, difficulty in economic growth, digital transformations, universities 4.0, new competencies, etc. These shifts and transformations have impacted us at work, within the family, with friends, within governmental institutions, and across cultures.

The challenge for organizations, institutions, corporations, and leaders is not about elaborated plans and strategies that often remain unattainable. It is not about searching for external resources and funds. It is mainly about tackling these aspects from within, considering particularly the human involvement. It is about creating a balance between organizational and personal transformations. Their alignment is the essence of bringing back harmony to a broken world.

The big debate today is how to lead this transformation, adopting a holistic perspective that encompasses healthy relations, exercise, mindfulness, spirituality, financial stability, romance, and many others. The aim of holistic living, inspired by many researches based on positive leadership and positive psychology, is to live a more fulfilling life with less stress by creating a harmony between the personal and the professional sphere. It also aims to develop more wisdom and forgiveness, to heal the body and the soul, allowing enhanced interpersonal relations. It is about endless benefits that prioritize the Human's wellbeing, positive thinking, and optimism, personal and spiritual growth.

Some practices like yoga and mindfulness proved to have a considerable impact on people's lives and happiness. A daily training will provide better conflict management, constructive cooperation, and interactions with the team. Mindfulness is part of the pillars of wellbeing from per-

---

sonal and professional perspectives. It can also improve our relations and develop more focus, especially in an environment often disrupted by the media and social networks. It triggers peoples' motivation so that they can handle the external challenges and make real projects from these transformations.

Every transformation should start from within. To make it successful, leaders' involvement is crucial. They must become Catalyzers of change with a future vision based on a holistic approach putting the human at the core, starting from inner transformation towards an external one.

Hanane Anoua, Global Goodwill Ambassador

What are the key ideas behind holistic living systems? The following list of Principles of Healthy Living Systems has been adapted from the work of Elisabet Sahtouris[157]:

» Self-refection—reserve time for inner contemplation and balance

» Self-maintenance—prioritize nutrition and exercise for physical body

» Engagement—involved in purpose and structure of organization

» Responsibility—balance internal and external stress or change

» Work-life balance—balance interests; serve what brings you joy

» Empowerment—channel your passion; propel your work

» Collaboration—augment and inspire yourself and others

» Reciprocity—give generously and serve others' needs

» Conservation—focus on what works well and uses less resources

» Innovation—change what does not work well

» Regeneration—monitor, evaluate, and rebalance your system

A good example of such an approach is the Zappos Happiness model.[158] The company encourages employees' balanced Healthy Living. It established a customer first attitude with an obsession for customer service. Its focus on employee culture is of "one mind" and laser-focused on optimizing the stakeholder experience. The Zappos culture is invested in really caring that everybody is happy—its customers, employees, and leadership. Or what we term Transformative Love, each stakeholder's needs are supported and harmonized with the organization. One way to sustain such a culture is to hire on two dimensions: experience/technical ability and personal values that match company's corporate culture. Zappos hires based on "just naturally living the brand." They figured out that people who don't fit the company culture are better off being paid to leave. Many organizational experts agree that Zappos' model is a new way to build and sustain a business.

Let's take a look at 10 Core Values of Zappos that define a holistic living philosophy:

1. Deliver Wow Through Service
2. Embrace and Drive Change
3. Create Fun and a Little Weirdness
4. Be Adventurous, Creative, and Open-Minded
5. Pursue Growth and Learning
6. Build Open and Honest Relationships with Communication
7. Build a Positive Team and Family Spirit
8. Do More with Less
9. Be Passionate and Determined
10. Be Humble

Just as marketing teams have adopted total customer experience as the gold standard, progressive organizations have focused on a holistic employee experience to attract, motivate, and retain superior talent. In a study[159], 80% of executives rated employee experience as important, but only 22% felt they were excellent at building such a holistic experience. This includes work-life balance, health and wellbeing, meaningful work, and positive work environment. Creating a holistic employee experience requires it to be an organizational priority incorporating active feedback, monitoring, and evaluation.

Obviously, it is necessary for Catalyzers governing innovative organizations to incorporate healthy living while working in an exciting transformative environment.

Transformative Economics

Transformative Economics realigns the "economy," the business model, and the related principles that guide the institution and organization to become the "servant" of its stakeholders rather than the "master" of them and the environment. This Transformative Economic model is inclusive and equitable, benefiting all stakeholders. It requires the exercise of power within the entire supply chain. It channels power as a transformative force for a collaborative economic model. All economic activities should be designed to generate social impact while contributing to the development of a sustainable society within resilient ecological systems. It contrasts the "green economy" with "ecological economics." The former attempts to reduce negative impacts (e.g., recycling) within the current capitalistic systems; the latter views the economic system as holistic and circular with products proactively designed to be reused.

Our broken world is fraught with non-sustainable and destructive economic behavior, reflecting the imperfections of the present capitalistic system. An example is the food and beverage industry as the power center of the market-place, both materially and ideologically. It is continuously marketing unsustainable/unhealthy foods while realizing great profits. Most of the manufacturers promote convenience, and promote entertaining foods, knowing that they contribute to obesity and illnesses such as diabetes and heart conditions. They have developed a lucrative niche market where junk food has become a habit and a necessity. Their role as a "purposeful" food company should be to nourish their targets as a "servant" to the people. Instead, they have become a powerful economic interest group solely dedicated to "serve" the shareholders.

In 2017 Indra Nooyi, CEO of PepsiCo addressed this discrepancy head-on with a new global corporate agenda, emphasizing health and social accountability. Its first action was "helping to improve health and wellbeing" through redesigning their products. She received this feedback "Don't be Mother Teresa. Your job is to sell soda and chips." Her response: "So this is not being disingenuous. We are trying to take a historical eating and drinking habit that has been exported to the rest of the world and make [it] more permissible."

According to the Transformative Economic principle, PepsiCo's role as a food company should be to nourish their targets as a "servant" to the people. At present, they are a powerful economic interest group at odds with the interests of their target population. Profit and sales revenue are old tools to measure success, and they must be replaced with Sustainable Impact Indicators (see Guidepost 11) to optimize results for all stakeholders. Such a change of measuring impact can begin to fix the broken world.

In a traditional economy, business is primarily about generating profits for its shareholders. All business actions, ethical or not, are based on their effect on shareholders. The rest of society is alienated from business decisions. It may suffer negative impacts but, if profits are realized, it is considered (wrongly) to be OK.

The digital revolution has shattered this outdated model. Due to the power and transparency of social media and digital technologies, consumers are no longer powerless puppets on the business-controlled stage. Businesses can no longer ignore the needs of the community or the planet over time if they wish to find success, sustainability, and profit. The goal of the new Transformative Economy is shared value for all stakeholders. Hence, return on investment (ROI), the pinnacle of traditional model, must be balanced with social and economic concerns. Such business efforts have culminated into *Creating Shared Value* (CSV), which focuses on creating business value by addressing social issues that directly or indirectly connect with one's business. CSV is a perfect model for businesspeople, entrepreneurs, and capitalists alike complementing a focus on profit while generating positive social impact.

Bringing Value to Individuals, Industries, and the Society

"Let the future tell the truth and evaluate each one according to his/her work and accomplishments. The present is theirs; the future, for which I have really worked, is mine," said the visionary Nikola Tesla. ICT professionals have a better understanding of Tesla and his legacy than his contemporaries, and for a good reason.

Our capacity for transformation is being tested daily. Challenges are many and they multiply ever faster. That is precisely where our personal and organizational agility and core values come to play as a major asset. Being able to reassess, recreate, and readapt ourselves, our offering, our business models, and our approach to innovation, while retaining the underlying principle of sustainability, is now more valuable than ever. Sustainability is not a choice; it is a matter of survival. It incorporates the capacity of looking beyond and capturing opportunities for ourselves and future generations.

The current challenge caused by rapid ICT technology development is to ensure a harmonious cooperation of people and technology. The time has come for us to surpass our fear of intelligent machines and to embrace a common future in which they support the development of our economy, society, and the environment in a sustainable way. Intelligent machines are opening opportunities for us to broaden our capabilities and experiences and to expand our potentials and use them for the advancement of humankind.

A leadership style that fosters true values nourishes a culture of innovation and relies on diversity and inclusion. It is the key to a sustainable value creation in our world that is continuously being reshaped by technology development. Such leadership gives people the opportunity, the support, and the empowerment they need to fulfill their potential, achieve their business and personal goals, and directly contribute to creating a sustainable networked world. The value that we create aims to serve a higher purpose, promoting social inclusion and sustainability. ICT technology is an essential part of our lives nowadays, and it is up to us to use it to make our lives easier and make our world a better place for all.

Gordana Kovačević, President of Ericsson Nikola Tesla, Croatia

Transformative Economics encourages companies to make a difference in the world, and to help fix what is broken. The new model, Strategic Harmony, views the economic system as holistic and circular with products proactively designed to be reused.

The world of Strategic Harmony is perfectly reflected in the concept of Global Ecological Footprint[160]. Its mindset and Transformative Economic models are best exemplified in Earth Overshoot Day (EOD). It's an illustrative calendar date on which humanity's resource consumption for the year exceeds Earth's capacity to regenerate those resources that year. Here is the map for the year 2020:

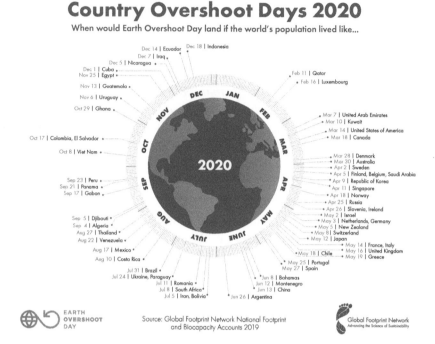

Country Overshoot Days 2020

When would Earth Overshoot Day land if the world's population lived like...

Dec 14 | Ecuador   Dec 18 | Indonesia
Dec 7 | Iraq
Dec 5 | Nicaragua
Dec 1 | Cuba   Feb 11 | Qatar
Nov 25 | Egypt   Feb 16 | Luxembourg
Nov 13 | Guatemala
Nov 6 | Uruguay
Oct 29 | Ghana   Mar 7 | United Arab Emirates
                                        Mar 10 | Kuwait
                                        Mar 14 | United States of America
Oct 17 | Colombia, El Salvador   Mar 18 | Canada
Oct 8 | Viet Nam
                                        Mar 28 | Denmark
                          2020   Mar 30 | Australia
                                        Apr 2 | Sweden
                                        Apr 5 | Finland, Belgium, Saudi Arabia
Sep 23 | Peru   Apr 9 | Republic of Korea
Sep 21 | Panama   Apr 11 | Singapore
Sep 17 | Gabon   Apr 18 | Norway
                                        Apr 25 | Russia
                                        Apr 26 | Slovenia, Ireland
Sep 5 | Djibouti   May 2 | Israel
Sep 4 | Algeria   May 3 | Netherlands, Germany
Aug 27 | Thailand   May 5 | New Zealand
Aug 22 | Venezuela   May 8 | Switzerland
                                        May 12 | Japan
                                        May 14 | France, Italy
Aug 17 | Mexico   May 16 | United Kingdom
Aug 10 | Costa Rica   May 18 | Chile   May 19 | Greece
Jul 31 | Brazil
Jul 24 | Ukraine, Paraguay   May 25 | Portugal
Jul 11 | Romania   May 27 | Spain
Jul 8 | South Africa   Jun 8 | Bahamas
Jul 5 | Iran, Bolivia   Jun 12 | Montenegro
                            Jun 13 | China
                   Jun 26 | Argentina

EARTH OVERSHOOT DAY

Source: Global Footprint Network National Footprint and Biocapacity Accounts 2019

Global Footprint Network
Advancing the Science of Sustainability

Figure 12.3 Global Map of Overshoot Days 2020

For example, in the case of the U.S., the sustainability balance was already destroyed on March 14, 2020. On that day, the country had produced more pollution and used more resources than it was able to reproduce until the end of the year.

Obviously, the shareholder approach, using profit and sales revenue, are old tools to measure success. They must be replaced by purposeful performance measurement or Sustainable Impact Indicators (SIIs) to optimize results for all stakeholders. On the positive side, there is a growing number of examples of Transformative Economic behavior. Take one more look at our favorite case, the Swedish company IKEA.[161] Its purpose is to create harmony for all people impacted by the business, and their vision states that more people can create a better everyday life at home.

IKEA's attempt to constantly improve its organizational culture are based on the notion that "Values Matter," paying great attention to togetherness, enthusiasm, cost-consciousness, and sustainability. The company is deeply committed to a *"People-Centric"* approach, focused on cooperation among all the stakeholders, customers, co-workers, suppliers, and other partners. In developing its Transformative Economy ecosystem, they cherish stakeholder cooperation through affordable prices by building long-term supplier relationships.

In another context, Unilever goes beyond traditional approaches to engage people using *"influencer marketing."* Executive Vice President Di Como[162] commented, *"We use it to build trust and credibility for our brands and to bring a really great brand experience to the people that we serve."* He suggested that its *"influencer efforts focus not just on a product, but on attempts to convey a brand's purpose—to talk about the brand value, of why the brand exists, and the purpose of the brand."* This is demonstrated by Dove Soap, the personal care line, focusing on *"real beauty."*

Transformation has always been a popular topic in literature and life. In quite a few tales, a prince or a princess turn into a Frog and could be re-transformed only by a magic kiss. In order to transform into a lady, Cinderella needs rich clothes. Exchange of suits causes major confusion in Mark Twain's Prince and the Pauper. In another traditional tale, the Beauty is confronted with a man transformed into a Beast. All these experiences talk about individuals, who eventually find out that outer beauty is not as important as inner beauty. Our Strategic Harmony model focuses on values, the best expressions of that "inner beauty."

The aim of this Guidepost has been to shed L.I.G.H.T. on the Strategic Harmony modules, and the impact of transformation on the marketplace, community, and society. As each of these components is illuminated, they augment the purpose and harmony of the evolving catalytic organization. They impact the inner dimensions and strength of the organization. Our wrap-up suggestion is that you reflect on the level of L.I.G.H.T. that your organization manifests.

PART V
DRIVE AND SCALE GLOBALLY

Guidepost 13

Reinventing

Strategic Harmony in Action

"Every sunset is an opportunity to reset. Every sunrise begins with new eyes."

Richie Norton

Following his lecture on Zen, a student said to a famous teacher Suzuki Roshi: "I've been listening to you for years but I still don't understand. Could you reduce your lectures to one phrase?"

Suzuki laughed and said: *"Everything changes."*

For 12 Guideposts, we have focused on how to design and build an organization that can deliver Strategic Harmony. We have shared examples of transformative leaders, their organizations, and businesses, which resonate with Strategic Harmony. In this Guidepost, we focus on *EmPower Us!*—the call to action for reinventing our world to thriving and sustainability. We focus on how to re-imagine ... portraying examples of Catalyzers and organizations that practice Strategic Harmony in name or form.

According to MIT Leadership Center[163], *"The world faces a host of systemic challenges beyond the reach of our existing institutions and their command-and-control hierarchies. Problems like climate change, ecosystem destruction, growing water scarcity, rising unemployment among younger generations, and embedded poverty and inequality. These serious issues require unprecedented collaboration – among different organizations, sectors, and even countries."*

Fixing what's broken requires self-reflection, obsessive listening, and true citizen participation to realize a set of mutual sustainable objectives.

Strategic Harmony is the HOW! Visionary enterprise leaders, entrepreneurs, and emerging influencers must become Catalyzers of change using the internal power of their values and Love of Purpose to generate social impact and harmony. It is a blueprint for an equitable economy, a regenerative society and life worth living. And it starts with a TEST: the four Values that make the difference: Trust, Empathy, Sustainability, and Transparency. Living these TEST Values translates into organizational strategies that realign and redirect our institutions towards sustainable goals. To achieve these goals, we need to develop collaborative working models across competitors and sectors that we can observe, learn from, refine, gain human-centered practices, and make successful. Since the journey is long and complicated, it requires Resilience, a new level of flexibility.

Who is to lead to achieve Strategic Harmony?

On a national level, we have examples of UAE (Dubai) committed to leading innovation, Japan building a model for Society 5.0, and China's Belt and Road project focused on building a modern-day "Silk Road." On corporate level, there are many inspiring cases.

In the Strategic Transformation space, we are faced with following questions:

» Will transformation be led by nation-states, global businesses (e.g., Alibaba, Amazon, Unilever, Royal Dutch Shell, or Google), strategic alliances, or all of the above?

» Which entities will adopt the TEST Values and generate the L.I.G.H.T. Impacts as the flame that needs to be stoked to burn through the resistances of Old Power?

» Which entities will have the courage and foresight to stoke the force of Transformative Power necessary to foster Strategic Harmony?

To *Reinvent*, we present a set of issues that require transformative solutions. We share seven working models developed by businesses and our team that strive to achieve Strategic Harmony. Each values-based model is focused on a specific issue including purpose, business model, stakeholder-centric culture, Strategic Transformation, Catalyzer network, social impact analysis, and global communications transformation platform. The models provide businesses and organizations a roadmap to build a sustainable response to disruption or crisis. The first is an application for a Post-COVID-19 Strategy.

Clarify Sustainable Purpose

If businesses are going to *Reinvent* in the Post-COVID-19 world, they have a powerful example in Unilever. In earlier Guideposts, we have discussed Paul Polman's decade of work setting the model for a purposeful global enterprise. Recently replaced by the new CEO, Alan Jope, Unilever has unified its 400 brands under one simple core concept and purpose: to make sustainable living commonplace. *The purpose is driven by four core values: integrity, responsibility, respect, and pioneering.*

The Purpose unifies their entire company, as Alan Jope recently discussed in a Bloomberg Breakaway Summit[164] interview: *"We've been operating a multi-stakeholders model for ten years believing that if we look after our employees and our customers, if we worry about society and the planet, and if we take care of our supplier partners, then ultimately our shareholders will be well rewarded."*

Unilever's performance[165] has proven that belief because 28 of its purposeful, sustainable brands, grew 69% faster than the rest of the business in 2018, compared to 47% in 2017.

The Transformative Power of Unilever's purpose was highlighted in Jope's immediate response[166] to the COVID-19 pandemic: *"We didn't honestly think it out. Our reflex was first of all to take care of our employees. On March the 12th our crisis team saying we should go into an immediate mandatory 100 percent indefinite global lockdown for all office employees. At the time it felt a little overwhelming but it was in the interests of protecting our employees. This response was ahead of any government suggestions of lockdown other than in China."*

In support of its global effort to help protect the lives and livelihoods of the communities in which it operates, Unilever USA donated[167] $20 million dedicating its workforce to one day of service in the local community and donating all the products manufactured at its factories that day or products of equal value to those impacted by COVID-19.

In the Post-COVID-19 world, businesses and organizations should take a lesson from Unilever to begin by reimaging a clear, sustainable purpose. Then their strategy and operations have an anchor and standard to follow.

Build A Transformative Business Model

The next step in *Reinventing* is to design and build a Transformative Business Model. This sustainable business model[168] describes how a company: (i) communicates its value proposition to its stakeholders, (ii) creates and delivers this value, (iii) captures economic value while maintaining or regenerating natural, social, and economic capital beyond its organizational boundaries.

With the COVID-19 pandemic significantly disrupting normal economic activity, there have been many suggestions to reshape the Linear Economic model that is inherently wasteful during production, consumption, and disposal. In response, the European Commission[169] has vowed to build a sustainable circular economy post-pandemic.

We incorporated the circular economy in this hybrid business model that synthesizes two lenses of the Catalytic Mindset–Think Circular and Think Connective. It integrates the intent of how value is captured and created via the circular economy with how value is delivered via digital economy.

Digital platforms augment social relationships via networks using the three Vs of big data—volume, variety, and velocity as they form the foundation for the shared economy. The Shared Economy[170] holds the promise for a more sustainable world by giving access to underutilized resources, at a fraction of the cost, to some who cannot or do not want to buy new products, and the chance of making an extra income for those who already own such underutilized resources. It is a peer-to-peer based sharing of access to goods and services, facilitated by a community-based online platform. For example, the sharing of transportation venues (e.g., cars, bicycles) has positive environmental impacts, reducing resources required, and pollutants, emissions, and carbon footprints.

Transitioning to sustainable circular economy radically transforms any business model. Circular Economy develops solutions based on efficient use of residual waste treating it as a resource for something else. The circular production models imitate nature's way and make sure that all waste is being reduced, reused, and recycled.

The Circular Economy delivers sustainable benefits for the future. *"Business models[171] based on reuse, leasing, repair, and remanufacturing could generate four times more jobs than waste treatment, disposal, and recycling. They generate local economic activity, helping to strengthen relations within communities."*

As previously discussed, our broken world faces the threat of climate change, major income inequalities, rise of popular movements, marginalization of people, increasing threats of terrorism, growth of fake news and corruption in business and governments. All can benefit from the holistic, systemic approach of the Circular Economy. This hybrid business model involves designing, promoting, consuming, and delivering products that can regenerate the environment. In a university study[172] of optimizing the value of a sustainable business model in the expanding digital environment, they concluded, *"The use of large data sets for a broad approach to sustainability is revolutionizing the world's economy."*

The Shared Economy model (e.g., eBay, Craigslist, Airbnb) for Strategic Harmony is the new business model for fixing the broken world. It has these conditions:

» Personalized product or service—deliver to customers' needs that harmonize with sustainable outcomes;

» Asset sharing—match two latent populations–a network of people with certain unused assets and needs and another network of people who have resources which are underutilized;

» Collaborative ecosystem—implement a digital platform that serves as a catalytic mechanism to match these networks, accellerate engagement, and reduce risk.

Through a digital platform these enterprises match two populations to create win-win for both. Let us explore an application of this digital model to communicate the needs of the Circular Economy.

Connecting Group 1 and Group 2

On one side of the broken world, we have a latent unconnected population of change agents, community organizers, and social entrepreneurs wanting and committed to a circular economy and striving to drive change and fix social problems (we call them Group 1). Often, their efforts are siloed not collaborative. In fact, they compete for scarce funding and resources to fulfill their vision and approach to social change. As independent "Rising Voices," their power for global change is fragmented as they are without a major constituency and network to scale and fulfill their dreams.

It is a population of disconnected change-makers - people that have a passion and intention for change and want to utilize efforts for the common good but have few venues to connect with the resources needed to drive sustainable change. If they had abundant resources, we would not be in the situation we are facing! They are like the latent population of people needing rides and efficient ways to get from place A to B, or people looking for affordable homes away from home which are friendly and hospitable but can't access them!

The second population (we call them Group 2) is a latent network with unutilized resources (time, money, skills, and passion). For a variety of reasons (too busy, other priorities, not educated to necessity of circular thinking, etc.) these people have neither been stimulated, nor motivated to act. Neither have they been provided an easy, convenient, affordable, low risk "pathway" to commit themselves to actively participate in creating change and driving Strategic Harmony.

Group 2 is like Airbnb owners of spare rooms who want to use their assets to gain additional income. Both have not realized the venue to transform their assets into Transformative Power.

Group 2 has the resources and often a compatible mindset (strong values, commitment to equality, representative justice). Most people of all religions believe in the above tenets, but they do not exercise them because of politics or corruption. Group 2 includes successful businesspeople and professionals; impact investors; those marginalized like the people of color, LBGTQ+, women, and the NextGen (14-39 years old). Often, they are on the sidelines, do not vote, or "vote for lesser of two evils"; do not express their dissatisfaction with the corrupt systems and myths perpetuated because they feel hopeless and powerless. They have strong values but have not found their place in society and the venue to transform their power to generate Strategic Harmony.

In order to connect the two groups, we need a global digital platform (catalyst to drive Strategic Harmony) that serves as the intermediary, integrating a series of venues such as strategic alliances, complementary grassroots efforts, or inspiring content (e.g., this book). This platform (like Airbnb) will reduce the resistance and activation energy required to efficiently connect, augment, and scale these latent networks. We need a venue that makes it easy and convenient to connect and mobilize to Make a Difference!

On one hand, there is Group 1—those who have a Love of Purpose and commitment to sustainable, circular solutions and have worked to innovate but do not have the resources and network to effectively aggregate and direct their power to facilitate change and operationalize their vision. On the other hand, there is Group 2—investors, business angels, committed professionals, marginalized people, women, and NextGen with strong values but without an organized venue to express and act. As untapped masses, they have resources and can be motivated to generate the power of their voices, votes, and purchasing power. The missing ingredient are Catalyzers throughout a global digital network, able to stimulate those of apathy to come forth and act, to exercise the Power of their views, their money, their love of values, their votes, and the purpose in meaning of life.

This transformation from a latent to an active network is a new source of Transformative Power which will challenge and disrupt the Old Power institutions to force them to listen and respond to change or they will become irrelevant and bankrupt. Such a hybrid sustainable business model of Strategic Harmony will empower a new movement of Global Catalyzers to ignite sustainable change globally—the mission of *EmPower Us!*.

A Few Working Models

On our journey to formulate the concepts and experiences that emulate Strategic Harmony, we have worked with many dedicated people globally from Groups 1 and 2 who have launched and executed working models of Strategic Harmony. These collaborative models address the systemic challenges of our broken world in which leadership and learning are transformed at every level. Our common mission is to prepare emerging leaders, entrepreneurs, and executives for the transformation that is challenging businesses and organizations in all sectors.

In the rest of this Guidepost, we will focus on issues challenging our broken world and present catalytic working models focused on contributing solutions.

1. Transition to Stakeholder Capitalism

The world is in the grip of a massive disruption. As we all seek ways to cope, global leaders are struggling to adopt to a new economic model that reflects a sustainable, equitable, and stakeholder-centric model (Quadruple Bottom Line). The Deloitte Global Millennial Survey 2019[173] of 13,000+ Millennials across 42 countries has shown that the Next Generation supports such a transition; 46% strive to make a positive impact on their communities or society at large.

But a major gap exists between the desire of the Next Generation to move toward stakeholder capitalism and the required infrastructure, training, and network necessary to connect with the resources (talent, money, experts) to successfully transition. To address the network need, The World Economic Forum[174] announced at Davos 2020 the collaboration with Salesforce, Deloitte, and LinkedIn to launch UpLink, an open, global platform to unleash entrepreneurs to scale up bright ideas and enterprises to our world's toughest problems and impact the Sustainable Development Goals (SDGs). As a crowd-engagement platform, *"it will connect the next generation of change-makers and social entrepreneurs to networks of leaders with the resources, expertise, and experience to create an impact."*

For the most part, our NextGen is brought up in a traditional, old school capitalistic model based on self-interest and siloed thinking. To reinforce this mindset, our emerging entrepreneurs are trained in business schools or incubators which promote this profit-first model with little regard to expand the impact to include the community at large. This is antithetical to our Strategic Harmony model and the global direction toward a more inclusive, stakeholder capitalism. Our emerging entrepreneurs require a purpose-driven learning framework to provide this foundation.

Entrepreneurship Redefined

After getting my bachelor's degree in 2012 I had to make a career choice; join one of the established multinationals or start my own company. I still remember the shock and confusion on the faces of my friends and family when I told them I was going to start my own venture and become an entrepreneur. No one in my generation; none of my classmates, none of my friends and none of my family members, have done anything similar.

Today, it seems almost unbelievable that people didn't see what personal and professional growth comes out of an entrepreneurial experience like running a start-up. The best and brightest of our new generations are either running start-ups or joining them at a rate that we've never seen before. This is both an incredible opportunity for growth, but it's also one of the most challenging stress tests for our business ecosystem, education, and values. Powered by technology and exponential growth, all these young and hungry people are experiencing the ultimate rollercoaster where the business highs are higher, but the lows are lower. All of the vulnerabilities in our legal, educational systems and in the business community are exposed even faster and they impose even bigger and more serious social ramifications than ever before.

The solution lies in combining the agility, technology, and growth mindset that we see among startups but also the values, ethics, and decision-making principles that we see among older institutions and companies that have been around for hundreds of years. It's not about replacing the old with the new - but it's about emulating the best of both worlds to create something that is flexible and aggressive but also leverages the wisdom of more experienced organizations to create a more stable, durable, and prosperous system for generations to come.

Obviously this will be a very challenging attempt, since it includes combining two completely opposite management and leadership styles, but as F. Scott Fitzgerald says, the test of a first rate intelligence is the ability to hold two opposed ideas in the mind at the same time, and still retain the ability to function. That is what I hope we will do, and Strategic Harmony is exactly the type of a model we will need along the way.

Josipa Majić, CEO at ID Guardian

To address the gaps in capacity building, Legacy International (*legacyintl.org*), in collaboration with Catalyzer Lab (*catalyzerlab.com*), has launched the Global Transformation Corps (GTC) (*gtcorps.com*). GTC has developed a values-based, impact-driven, capacity-building platform to empower NextGen entrepreneurs to create projects that support the UN SDGs. It enables them to effectively realign our economic system from the short-term focus on profit optimization to values-driven equitable, sustainable outcomes. Its Purpose is to catalyze conscious NextGen entrepreneurs to generate more inclusive, equitable, and compassionate solutions to power fast-track sustainable trans-formation.

The aim of GTC is to redirect entrepreneurship to a stakeholder centric model. It offers emerging entrepreneurs globally the training and resources (Catalytic Mindset, human-centered management practices, social impact analytics, impact investment) to build and sustain transformative ventures that foster a trusting and enlightened world, nurturing Strategic Harmony. It transforms the entrepreneurs' goal from solely material success to a Quadruple Bottom Line (people, planet, profit, prosperity), fully aligned with the SDGs. The initiative focuses on driving large-scale change by creating a worldwide network of social entrepreneurs to collaborate with impact investors and purposeful experts to create practical, sustainable solutions to the world's most pressing problems.

GTC is born with one laser-focused intention—the necessity to empower and scale sustainable ventures globally in business and social sectors. Its four-module entrepreneurial capacity-building program propels NextGen entre-preneurs to collaborate on social solutions; use design thinking to build radical innovative business models; and gain the training and resources necessary to generate success for their startups and sustainable business initiatives.

It includes: Module 1. UNVEIL Your Entrepreneurial Potential (for begin-ners to outline a new venture); Module 2. Catalytic Leaders Lab (for emerging entrepreneurs to build a fundable business plan); Module 3. GTC Accelerator (for startups to gain funding and execute their prototype); and Module 4. Scale Up to Drive Impact (for proven ventures to expand and support social impact goals).

GTC's deliverables are:

1. Mobilize values-based, emerging leaders giving them the skillset and support necessary to build resilient, circular businesses and social impact ventures; they emerge as Catalyzers.
2. Connect these Catalyzers via global networks with impact inves-tors, expert coaches, and social pioneers that want to impact their local communities.
3. Incorporate Sustainable Impact Indicators (SIIs- social, economic, environmental, and community metrics) to evaluate the impact of the ventures based on the TEST Values.
4. Certify participants completing Module One and Two.

5.   Augment funding for Module Three social impact startups with GTC values-based, impact-driven coaching.

6.   Scale incubated ventures (Module Four).

GTC's anticipated impacts:

1.   Provide HOPE! Invest in emerging leaders as a catalytic force for regeneration.

2.   Reduce the failure rate of startups from 90% to 60%.

3.   Reimagine "corporate capitalism" as a more equitable and sustainable economic system, responsive to the demands of our crises-driven planet.

4.   Move away from the "dependence" on international aid toward collaborative funding from public/private sources within the context of sustainable enterprise development.

5.   Circumvent the inefficiencies rampant in existing governmental and philanthropic funding.

6.   Facilitate continuous social innovation to fuel sustainable economic models.

7.   Support young entrepreneurs with an alternative to old school thinking by coaching their innovations and dreams.

8.   Help build the world of Strategic Harmony.

2. Roadmap for Strategic Harmony

In the contemporary world of chaos and uncertainty, the business community is searching to determine the New Normal, a comfortable, low-risk state of incremental change. Instead, there is an imperative that business and organizations strive to define as a dynamic, exponential approach to *EmPower Us!* on the path to Strategic Harmony.

In response, *Catalyzer Lab* (*catalyzerlab.com*) designed Strategic Harmony, bridging the internal force of Love (Harmony) with the external force of Power (Strategy) to transform organizations' business models and social impact. It turns a crisis 180° from an enemy to an opportunity; from corporate chaos to catalytic transformation; and from disruption to a strategic direction.

Catalyzer Lab provides an organizational reinvent using the ABCD's of Transformation to address the enterprise's challenges to become a sustainable business. Its values-driven, blended learning platform prepares executives, entrepreneurs, and emerging leaders for disruption and uncertainty—aligning purpose with mindsets, uncovering stakeholder-centric strategies, and propelling collaborative action. It guides your team to direct scarce resources to sustainable impact.

Strategic Harmony is ongoing transformation—reinventing how we transform internally (as an individual and organization) and how to translate that change externally (through business models, offerings, and impact). The aggregation of how each of us and our organization's share value(s) in responding to a crisis (e.g., climate threat, pandemic, exponential technology) will determine the state of New Harmony.

Below is a snapshot of the six interactive units of the Catalyzer Master Lab presented in Figure 13.1. It is designed for leaders to respond to the uncertainty of a crisis. The immersion in this blended learning platform guides the transformation of the self (leader), the organization (culture), business model (value), and impact (sustainable performance).

Catalyzer Master Lab
Building Strategic Harmony

INTERNAL HARMONY			EXTERNAL STRATEGY		
Transformative Love	Intent	Process, Methods	Transformative Power	Intent	Process, Methods
1. Reinvent INDIVIDUAL Intention Quantum thinking Self-Reflection Self-Identity	Inspire Leaders	*Unlearn habits, Learn to Learn. Apply* ······· Self-assessment Human potential assessment Boundaries Building	**4. Reinvent BUSINESS MODEL** Circular Thinking "Liquid People" Segmentation Catalytic Mindset Brand Pivot Stakeholder Centric Social Impact	Transform Value	*Holistic, authentic, framework* ······· Bus Model Assessment Transformative Why Value Proposition Brand Blueprint Life Centered Design Rapid Prototyping
2. Reconstruct ORGANIZATION Intention Values Collaboration Empowerment	Align Team Culture	*Build Cultural Harmony* ······· TEST Values Purpose Anchor Mindset Change	**5. Reconstruct OPERATIONS** Cross Boundary Management Strategy-Culture Alignment Cross Functional Transformation Trust Networks Supply Chain Agility Quadruple Bottom Line	Create Value	*Trusted, resilient capacity* ······· Trust Diagnostics Talent Driven Impact Inclusive Design Stakeholders Analysis LIGHT Impacts
3. Redesign FUTURE DIRECTION Organization Policy Stakeholder Capitalism Circular Economy Risk Management	Inspire Direction	*Generate Harmony* ······· Future Mind Map Risk Survey Sustainability Plan Gap Analysis Scenario Planning	**6. Reinvent SCALE IMPACT** Reputation Engagement Disruption Strategy Digital Accelerator Strategic Partnerships All driven Networks	Impact Value	*Strategic uncertainty, Scale Social Impact* ······· Agile Strategic Plan Advocacy Strategy Leveraging the Edge Exponential Trend Strategy

Figure 13.1 Catalyzer Master Lab

The Master Lab is a two-stage process. Stage 1 develops the internal harmony of the leadership and their team based on Love of Purpose and Values. Stage 2 translates this transformation into external (harmonious) strategies based on the Power of human-centered business practices. Its six units apply methodologies to reinvent and reimage the "leader" and organization including:

» Reinvent Individual–inspires leaders to open themselves up to new possibilities through self-reflection and self-identity. It drives them to challenge their biases and assumptions, breakdown boundaries and siloes, and unlearn their practices that cause disharmony and inhibit innovation in the organization.

» Reconstruct Organization–aligns the team to build cultural harmony within the organization. It clarifies their values and empowers their Purpose to foster a Catalytic Mindset and trusting environment necessary to fuel transformation initiatives.

» Redesign Future Direction–inspires and propels the direction of the organization toward harmonious, yet exponential outcomes. It analyzes emerging and disruptive trends in the context of an interconnected circular economy. It incorporates risk and scenario planning, as well as, gap analysis to reduce uncertainty and generate sustainable outcomes.

» Reinvent Business Model–transforms the organization's Purpose into shared value for all stakeholders. The business model, anchored in an interconnected, Catalytic Mindset, is stakeholder-centric. The Lab provides a holistic framework to generate a life-centered design for an authentic brand, product, or service, and impact business model canvas.

» Reconstruct Operations–translates the business model into operations that create value. It incorporates a cross-boundary management structure which aligns strategy with organizational culture. It builds Trust and authenticity across stakeholders' networks facilitating effective work across functions and generations. It encourages new talent to drive design and innovation fueling social impact and a Quadruple Bottom Line.

» Redesign Scale Impact–addresses the strategic uncertainty of the marketplace to scale social impact. It develops Trust strategies to leverage exponential trends that assess and generate sustainable impact. The scaling strategy builds reputation through advocacy, digital acceleration, and artificial intelligence driven networks.

Each unit is a mini lab that builds upon one another empowering the team to translate its values and Purpose into a transformative business model and the operations to execute and scale.

Catalyzer Lab is a vehicle for gaining the mindset and skills necessary to catalyze and sustain our institutions.

3. Network of Change-oriented leaders, Catalyzers

For the world to be fixed, we need a critical mass of Catalyzers in all segments of our life – politics, business, culture, religion, education, sport. We need ambassadors of Strategic Harmony.

To have real impact, such Catalyzers must be networked. It is not just to provide leaders and change agents to move in the right circles, to socialize with important people, and to have connections in the right places. It is not just to be well informed and to communicate with the most successful among colleagues. Such networking must be intended to provide a critical mass for transformation.

It is of great importance to regularly meet authorities like consultants or professors who are in touch with theory and research. It is vital to systematically contact people in government positions close to your line of work, as well as your suppliers and customers in order to learn what problems they face. But it is even better when all the people you network with are committed to fixing the broken world and leading it to Strategic Harmony.

Such networking also enables you to spend time with the best inputs, and it puts you on the edge. It enables you to deal with tough challenges; it sets your goals high, creates opportunities, and provides you with valuable information and encouraging experiences. Also, it sharpens your instincts. Our book is an example and an outcome of such networking, because it is a product of more than 40 highly competent Catalyzers, spread across the globe, all on their respective paths to Strategic Harmony.

The network in question, aimed at helping reinvent is named ELITE (Excellence in Leadership, Innovation, and Technology) (*velimir1.wixsite.com/elite*). It is an international network of Catalytic Leaders, established to *empower* a growing meeting point of recognized leaders in science, education, business, politics, and consulting interested in fostering sustainable and harmonious innovation and change.

ELITE[175] is intended to become a global network of change-oriented leaders, catalysts of the Strategic Harmony who want to make the world a better place.

It's mission is to lead the preparation and transformation of leaders to generate innovative and social impact solutions in business and government. Members of ELITE are on the mission to help individuals and organizations on their journey to values-driven, sustainable development.

The network was established in November 2016. Its founders are Croatian members of the European Academy of Arts and Sciences with international partners from politics, consulting, business, and academia.

4. Social Impact Analysis—*Trust-Love-Care Index*

To address the global call for a consistent approach to measuring and assessing social impact, the World Economic Forum developed a collaborative, consultative approach, *Toward Common Metrics and Consistent Reporting of Sustainable Value Creation*[176], stating

"A company is more than an economic unit generating wealth. It fulfills human and societal aspirations as part of the broader social system. Performance must be measured not only on the return to shareholders, but also on how it achieves its environmental, social, and good governance objectives."

The SDGs are increasingly seen by investors as a framework for assessing the environmental and social impact of their responsible investment approaches. However, impact investors agree that the traditional financial tools and investment structures are restricting innovation and sustainable investment. Tools and methodologies are being developed to allow investors to determine the capacity of the companies analyzed to contribute to the 2030 SDG Agenda. But none of these methods are able to offer an exhaustive view of products and operations, contribution and obstruction, varying levels of commitment and impact—with robust indicators.

The missing link is to approach the challenge through the lens of intention and the TEST Values. The best way to deliver impact is to make it intentional, declare it, steer all resources towards it, constantly track it and make reports transparent and accountable to your values. Organizations must deliver the efforts commensurate to their stated intentions. This approach guarantees integrity, truth, loyalty; therefore, it deserves trust.

In this context the *SDG Transformation Accelerator Index* (STrAX) (Figure 13.2) was developed to revolutionize the space of social impact measurement. It focuses on intent and purpose, building a strong bridge and link between intent and impact while incorporating the intention and methodologies of Strategic Harmony and suggesting a values-based model to integrate its three indices: *Trust - Love - Care.*

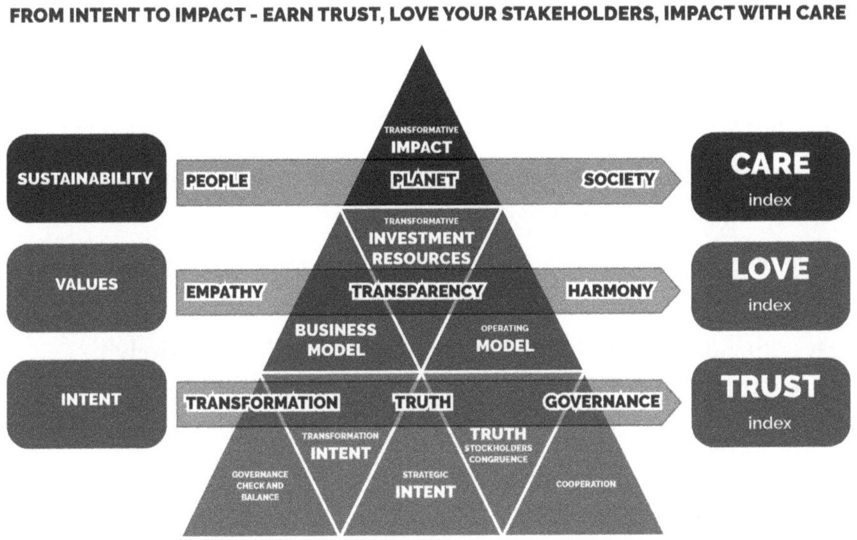

FROM INTENT TO IMPACT - EARN TRUST, LOVE YOUR STAKEHOLDERS, IMPACT WITH CARE

Figure 13.2 Trust-Love-Care Index

Designed by Aissa Azzouzi[177], (*thinkcatalytic.com/social-impact-analysis-809acdcc45cb*) STrAX incorporated the concepts of Strategic Harmony in designing the three indices to benchmark organizations, monitor progress and momentum, and identify associated risks. The framework and model begins by assessing the leadership intent. Leadership intent is fundamental to drive the necessary Strategic Transformation for all stakeholders. The level of authenticity or truth in the intention to deliver the SDG agenda drives the level of Trust the stakeholders can have in the leadership.

TRUST INDEX

Most companies mention the SDGs as part of their goals, yet they are rarely mentioned by the leadership. The CEOs lack the intent to incorporate SDGs in their impact strategy (which incidentally is rarely formulated). STrAX addresses this discrepancy by requiring every company that claims to be compliant with the current norms and standards (CSR, ESG, SDG) to publish a Leadership Intent Statement. This explains the transformation the company intends to perform through its strategy and operations, business model, stakeholder relationships, and external impact of its operations on people, the planet, and communities. The congruency between this statement and how the intention manifests positively influences the TRUST Index.

This index addresses leadership intent through a series of questions. If the answers to the following questions are positive, this would result in a high rating for the TRUST Index.

Does your leadership intend to contribute to the 2030 SDG Agenda by:

- » demonstrating that its purpose is to radically transform itself and/or its strategy to meet the Agenda?
- » providing evidence of integrity in its behavior to radically contribute to the Agenda?
- » taking full responsibility and accept accountability to actively contribute to the Agenda?

LOVE INDEX

The level of intention and implementation of core values (e.g., empathy) with the impacted stakeholders will influence the LOVE Index.

Does your Business Model manifest and demonstrate…

- » *Empathy* in considering and taking care of all the directly or indirectly impacted stakeholders (being stakeholder-centric)?
- » *Transparency* across all the directly or indirectly impacted stakeholders in considering all the externalities?
- » *Inclusivity and Equality* across all the directly or indirectly involved and/ or impacted stakeholders?

If your Business Model is stakeholder-centric and SDG friendly, then it qualifies for a high rating for LOVE Index.

CARE INDEX

If the aim of your strategy is to align your intent to your business and operating model, this will result in your impact being directly connected to your intent. The focus will reside in measuring the degree of impact your strategy has achieved rather than trying to identify what the actual impact of your strategy is. Here are selected questions that determine the CARE Index:

» Does the impact this strategy delivers align with the SDGs?

» Does your strategy harm the planet or any of your stakeholders?

» Is your strategy sustainable (e.g., produces externalities that are positive or negative to any constituency), or does it alienate any constituency (e.g., transforms into negative forces amongst the ecosystem)?

» Does your strategy have a net positive impact in terms of livability and quality of life for these constituencies: the planet, peoples' lives, society?

» Does your strategy, plan, operation, business model, enterprise risk management, investments, and multiple capitals produce a *Net Impact* that

   » Cares for the environment and is planet-friendly?

   » Cares for the overall well-being of individuals and is people-friendly?

   » Generates a transformative *Net Impact* that benefits society in general and is society-friendly?

If the answers to these questions are positive, this will result in a high rating for the CARE Index.

5. Transforming Enterprise Leaders into Catalyzers

Humanity, Inc (*www.soulbranding.com/humanity-inc*) is the boutique advisory firm that has been innovating in the practice of Strategic Harmony for decades. It guides pioneering businesses to align their operations with their particular sweet spot of profitable social impact. Love, integrity, impact are the driving values of Humanity, Inc. Its signature service is The SoulBranding™ System, an enterprise process of rigorously aligning corporate behaviors with human values, profitably. Its work is transforming enterprise leaders into Catalyzers for whole-system wellbeing by:

1. Fostering their personal congruence with holistic wellbeing in body, mind, spirit
2. Building enterprise ability to self-organize and innovate for systemic wellbeing
3. Infusing the critical business practices and policies with System Gaze

4. Sharing insights into emergent trends in the outer ecosystems
5. Ongoing counsel around mission-critical milestones, collaborations, and Board and investor engagement

---

CONGRUENCE

Business as usual is a clear and present existential threat.

Now is our second chance at the Pivot that matters. Twenty years of "sustainable branding" veiled the endemic inequity and predation that have finally rotted through the social fabric and spun Nature off course, too. Now it's time to turn to each other, to discover and generate the outcomes that matter to each's wellbeing. Let's not again swap one veneer of share-owner capitalism for another, ready palliative. Now is the chance to make the difference that matters — to invent a shared destiny of wellbeing for all, in communion with the whole living system.

Pioneering organizations foresaw this over the past few decades. And they got ahead of the 'selective sustainability' curve that devoured so much resource and goodwill. These companies are the profitable front-runners in today's migration to what's called stakeholder capitalism, and other labels that suggest a focus on systemic wellbeing.

It's useful to have those examples handy especially today. Now's the time to rise into the new model, when the appetite for meaning and the necessity to restore equilibrium in economic and natural systems is widely characterized as urgent.

Perhaps our collective will for substantive, systemic change finally is tipping into critical mass. Certainly now, our felt sense of humanity and shared fate is activated. But we have yet to upscale relational- and system-collaboration skills and to allocate the resources at scale to be effective.

Two watchwords might be useful for the leader on this transition path now: A Felt Sense of Humanity, and Congruence.

First, motivation matters: prepare to manage your internal state. You may notice the pull of habit, implicit biases, the tug of your legacy expertise, and old identity rising to soothe uncertainty and fear and divert your path. We can count on such very human resistance to change.

But we have each other as champions as we move ahead together. And in our own souls sits the wisdom of all peoples to keep us from turning back from our human family: The Golden Rule, treat others as you would want to be treated.

Alive with this intrinsic motivation to support the wellbeing of humanity, the leader will intentionally manage the congruence of their own behavior.

Second, that's when the leader empowers others' congruence with supportive tools, skills, and above all, systems. One of the essential systems to create right now is Brand Congruence/Corporate Governance: to reconstitute the trustworthiness of what a company's brand 'says' and the impact of what the corporation actually does behind the scenes. In another fraught period the master of system change, W. Edwards Deming made it clear why: 'A bad system will beat a good [person] every time'."

Elsie Maio CEO, Humanity, Inc, The SoulBranding Institute

6. Global Communications Transformation Platform

MAD Talks *(madtalks.com, xponentialtalks.com)* is a global communications platform that fuels transformation through business storytelling and people who are making a difference. MAD Platform is closely associated with the vision, the purpose, and the values of Strategic Harmony; it is dedicated to telling transformation stories. The stories fit into one or more categories: events, failures, leaders, learning, and media. A special story channel is dedicated to MAD Fintech presenting living examples associated with the newest tsunami of digital change in the global environment, the role of cryptocurrencies and blockchain in the financial world.

Obviously, the core purpose and mission of MAD Talks is to *Make A Difference.* They claim to be MAD in everything they do, in business and in life, and they are proud to serve humanity. Such an approach is called "Massive Transformative Purpose" (MTP). The ambitious MAD vision is to reach and empower a billion people through the MAD Channels and Talks platform. They are doing it through the transformative power of digital and the "intelligence" revolution. Also, they are doing it through projecting everything into the future, while engaging with today's issues. Their goal is to support and promote genuine innovation, empowering the youth & entrepreneurial thinking.

MAD Talks has branded channels to generate greater reach. These channels are franchisable and can grow internationally quite seamlessly and scale with ease.

MAD Talks has created a separate entity, Xponential, which is focused only on the future: the transformation, mindset, toolsets, and fundamental metamorphosis of both the individuals and companies. Xponential, has adopted the ExO model (Exponential Organizations leverage exponential technologies to shift the global business mindset and transform corporations.). Xponential has created an X-Academy, X-Talks and X-World community to engage with the future and its exponential dynamics. This empowers the MAD platform.

This platform was founded by Tariq Qureishy, a visionary Dubai-based businessman, who launched a social enterprise to revolutionize philanthropy and change some habits for the way people donate money to charity by making it very simple, transparent, and seeing the contribution reaching the beneficiary. The initial idea was to raise US$1 billion in micro-donations (the price of a cup of coffee), through the storytelling platform, events, and content, turbocharged by the podcast revolution, and always giving the full 100% to charity through a social venture 100% MAD. The administration costs are absorbed by the commercial arm, thus keeping the donations untouched and pure. Many new payment methods are making this dream much more viable now as the NextGen are quite focused on Making A Difference.

Focusing on the future, innovation, entrepreneurship, and youth, the MAD Platform provides a mirror to the values and models presented throughout this book, from TEST to L.I.G.H.T., and they prove to be fueled by Transformational Power and Love.

The growing number of such networks, initiatives, and actions is a burning sign that the time has come for Strategic Harmony. The new mindset opens a path to a new business and political ecosystem built on cooperation, collaboration, and alliances.

Strategic Alliances: Cooperate or Perish!

We all grew up with the Social Darwinian idea that "survival of the fittest" determined success. Few of us ever questioned what "fittest" really meant. After all, Darwin examined the animal world and demonstrated that this dictum was true. Or was it? Must it follow that human social systems obey the same rules as the animal world? Must the strongest and most aggressive always win? Suppose for a moment that human beings dominated the rest of life on Earth, not because they were the strongest BUT because they were the best at cooperating to reach their objectives.

Unfortunately for most of the 20th century, in male-dominated business schools and economic institutions, the opposite idea took hold. Namely, as Darwin suggested, competition was the key to economic and social success – "the strongest win and winner takes all."

In the 20th and 21st centuries, women entered the traditional male bastions of economics and business. They introduced new business strategies into our hyper-connected world. As more women began moving into positions of power, they started touting cooperative strategies as superior to the older simplistic, competitive models. They showed us that, in the long run, cooperative teams often unleash much greater innovation than competitive teams.

Today, the search for continuous innovation has become the holy grail of most successful global businesses. Across the business spectrum, "strategic alliances" are in and the old "dog eat dog" mentality is being shown the exit. From 1990 to 2018, strategic alliances went from accounting for just 5% of the total revenue of the Global 1000 companies to nearly 40%.

It has also become clear that you cannot successfully manage strategic alliances by the old hierarchical rules. Instead, you must employ a values-driven strategy of "mutual trust," "shared risks and rewards," and "mutual respect" to resolve differences and achieve synergy. While not easy, cooperation leads to a "triple win" for their businesses, customers, and the world at large. The new mantra is "Cooperation as the new Competitive Advantage".

In this era of predatory capitalism and rampant global warming, humanity has come to a major survival decision point. The reality today is that humans have a stark and simple choice to make, "Cooperate or Perish." What are we going to choose?

Stephen L. Gomes, Ph.D.

KINS Innovation Networks

KINS Innovation Networks are self-organizing networks of well connected, high-integrity leaders in widely diverse fields who are invited to come together to achieve inspiring innovations and critical transformations while enjoying their kindred spirits. These collaborative networks are synergistic leveraging existing 'conscious sustainable' initiatives with powerful new ventures. They manifest innovations faster and less expensive and expand resource base, with higher impact and more fun.

The KINS Innovation method was first developed in 1979 by the Chicago Network, whose members were top women leaders in each of 100 different fields. It was so successful that we replicated this collaboration method based on extremely diverse groups. It's been evolved through 30 sequential networks over 40 years. Each network has improved taking advantage of global advances in both technology and consciousness. The method has proven success in social enterprises across all sectors: social venture capital, socially-responsible business, women's leadership, solar, organics, local living economies, microenterprise, and local-foreign collaboration.

There were two secrets to the success of KINS networks. First, we used 'search firm' practices to find influential and visionary people who were drawn to a path of service rather than a career path of glory. Second, network members delved into the unknown, including their personal spiritual practice, for breakthroughs and uncovering new possibilities.

Take a look at the criteria our 'search' uses to choose members:

» *Have high credibility in their field*

» *Give back the most in their field*

» *Have a reputation for integrity*

» *Have advanced collaboration skills*

> *» Have a heartfelt spiritual practice and believe that "we are all united as one"*

> *» Are passionate about the network's mission*

Our strategy is generosity. A deal is only good if it pleases all concerned, especially the Earth. Everyone does what we love to do and do well, without charge... and little else. We sit at the table of unknown solutions and invite support from members to co-create innovations; discover expert and financial resources; and drive mutually advantageous solutions for the highest good for all concerned. Everyone gets equal time to discuss their reflections. All information is open and transparent, available to all members, all the time.

The members quickly become deeply engaged realizing that experts have done the research to "gift each one" with solutions which harmonize with the member's needs. With consciousness now rising measurably on Earth, it seems time for this tested innovation method to go mainstream and support those on the path to Strategic Harmony.

Susan Davis, Founder KINS Innovative Network

Of course, we are going to choose cooperation. In order to build the model of Strategic Harmony, we require businesses, organizations, and governmental agencies to collaborate based on the TEST Values.

More examples and cases

We have presented selected models that are striving to build a more equitable and harmonious society. We are still living in World 4.0, also called the Information Age, which is a manifestation of exponentially emerging technologies and a changing narrative in our business-political ecosystem. COVID-19 has confronted our institutions and businesses with the reality that a New Harmony is a necessity, transforming mindsets among our leaders, and an integration of values and purpose among the stakeholders of organizations as they enter World 5.0, the Smart Age. This is the path to Strategic Harmony.

We can learn much from the pandemic, and many articles have been written on the topic.[178] Many people argue that COVID-19 will reverse globalization and urbanization trends[179], increasing the distance between countries and between people. The crises will force Us to face the prevailing lifestyle choices, consumption of goods and services, and common definitions of prosperity.

Pandemics reveal several important things that we must consider on the path to Strategic Harmony. Firstly, we are all interconnected, for better or worse, and there is no practical way to cut communities and nations off from the rest of the world. At the same time, the seamless globalization of trade has left countries vulnerable to supply chain disruptions. Also, in a pandemic, nation-states turn out to be indispensable actors in coordinating a response. The wildly varied success rates in taming the pandemic in different countries provide stark evidence that competent governments are still essential to the well-being of their people. Finally, sub-national responses by cities and states also vary in their effectiveness.

Completing the discussion on emerging models of institutions on the path to Strategic Harmony, we share a few nation states models to generate global transformation. The trajectory and direction of these initiatives have been significantly altered with the onset of COVID-19. In addition to the post-ponement of in-person global events due to the pandemic and downturn of the global economy, there has been a refocus on local initiatives:

» Dubai is targeting to become Gateway to Global Trade, the innovation and technology hub. It is hosting Expo 2020 which Dubai postponed to 2021 gearing up to help shape a post-pandemic world and create a better future. The World Expo[180] will focus on a *"collective desire for new thinking to identify solutions to some of the greatest challenges of our time."*

» The Japanese government is expecting to host Expo 2025 Osaka to showcase a model of Society 5.0.[181]

» China unveiled in 2013, the Belt and Road Initiative (BRI)[182], aimed at building the modern "New Silk Road." This effort was to finance nearly half a trillion dollars in new infrastructure across Asia, Africa, Europe, and Latin America. Its objective was to connect China by land and sea to Southeast Asia, Pakistan, Central Asia, and beyond to the Middle East, Europe, and Africa. " It was considered the largest project of the century — building a network of railroads and shipping lanes linking 70 countries.

With the impact of COVID -19 on global economic stability, BRI[183] has been suspended with many countries unable to fulfill their loan obligations to China. Last year, President Xi unveiled a more modest vision of the Belt and Road, one with higher standards of economic sustainability, transparency, and environmental protection.

The newest 2019 World Economic Forum's[184] project, Globalization 4.0, is addressing the competing narratives facing our globe. WEF is striving to use the spirit of Davos to build the future in a constructive, collaborative way—the path to Strategic Harmony.

As stressed in its document, *"We are shifting from a world order based on common values to a 'multi-conceptual' world shaped by competing narratives seeking to create a new global architecture. We live in a world with new planetary boundaries for its development."*

Globalization 4.0 plans to offer a new narrative to replace the abusive, extractive, and sexist neoliberalism of the past few decades. Our broken world needs far more cooperation among governments to rewrite the rules of finance, trade, wages, and taxation. Only then can we ensure that the Fourth Industrial Revolution (4IR) benefits ordinary people.

Maybe the most interesting of such national and global activities is Society 5.0[185], Japan's effort to reinvent society based on Strategic Harmony. The core idea is that economic growth driven by new technologies cannot be allowed to take place in a vacuum, but must be accompanied by sustaining the needs of all stakeholders and ensuring the equitable distribution of the benefits. In this regard, Japan plans to lead the way with its concept of Society 5.0. It puts people and society — and not industry per se as the focus of necessary and unstoppable technological change.

There is an old saying that teachers can change lives with just a right mix of chalk and challenges. There should be a new saying that *Catalyzers can change lives with just a right mix of values and technology, assisted by institutions dedicated to support the process.*

The cases, individuals, social enterprises, organizations, and national strategies presented in this book are still a small tip of a growing Strategic Harmony narrative. It is not a representative sample; it is just a reflection of author's views, knowledge, activities, and personal experiences. Join us or build your own catalysts of change.

The broken world needs to be *Reinvented*, which is the intention of *EmPower Us!*. The future belongs to the Catalyzers who believe in the Power of Us to full-fill their dreams and transformative strategies, but also in the power of their actions!

Guidepost 14

New Emergence

New Harmony

"Every new beginning comes from some other beginning's end."

Seneca

Since the financial crisis of 2007-2008, the New Normal has become a common phrase for the outcome of something that most people don't really like but are forced to accept. In politics, it was most often associated with the Donald Trump era. In our current environment, it has been mostly the COVID-19 pandemic. The cynics would comment on the situation by saying that, in both cases, the weird is good, and the normal is overrated. Others would say that the New Normal is a misnomer, because the Old Normal did not work. Rather, the Old Normal created the climate crisis, the inequities between peoples, mass immigration, ineffective response to the COVID-19, intense racial tensions (exacerbated by the death of George Floyd at the hands of police), and an outdated and greed-oriented capitalistic system.

We see all these issues as opportunities through the lens of transformation. They are triggers that fuel the transition from the New Normal to New Harmony, or as Confucius once noted *"open-mindedness and a balance of firmness and gentleness...a proper equilibrium."* This driving force for equilibrium is the path to Strategic Harmony.

As our world faces a turning point, we need to visualize our New Harmony, the emergence of new beginnings, and to work to bring our planet from a state of "Darkness into Light." If we don't have a dream, we are unable to make it come true. The last time the whole world was dreaming, it was in the counter-cultural 1960s, when all possibilities seemed open and inviting. But only now are we about reinventing our institutions to realize some of these fantasies. It is our responsibility to respond to the urgency and to fuel sustainable solutions.

EmPower Us! provides Guideposts for each of us to actively participate in moving our planet from ongoing crises to Strategic Harmony. It's a roadmap for realizing the needs of our broken world, navigating and reinventing solutions to restructure our planet. *Now everyone who accepts this roadmap has a responsibility for acting to make a difference.*

Rising Voices for Transformation

In the last few years transformation is continuing to reverberate globally, bringing on a rediscovering of values and new directions. These impacts are more than just talk and protests; they're Rising Voices generating real changes. Here are just a few resilient signs of the New Transformational Order of values driving change. Strategic Harmony is beginning to evolve across sectors:

Socio-economic Policy

» In 2020 Luxembourg became the first country in the world to make all public transport in the country (buses, trams, and trains) free for all passengers.

» J.P. Morgan Chase CEO, Jamie Dimon, urged business and government to use the coronavirus as an opportunity to create a fairer economy: *"This crisis must serve as a wake-up call and a call to action for business and government to think, act, and invest for the common good and confront the structural obstacles that have inhibited inclusive economic growth for years."*

» American politician and philanthropist, Andrew Yang, advocates the Freedom Dividend, a rebranded universal basic income of $1,000 a month to every American over 18. *"When we put the money into our hands,"* he said, *"we can build a trickle-up economy from our people, our families, and our communities up."* Several other nations are also considering versions of a universal basic income.

Citizen Action

» The Yellow Vest movement keeps on organizing a series of protests in Paris and other parts of France against insensitive government and economic injustice.

» The Parkland, Florida, USA school shooting marked the active response of Generation Z students and the rise of the #NeverAgain movement. It organized nation school walkouts and *March for Our*

Lives protests in Washington, D.C. drawing 800,000 people, and galvanized gun-control supporters. The result was that U.S. States, including 14 with Republican governors, enacted 50 new laws restricting access to guns.

» Such movements have accelerated the U.S. voter registration drive for those 18 years and over. The Center for Information and Research on Civic Learning and Engagement at Tufts University reported that the voter turnout among 18 to 29-years-olds in the U.S. 2018 mid-term elections was 31%, a 10 point increase from 2014's mid-term elections. In the 2020 election, the turnout is at record levels.

» The #MeToo Movement surfaced to address the sexual abuse of women by men in power. Its impact has increased the role, equity, and participation of women on a global basis. This movement reflects Transformative Love and the redefining of Transformative Power. They are egalitarian and earned, rising from the ground up instead of the top down. In elections globally, there are a record number of women running for office.

» Joe Biden was elected the 46th U.S. President declaring that America was in a "Battle for the Soul of the Nation." His platform and statements reflect values-based themes common to Strategic Harmony:
"Be an ally of the light, not the darkness"
"Treating people with dignity and respect should be the baseline for how we act to one another"
"Everyone is your equal, and everyone is equal to you"
"You always put yourself in the other person's position, and then also to understand where they're coming from"
"Failure is at times inevitable but giving up is unforgivable"
"You've got to find purpose"
"Target resources in a way that is consistent with prioritization of environmental and climate justice"

Values-driven Business

» Based on the *Report on U.S. Sustainable, Responsible and Impact Investing Trends*[186], one in four dollars of invested assets is invested sustainably. With $12 trillion now invested in the United States, sustainable investing is not just a trend; it's becoming part of the fabric of investing.

» According to the Edelman Trust Barometer, 76% of people believe that the best answer to climate change are purposeful corporations and the leading role of their CEOs. More than 400 of the world's biggest companies have already committed to align their strategies with the ambition of the Paris Agreement through the Science-Based Targets initiative aimed at reducing GHG (greenhouse gases).

» A senior GOOGLE research scientist has quit the company in protest over its plan to launch a censored version of its search engine in China. He felt it was his ethical responsibility to resign in protest of the forfeiture of our public human rights commitments as Google's actions are crossing their ethical red lines.

» The *"Inspiring Purpose-Led Growth"* report[187] notes Purposeful Brands have experienced a brand valuation increase of 175% over the past 12 years, compared to the median growth rate of 86% and the 70% growth rate for brands with a low sense of purpose.

» As an outcome of COVID-19, Brian Chesky, CEO of Airbnb, was forced to fire 25% of his workforce, he shared his purpose and struggle in an open letter: *"Our mission is not merely about travel. When we started Airbnb, our original tagline was, "Travel like a human"...The human part was always more important than the travel part. What we are about is belonging, and at the center of belonging is love."*

As we were writing this conclusion, two global crises erupted advancing transformation—the COVID-19 and the Protests for Racial Justice. The Rising Voices described in Guidepost 6 were protesting for 60+ days the police murder of George Floyd and other people of color. A growing wave of young activists were organizing protests across the U.S. In San Francisco a 17-year-old's efforts drew more than 10,000 people, while four 14 to 16 year old girls in Nashville, Tennessee USA organized a Black Lives Matter protest that drew 10,000 people.

For centuries, people of color have suffered racial injustice, police brutality, and social inequities with minimal change. The same issues provoked sister demonstrations across 20 countries (Europe, Asia, Australia, Latin America) calling out for transformative change of systemic inequities and racial discrimination.

This is a further example of the broken world and the Rising Voices opening the window of hope. Hundreds of thousands of people across generations and ethnicities responded, running to the streets to support that hope for transformation.

The second marker was *Edelman Global Trust Study*[188] in 12 markets on the role brands are expected to play during COVID-19. The pandemic catalyzed a powerful response across the global citizenry demanding business to be more actively responsible.

» *"71% agree that if they perceive that a brand is putting profit over people, they will lose trust in that brand forever."*

» *"65% said that a brand's response in the crisis will have a huge impact on their likelihood of purchasing it in the future."*

» *"60% said that they are turning to brands that they absolutely can trust."*

» *"One-third of respondents have already convinced other people to stop using a brand that was not responding well during the pandemic."*

We are enthusiastic about the momentum toward transformation. But this passion and Love of Purpose must be met with a clear plan and strategies to pierce the old abusive power and generate sustainable transformation.

The above responses helped us to reinforce the following takeaways:

1. The world is in a deep state of trouble and desperately needs inspiring models to regenerate and transition.
2. Strategic Transformation begins with leaders focused on purpose and targeting values.
3. Trust is the currency of transformation and the foundation of authentic relationships necessary to fix our planet.
4. Rising Voices are engaged, entrepreneurial, and acting out their values.
5. Building collaboration between generations is necessary to address our global problems.
6. Leaders must transform to become Catalyzers of transformation.
7. Business leaders must be held accountable on their proclamations to realize stakeholder capitalism.
8. Transformation is accelerated by reducing resistance rather than pushing a message.
9. Seeing change through the "eyes of a network" scales all efforts.
10. Strategic Harmony is achieved by augmenting Love and Power as transformative forces.

The chosen examples and the suggested takeaways may serve as scalpels used to cut into our "normal" mind, as hammers used to shatter our fixed thinking, or as Rubik's Cubes of ideas for our mind to unravel. Basically, the purpose that fueled our journey to write this book is discovering and applying Strategic Harmony. *EmPower Us!* is the roadmap for transformation. *We repeat—now everyone who accepts this roadmap has a responsibility for acting to make a difference.*

In 1971, a young man dreamed of peace and a new way of doing things. He asked us in a well-loved song to Imagine a world of Harmony, Love, and Oneness.

John Lennon did not live to see his dreams come true, but his son Julian in his own songs of peace and transformational change, such as "Someday," shows us that the time is ripe now. The global crisis is a catalyst for our unprecedented opportunity, our road to activate this imaginary world into a real world. Are we going to dare travel there?

In searching for answers, we offer a concluding story from ancient mystics.

A man was traveling through the desert, hungry, thirsty, and tired, when he came upon a tree bearing luscious fruit and affording plenty of shade, underneath which ran a spring of water. He ate of the fruit, drank of the water, and rested beneath the shade.

When he was about to leave, he turned to the tree and said: "Tree, O tree, with what should I bless you?"

"Should I bless you that your fruit be sweet? Your fruit is already sweet."

"Should I bless you that your shade be plentiful? Your shade is plentiful. That a spring of water should run beneath you? A spring of water runs beneath you."

"There is one thing with which I can bless you: May it be God's will that all the trees planted from your seeds should be like you ..."

Are we going to allow ourselves to be the seeds of that life-giving tree?

Can we mobilize ALL the branches and seeds to *empower us* to drive the Strategic Harmony necessary to realign our planet?

We leave you with this challenge.

Strategic Harmony Snapshot

Purpose

Reinvent the world's institutions driven by values as the currency of decision-making and emerging technologies to drive sustainable impact.

Guiding Principles

1. Catalyzers are driven by Transformative Love and Transformative Power.
2. Catalyzers hold themselves accountable to the TEST Values—Trust, Empathy, Sustainability, and Transparency.
3. Catalyzers lead their organizations with a Catalytic Mindset—think Quantum, think Circular, think Connective, and think Intelligence.
4. A catalytic institution, organization, or enterprise is designed around five L.I.G.H.T. Impacts—Lifelong Learning, Innovation Engine, Good Governance, Holistic Living, and Transformative Economics.

Imperatives

1. Drive current leaders and entrepreneurs to adopt inclusive growth, stakeholder-centric business models to generate a sustainable future.
2. Build an inclusive, social impact measurement and transparent rating methodology focusing on intent and purpose, incorporating the TEST Values to hold institutions accountable for their actions.
3. Introduce the L.I.G.H.T. Impacts in your personal and organizational environments to attain and sustain Strategic Harmony.
4. Ignite a collaborative, intergenerational movement of Global Catalyzers—Rising Voices (Next Generation, Women, Marginalized), entrepreneurs and progressive leaders to drive social impact.

Join Us

Next Steps to Strategic Harmony

Join us at

www.EmPowerUs.world

Endnotes

Guidepost 1

1 https://iop.harvard.edu/youth-poll/fall-2017-poll

2 https://sustainabledevelopment.un.org/post2015/transformingourworld

3 https://www.brainyquote.com/quotes/albert_einstein_121993

4 https://www.goodreads.com/quotes/33541-it-has-always-seemed-strange-to-me-the-things-we-admire

5 https://www.edelman.com/research/2018-edelman-trust-barometer

6 https://www.proserveit.com/blog/five-monkeys-experiment-lessons

Guidepost 2

7 http://www.dltk-teach.com/rhymes/sleeping-beauty/story.htm

8 https://nice-inspiration.blogspot.hr/2011/09/chinese-story-about-harmony.html

9 https://www.thoughtco.com/what-is-a-paradigm-shift-2670671

10 https://www.lombardodier.com/manifesto

11 https://www.algora.com/449/book/details.html

12 https://en.wikipedia.org/wiki/Nicholas_Sparks

13 https://deming.org/quotes/

14 https://www.lombardodier.com/rethinksustainability

Guidepost 3

15 https://www.striveleadership.org/sl-blog/lack-of-leadership-is-on-the-global-agenda-test2

16 https://ourworldindata.org/trust

17 https://www.edelman.com/research/2019-edelman-trust-barometer

18 https://www.people-press.org/2015/11/23/1-trust-in-government-1958-2015/

19 https://www.edelman.com/post/an-implosion-of-trust

20 http://epress.lib.uts.edu.au/journals/index.php/AJCEB/article/view/4811/5244

21 http://www.azquotes.com/quote/935758

22 http://blog.readytomanage.com/how-can-individual-and-organizational-values-be-better-aligned/

23 https://hbr.org/2013/05/creating-the-best-workplace-on-earth

24 http://www.haygroup.com/

25 https://www.youtube.com/watch?v=Thfm3pTtymQ

26 https://www.cnbc.com/2016/05/25/vietnam-thp-ceo-founder-tran-qui-thanh-says-inheriting-the-family-business-must-be-earned.html

27 https://sustainablebrands.com/read/organizational-change/these-8-core-values-helped-my-business-achieve-long-term-growth

28 http://www.ijaiem.org/volume2issue12/IJAIEM-2013-12-06-011.pdf; https://www.cfps.org.uk/trust-in-government/

29 https://techcrunch.com/2016/04/24/the-future-is-the-trust-economy/

30 https://wealthygorilla.com/10-most-inspirational-short-stories/4/#ixzz5963Vg8mz

31 https://venturebeat.com/2018/09/18/apple -itunes-device-trust-score-based-on-calls-and-emails/

32 https://www.accenture.com/_acnmedia/thought-leadership-assets/pdf/accenture-competitive-agility-index.pdf

33 https://philipchircop.wordpress.com/category/zen-stories/

34 https://en.wikipedia.org/wiki/Sustainability

35 http://www.me-to-we.org/ how_to_create_a_positive_future_for_the_clima_107233.htm

36 https://en.wikipedia.org/wiki/Circular_economy

37 https://en.wikipedia.org/wiki/Cradle-to-cradle_design

38 http://www.capsulamundi.it/en/

Guidepost 4

https://en.wikipedia.org/wiki/Jim_Rohn

https://www.dailymail.co.uk/news/article-3482978/Penguin-returns-home-year-Brazilian-man-saved-it.html

https://hbr.org/2014/12/understanding-new-power

https://thisisnewpower.com/

https://www.wiley.com/en-us/Maslow+on+Management-p-9780471247807

https://www.tampabay.com/florida-politics/buzz/2018/08/25/u-s-12th-district/

https://www.amazon.com/New-Power-Works-Hyperconnected-World/dp/0385541112

https://buddhaimonia.com/blog/zen-stories-important-life-lessons

http://www.altfeldinc.com/pdfs/maslow.pdf

https://www.wiley.com/en-us/Maslow+on+Management-p-9780471247807

https://beatricebenne.com/2009/12/27/the-transformative-power-of-love/

https://www.fastcompany.com/3041948/why-engagement-happens-in-employeess-hearts-not-their-minds

http://www.thekinglegacy.org/books/where-do-we-go-here-chaos-or-community

https://www.theguardian.com/commentisfree/2013/jan/25/lincoln-wisdom-swamp-ridden-politics

https://www.japanindustrynews.com/2017/08/japans-society-5-0-going-beyond-industry-4-0

https://www8.cao.go.jp/cstp/english/society5_0/index.html#

https://www.brainyquote.com/quotes/jimi_hendrix_195397

http://www.rethinkchurch.org/articles/recent-posts/black-panther-power-and-love

Guidepost 5

https://www.scribd.com/document/336621519/2017-Edelman-Trust-Barometer-Executive-Summary

https://www.passiton.com/inspirational-quotes/3260-i-am-personally-convinced-that-one-person-can

https://en.wikipedia.org/wiki/Great_man_theory

https://www.accenture.com/_acnmedia/thought-leadership-assets/pdf/accenture-strategy-whole-brain-leadership-new-rules-of-engagement-for-the-c-suite.pdf

https://www.forbes.com/sites/anadutra/2012/09/27/filling-the-leadership-void-from-the-middle/#3f9f192c7219

https://www.linkedin.com/pulse/20140622153547-11845485-teamwork-are-you-an-annoying-maverick-or-a-welcome-initiator/

https://www.ey.com/en_bg/trust/how-building-trust-is-crucial-for-business-transformation

https://transformationsforum.net/our-leaders-have-failed-the-challenge

https://www.adrianswinscoe.com/2020/01/customer-experience-has-a-senior-leadership-problem-new-research-shows-how-to-fix-it

http://www.sasb.org/wp-content/uploads/2014/06/FT-Branded-File.pdf

http://www.altfeldinc.com/pdfs/maslow.pdf

Guidepost 6

https://www.americanprogress.org/issues/women/reports/2018/11/20/461273/womens-leadership-gap-2/

https://www.scientificamerican.com/article/women-may-find-management-positions-less-desirable/

Srića V., In Search for Harmony in a Disharmonious World, Algora Publishing, NY, 2014, p. 117

https://www.pewsocialtrends.com/essay/on-the-cusp-of-adulthood-and-facing-an-uncertain-future-what-we-know-about-gen-z-so-far

https://www.macleans.ca/opinion/what-fights-about-erasing-history-are-really-about

http://www.pewresearch.org/fact-tank/2017/06/13/5-key-findings-about-lgbt-americans

https://wearesocial.com/blog/2018/01/global-digital-report-2018

http://geh.ucsd.edu/wp-content/uploads/2019/05/2019-metoo-national-sexual-harassment-and-assault-report.pdf

https://www.amazon.com/Journey-into-Europe-Immigration-Identity/dp/0815727585

https://www.amazon.com/Applied-Sufism-Ahmed-Abdur-Rashid/dp/1595941215

http://13.251.163.42/wp-content/uploads/2019/02/ThomsonReuters-stateoftheGlobalIslamicEconomyReport201617.pdf

https://money.cnn.com/2016/11/11/technology/alibaba-by-the-numbers/index.html

Guidepost 7

80 https://www.brainyquote.com/quotes/sydney_j_harris_105451

81 https://medium.com/leadership-motivation-and-impact/the-power-of-starting-with-why-f8e491392ef8

82 https://www.amazon.com/Corporate-Culture-Performance-John-Kotter/dp/1451655320

83 https://www.thebodyshop.com/

84 http://www.ellaskitchen.com/

85 https://www.youtube.com/watch?v=laTIbNVDQN8

86 https://www.dove.com/us/en/home.html

87 https://www.goodreads.com/quotes/5911-this-is-the-true-joy-in-life-the-being-used

88 https://assets.ey.com/content/dam/ey-sites/ey-com/en_gl/topics/digital/ey-the-business-case-for-purpose.pdf

89 https://www.starbucks.com/

90 https://www.theguardian.com/business/2010/apr/05/unilver-paul-polman-shareholder-value

Guidepost 8

91 https://www.diygenius.com/the-creative-mindset/

92 https://en.wikipedia.org/wiki/Catalysis

93 http://www.jimcollins.com/article_topics/articles/good-to-great.html

94 https://www.chobani.com/

95 http://www.brainyquote.com/quotes/authors/p/phil_knight.html

96 http://www.britannica.com/biography/Oda-Nobunaga

97 http://www.butler-bowdon.com/meditat

98 http://www.gore.com/en_xx/aboutus/

99 https://www.entrepreneur.com/article/273207

Guidepost 9

100 https://www.brainyquote.com/quotes/henry_ford_145978

101 http://www.salimismail.com/

102 https://medium.com/pronouncedkyle/quantum-thinking-a-new-mental-superpower-as-explained-by-huge-nerds-1641cfd8e7f9

103 http://fortune.com/ikea-world-domination/

104 https://www.ingwb.com/media/2692501/ing_us-circular-economy-survey-05-02-2019.pdf

105 https://www.gailfosler.com/networks-making-unconventional-politics-interview-joshua-cooper-ramo

106 https://www.warbyparker.com/buy-a-pair-give-a-pair

107 https://www.forbes.com/sites/ciocentral/2015/03/09/the-rise-of-digital-ecosystems-in-the-we-economy/#7954aa415514

108 https://www.brainyquote.com/quotes/olaf_carlsonwee_851386

109 https://www.brainyquote.com/quotes/tim_bernerslee_373116?src=t_data

110 https://www.oliverwyman.com/our-expertise/insights/2017/may/transforming-into-a-data-driven-organization.html

111 https://www.inc.com/brent-gleeson/benefits-of-leading-data-driven-organizational-change.html

112 https://programs.online.utica.edu/articles/data-driven-decisions

113 https://www.sfu.ca/continuing-studies/programs/executive-leadership-certificate/mindsets.html

114 https://www.inc.com/sonya-mann/dara-khosrowshahi-first-month.html

115 https://medium.com/project-breakthrough/tomorrows-business-models-will-be-x-rated-f654a7c690f5

116 http://businesscasestudies.co.uk/ikea/meeting-the-needs-of-the-consumer/introduction.html

Guidepost 10

117 https://www.goodreads.com/book/show/485894.The_Metamorphosis

118 https://www.forbes.com/sites/brucerogers/2016/01/07/why-84-of-companies-fail-at-digital-transformation/?sh=240beded397b

119 https://www.jabil.com/dam/jcr:41ad85b0-b74b-4004-807d-bc42b56c9e41/jabil-2018-digital-transformation-report.pdf

120 https://www.weforum.org/agenda/2018/01/18-technology-predictions-for-2018/

https://www.edelman.com/research/2018-edelman-trust-barometer

http://d2f5upgbvkx8pz.cloudfront.net/sites/default/files/inline-files/Freeman%20Verizon%20Monograph%2C%20Proof5-Final.pdf

https://www.wiley.com/en-us/Maslow+on+Management-p-9780471247807

https://www.forbes.com/sites/stevedenning/2013/08/05/the-golden-age-of-management/#89630da5692f

http://www.amazon.com/gp/product/B004GXAU3E

https://www.forbes.com/sites/stevedenning/2013/08/05/the-golden-age-of-management/

https://www.forbes.com/sites/stevedenning/2013/05/30/the-management-revolution-thats-already-happening/#40c974f47091

http://online.wsj.com/article/SB10001424052748704476104575439723695579664.html

https://www2.deloitte.com/us/en/insights/economy/covid-19/heart-of-resilient-leadership-responding-to-covid-19.html

https://www.3m.com/3M/en_US/careers-us/full-story/~/inge-thulin-3m-ceo-diversity-for-change-founding-member/?storyid=f31e59d2-6e6b-417c-816c-ce747ae56334

https://www.cohnreznick.com/insights/digital-transformation-leading-success-at-growth-companies

https://www.forbes.com/sites/stevedenning/2013/05/30/the-management-revolution-thats-already-happening/#42ed5d467091

https://hbr.org/2017/11/the-future-economy-project-qa-with-paul-polman

https://www.benedictine.edu/academics/departments/economics/centesimus-annus-and-key-elements-john-paul-iis-political-economy

https://www.passiton.com/inspirational-quotes/6501-life-isnt-about-waiting-for-the-storm-to-pass

uidepost 11

https://www.penguinrandomhouse.ca/books/294806/qbq-the-question-behind-the-question-by-john-g-miller/9780399152337/excerpt

https://www.forbes.com/sites/christinecomaford/2017/01/28/63-of-employees-dont-trust-their-leader-heres-what-you-can-do-to-change-that/#319bdc9b7de4

https://www.edelman.com/research/2018-edelman-trust-barometer

https://hbr.org/2015/09/empathy-is-still-lacking-in-the-leaders-who-need-it-most

https://www.theguardian.com/sustainable-business/sustainability-key-corporate-success

https://globescan.com/insight/

https://www.thenationalnews.com/business/vuca-volatile-uncertain-complex-and-ambiguous-era-for-brands-1.184214

https://advisory.kpmg.us/articles/2017/dms-design-thinking-fail-transformation.html

https://www.edelman.com/research/the-shifting-of-power

https://www.cio.com/article/3183552/how-design-thinking-can-boost-digital-transformation.html

https://www.blackrock.com/corporate/investor-relations/larry-fink-ceo-letter

https://www.academia.edu/2917910/Measuring_Shared_Value

http://www.youaresocool.net/2013/01/16/a-zen-story-on-change/

uidepost 12

https://www.mckinsey.com/featured-insights/future-of-organizations-and-work/the-digital-future-of-work-what-skills-will-be-needed

https://fortune.com/change-the-world/

http://www.globalhealthmgh.org/camtech

https://www.innovatorsmag.com/innovation-key-to-achieving-sdgs/

https://www.coe.int/en/web/good-governance/12-principles

https://policyoptions.irpp.org/magazines/april-2020/crisis-shows-that-good-governance-and-strong-institutions-matter/

http://peacebuildingcentre.com/pbc_documents/Five_Principals_of_Good_Governance.pdf

https://www.goodreads.com/quotes/28440-the-greatest-wealth-is-health

https://en.wikipedia.org/wiki/Elisabet_Sahtouris

https://www.fastcompany.com/1657030/happiness-culture-zappos-isnt-company-its-mission

https://www2.deloitte.com/us/en/insights/focus/human-capital-trends/2017/improving-the-employee-experience-culture-engagement.html

https://www.overshootday.org/newsroom/country-overshoot-days/

https://www.ikea.com/ms/en_JP/about_ikea/the_ikea_way/our_business_idea/index.html

https://www.warc.com/newsandopinion/news/unilevers-rules-for-influencer-marketing/41407

Guidepost 13

163 http://leadership.mit.edu/no-heroes-peter-senge-system-leadership/

164 https://www.youtube.com/watch?v=GJQDbOvA1rI

165 https://www.unilever.com/Images/unilever-annual-report-and-accounts-2018_tcm244-534881_en.pdf

166 https://www.youtube.com/watch?v=GJQDbOvA1rI

167 https://www.unileverusa.com/news/press-releases/2020/unilever-united-for-america-initiative-helps-protect-lives-and-livelihoods.html

168 https://www.mdpi.com/2071-1050/10/9/3113

169 https://theconversation.com/what-a-sustainable-circular-economy-would-look-like-133808

170 https://www.mdpi.com/2071-1050/10/9/3113

171 https://theconversation.com/what-a-sustainable-circular-economy-would-look-like-133808

172 https://www.mdpi.com/2071-1050/10/9/3113/htm

173 https://www2.deloitte.com/global/en/pages/about-deloitte/articles/millennialsurvey.html

174 https://www.weforum.org/agenda/2020/01/uplink-young-leaders-global-platform-sustainable-development-davos/

175 http://velimir1.wixsite.com/elite

176 http://www3.weforum.org/docs/WEF_IBC_ESG_Metrics_Discussion_Paper.pdf

177 https://www.linkedin.com/in/aissa-azzouzi-95490510/

178 https://www.aspeninstitute.org/blog-posts/how-covid-19-is-changing-global-business/

179 https://knowledge.wharton.upenn.edu/article/post-covid-19-world-will-less-global-less-urban/

180 https://www.expo2020dubai.com/en/whats-new/expo-stories/bie-announcement

181 https://www.i-scoop.eu/industry-4-0-society-5-0/

182 https://www.businessinsider.com/what-is-belt-and-road-china-infrastructure-project-2018-1

183 https://www.latimes.com/world-nation/story/2020-05-20/coronavirus-strikes-chi%ADnas-belt-and-road-initiative

184 http://www3.weforum.org/docs/WEF_AM19_Meeting_Overview.pdf

185 https://www.i-scoop.eu/industry-4-0-society-5-0/

186 https://www.ussif.org/files/Trends/Trends%202018%20executive%20summary%20FINAL.pdf

187 https://consulting.kantar.com/wp-content/uploads/2019/06/Purpose-2020-PDF-Presentation.pdf

188 https://www.edelman.com/research/brand-trust-2020